A HAGUE CONVENTION ON JURISDICTION AND JUDGMENTS

A HAGUE CONVENTION ON JURISDICTION AND JUDGMENTS

Why did the Judgments Project (1992–2001) Fail?

Eva Jueptner

INTERSENTIA
Cambridge – Antwerp – Chicago

Intersentia Ltd
8 Wellington Mews
Wellington Street | Cambridge
CB1 1HW | United Kingdom
Tel: +44 1223 736 170
Email: contact@larcier-intersentia.com
www.larcier-intersentia.com

Distribution for the UK and
Rest of the World (incl. Eastern Europe)
NBN International
1 Deltic Avenue, Rooksley
Milton Keynes MK13 8LD
United Kingdom
Tel: +44 1752 202 301 | Fax: +44 1752 202 331
Email: orders@nbninternational.com

Distribution for Europe
Lefebvre Sarrut Belgium NV
Hoogstraat 139/6
1000 Brussels
Belgium
Tel: +32 (0)2 548 07 13
Email: contact@larcier-intersentia.com

Distribution for the USA and Canada
Independent Publishers Group
Order Department
814 North Franklin Street
Chicago, IL 60610
USA
Tel: +1 800 888 4741 (toll free) | Fax: +1 312 337 5985
Email: orders@ipgbook.com

A Hague Convention on Jurisdiction and Judgments. Why did the Judgments Project (1992–2001) Fail?

ISBN 978-1-83970-432-1
D/2024/7849/28
NUR 822

British Library Cataloguing in Publication Data. A catalogue record for this book is available from the British Library.

PREFACE

The 'Judgments Project' was a process of multilateral discussions and negotiations between the members of the Hague Conference on Private International Law between 1992 and 2001. Its aim was to create unified legal provisions regulating the exercise of international direct jurisdiction and ensuring the recognition and enforcement of judgments in civil and commercial matters. This project was a remarkable and important project for various reasons. By creating a global regime enabling the recognition and enforcement of judgments in civil and commercial matters across borders between the Hague Conference members (including, among others, the United States of America and the Member States of the European Community) and third States, it would have filled a massive gap in the international legal order at the time. In addition, the Hague Judgments Project was the first serious attempt by the Hague Conference since the 19th century to unify rules of international (direct) jurisdiction (sometimes simply referred to as 'jurisdiction'), concerning the power of courts to hear civil and commercial proceedings with an international element and render a judgment against the defendant, on a large scale. This ambitious project to create a global convention on jurisdiction and judgments failed, however, after almost 10 years of preparatory work, and an enormous amount of resources on the part of both the Hague Conference Member States and the secretariat of the Hague Conference, the Permanent Bureau, had been spent. This book shows that the preparation and management of this project by the Permanent Bureau (the organisers of the multilateral negotiation process) was not commensurate to the complexity of the endeavour, and it is likely that the main reasons for the failure of the project are linked to its preparation and management. Moreover, the book demonstrates that in order for the Hague Conference to create unified rules on international direct jurisdiction successfully in the future, it will be vital for the Permanent Bureau as well as for the Hague Conference members to draw lessons from the failure of the original Judgments Project. In particular, it will be essential that the Permanent Bureau exercises leadership by expanding and managing the preparatory work on international direct jurisdiction in the course of the Hague

Jurisdiction Project. The Permanent Bureau should recommend working towards creating a true 'mixed convention' as envisaged by the American scholar Arthur T von Mehren as the only convention type with the potential to regulate the recognition and enforcement of foreign judgments *and* the question of international direct jurisdiction at the same time.

ACKNOWLEDGEMENTS

The author would like to thank Ms Aude Fiorini and Professor Peter McEleavy (University of Dundee) for their continuous support and guidance as supervisors of the PhD thesis on which this text is based. Moreover, the author would like to thank her mother, Christa Elisabeth Jüptner and her father, Dr Roland Jüptner, without whom writing this text would not have been possible, her brother Jakob and his family Kathrine, Lilith and Magnus, and her grandmothers, Theresia and Adeltraud. Professor Colin T Reid, Professor Etienne Pataut, and Dr Sean Whittaker provided valuable comments on the text of the PhD thesis. Ahmed Hegazi, Margit Bal, Rebecca Moffat, Ella Brice-Jeffreys, Francesca Ramadan, and the editorial team from Intersentia provided excellent support during the publishing process. The author would also like to thank Professor Alexander R Markus (University of Bern) for supporting the initial stages of the PhD thesis, as well as Professor Sarah Hendry, who enabled the author to finalise the text of this book. Finally, the author would like to thank her friends Ulrike, Lucas, and Jill for their support over the years, as well as Camille, Finlay, Alan, Evy, Anthonia, Misan, Pontian, Bérénice, and her colleagues from Dundee Law School.

CONTENTS

LIST OF CASES

COURT OF JUSTICE OF THE EUROPEAN UNION

NATIONAL

ENGLAND AND WALES

FRANCE

UNITED STATES OF AMERICA

LIST OF LEGISLATION AND LEGAL INSTRUMENTS

LEGISLATION

EUROPEAN UNION

Council Regulation (EC) No 44/2001 of 22 December 2000 on jurisdiction and the recognition and enforcement of judgments in civil and commercial matters [2001] OJ L 12/1 (Brussels I Regulation)

Regulation (EU) No 1215/2012 of the European Parliament and of the Council of 12 December 2012 on jurisdiction and the recognition and enforcement of judgments in civil and commercial matters (recast) [2012] OJ L351/1 (Brussels Ibis Regulation)

UNITED STATES OF AMERICA

The Constitution of the United States of America (as amended)

OTHER

Austria

Gesetz vom 27. Mai 1896, über das Exekutions- und Sicherungsverfahren (Exekutionsordnung – EO)

Belgium

Judicial Code (Code Judiciaire)

Canada

1985 Canada-United Kingdom Civil and Commercial Judgments Convention Act (RSC, 1985, c C-30)

France

Civil code (code civil)

Germany

Civil Code 1896
Code of Civil Procedure

Italy

Civil Procedure Code (Codice di procedura civile 1942)
Reform of the Italian System of Private and Procedural International Law Act of 31 May 1995 (legge 218/95)

Liechtenstein

Gesetz vom 24. November 1971 über das Exekutions- und Rechtssicherungsverfahren (Exekutionsordnung; EO)

Netherlands

Code of Civil Procedure

Spain

Civil Procedure Code

United Kingdom

Civil Procedure Rules
Practice Direction 6B

INTERNATIONAL INSTRUMENTS

EUROPEAN UNION

Convention on the accession of the Kingdom of Spain and the Portuguese Republic to the Convention on jurisdiction and the enforcement of judgments in civil and commercial matters and to the Protocol on its interpretation by the Court of Justice with the adjustments made to them by the Convention on the accession of the Kingdom of Denmark, of Ireland and of the United Kingdom of Great Britain and Northern Ireland and the adjustments made to them by the Convention on the accession of the Hellenic Republic (89/535/EEC)(1) [1989] OJ L285/1 (1989 San Sebastián Convention)

Treaty of Amsterdam amending the Treaty on European Union, the Treaties establishing the European Communities and certain related acts – Final Act [1997] OJ C340/115

Treaty establishing the European Community (Amsterdam Consolidated Version) [1997] OJ C340/173

Treaty establishing the European Community (Maastricht Consolidated Version) [1992] OJ C224/6

Treaty establishing the European Community (Consolidated Version), Protocol (No 5) on the position of Denmark (1997) [2006] OJ C321/201

Agreement between the European Community and the Kingdom of Denmark on jurisdiction and the recognition and enforcement of judgments in civil and commercial matters [2005] OJ L299/62

Treaty establishing the European Economic Community (adopted 25 March 1957, entered into force 1 January 1958) 298 UNTS 3 (EEC Treaty or Treaty of Rome)

Convention establishing the European Free Trade Association (signed 4 January 1960, entered into force 3 May 1960) 370 UNTS 5 (EFTA Convention)

Treaty on European Union (signed 7 February 1992, entered into force 1 November 1993) (Maastricht Treaty) 31 ILM 253

Treaty on European Union (Consolidated version 2016) (TEU) [2016] OJ C 202/13

Consolidated Version of the Treaty on the Functioning of the European Union (TFEU) [2016] OJ C202/47

Convention on jurisdiction and the enforcement of judgments in civil and commercial matters [1972] OJ L299/32 (1968 Brussels Convention)

Convention on jurisdiction and the recognition and enforcement of judgments in civil and commercial matters (adopted 16 September 1988, entered into force 1 January 1992) SR 0.275.11 (1988 Lugano Convention)

Convention on jurisdiction and the recognition and enforcement of judgments in civil and commercial matters (concluded 30 October 2007, entered into force 1 January 2010) SR 0.275.12 (2007 Lugano Convention)

Treaty of Lisbon Amending the Treaty on European Union and the Treaty Establishing the European Community [2007] OJ C306/1

HAGUE CONFERENCE ON PRIVATE INTERNATIONAL LAW

Convention on the Civil Aspects of International Child Abduction (adopted 25 October 1980, entered into force 1 December 1983) 343 UNTS 89 (1980 Child Abduction Convention)

Convention on Jurisdiction, Applicable Law and Recognition of Decrees Relating to Adoption (adopted 15 November 1964) (1964 Convention on Intercountry Adoption)

Convention on Choice of Court Agreements (adopted 30 June 2005, entered into force 1 October 2015) 44 ILM 1294 (2005 Hague Choice of Court Convention)

Convention sur la compétence du for contractuel en cas de vente à caractère international d'objets mobiliers corporels (adopted 15 April 1958), in Hague Conference on Private International Law, *Collection of Conventions (1951–2009)* (2009) 27

Convention on the Law Applicable to Agency (concluded 14 March 1978, entered into force 1 May 1992) (1977) 16 ILM 775

Convention on Protection of Children and Co-operation in Respect of Intercountry Adoption (adopted 29 May 1993, entered into force 1 May 1995) (1993) 32 ILM 1134 (1993 Intercountry Adoption Convention)

Convention on the Recognition and Enforcement of Foreign Judgments in Civil and Commercial Matters (adopted 1 February 1971, entered into force 20 August 1979) 1144 UNTS 249 (1971 Hague Judgments Convention)

Convention on the Recognition and Enforcement of Foreign Judgments in Civil or Commercial Matters (adopted 2 July 2019; entered into force 1 September 2023) (2019 Hague Judgments Convention)

Rules of Procedure for Plenary Meetings, reprinted in Hague Conference on Private International Law, *Proceedings of the Seventeenth Session 10 to 29 May 1993, Tome I, Miscellaneous Matters* (SDU Publishers 1995) 20 (Original Rules of Procedure)

Rules of Procedure (as amended in 2005), in Hague Conference on Private International Law, *Proceedings of the Twentieth Session, 14 to 30 June 2005, Tome I, Miscellaneous Matters* (Intersentia 2015) 57 (2005 Rules of Procedure)

Rules of Procedure of the Hague Conference on Private International Law (as amended in 2005 and subsequently amended in 2012) (2012 Rules of Procedure) (on file with author)

Rules of Procedure of The Hague Conference on Private International Law (HCCH) (2020 Rules of Procedure) <https://assets.hcch.net/docs/52b9ea0d-dce2-4528-aeda-77a746f5fa14.pdf>

Statute of the Hague Conference on Private International Law (adopted 31 October 1951, entered into force 15 July 1955) 220 UNTS 121 (Original Statute Hague Conference)

Statute of the Hague Conference on Private International Law (adopted 1 October 1951, entered into force 15 July 1955, as amended) (Statute Hague Conference)

Supplementary Protocol to the Hague Convention on the Recognition and Enforcement of Foreign Judgments in Civil and Commercial Matters (adopted 1 February 1971, entered into force 20 August 1979) 1144 UNTS 271

UNIDROIT

Convention on International Interests in Mobile Equipment (concluded 16 November 2001, entered into force 1 April 2004) 2307 UNTS 285 (Cape Town Convention)

UNITED NATIONS

United Nations Convention on the Carriage of Goods by Sea (concluded 31 March 1978, entered into force 1 November 1992) 1695 UNTS 3 (Hamburg Rules)

DRAFT CONVENTIONS

Convention on the reciprocal recognition and enforcement of judgments in civil matters [ad referendum text, initialed at London, October 26, 1976] [1977] 16 ILM 71–87 (1976 UK-US draft Convention)

MODEL RULES

ALI/UNIDROIT Principles of Transnational Civil Procedure (2004) 4 Unif L Rev 758
Foreign-Country Money Judgments Recognition Act (2005) (USA)
Uniform Foreign Money Judgments Recognition Act (1962) (USA)

LIST OF ABBREVIATIONS

Alb L Rev	Albany Law Review
ALI	American Law Institute
Am J Comp L	American Journal of Comparative Law
ATS	Australian Treaty Series
Berkeley J Int'l L	Berkeley Journal of International Law
Brook J Int'l L	Brooklyn Journal of International Law
BUP	Brussels University Press
CJEU	Court of Justice of the European Union
Cornell Int'l L J	Cornell International Law Journal
Cornell L Rev	Cornell Law Review
Doc prél	Document préliminaire
Duke J Comp & Int'l L	Duke Journal of Comparative and International Law
EC	European Community
ECJ	European Court of Justice
EDA	Eidgenössisches Departement für auswärtige Angelegenheiten
EEC	European Economic Community
EFTA	European Free Trade Association
EU	European Union
Geo Wash Int'l L Rev	The George Washington International Law Review
Harv L Rev	Harvard Law Review
Hous J Int'l L	Houston Journal of International Law

ICLQ	International and Comparative Law Quarterly
ILM	International Legal Materials
Info Doc	Information Document
Int'l L	The International Lawyer
IPRax	Praxis des Internationalen Privat- und Verfahrensrechts
J Comp L	Journal of Comparative Law
J Dr Int'l Prive & Juris Comparee	Journal du Droit International Privé et de la Jurisprudence Comparée
J Int'l Econ L	Journal of International Economic Law
JL & Com	Journal of Law and Commerce
JPIL	Journal of Private International Law
Law & Contemp Probs	Law and Contemporary Problems
Law & Pol'y Int'l Bus	Law and Policy in International Business
Monthly Lab Rev	Monthly Labor Review
NCJ Int'l L & Com Reg	North Carolina Journal of International Law and Commercial Regulation
NiPR	Nederlands Internationaal Privaatrecht
Nw J Int'l L & Bus	Northwestern Journal of International Law & Business
NYUJ Int'l L & Pol	New York University Journal of International Law and Politics
OJ	Official Journal
PMJ	Project Management Journal
Prel Doc	Preliminary Document
RabelsZ	Rabels Zeitschrift für ausländisches und internationales Privatrecht
RCDIP	Revue critique de droit international privé
REIO	Regional Economic Integration Organisation
Rev Litig	The Review of Litigation
RSC	Revised Statutes of Canada

SR	Systematische Rechtssammlung
UC Davis L Rev	University of California, Davis Law Review
UN	United Nations
UNCITRAL	United Nations Commission on International Trade Law
UNIDROIT	International Institute for the Unification of Private Law
Unif L Rev	Uniform Law Review
UNGA	United Nations General Assembly
UNTS	United Nations Treaty Series
U Pa J Int'l Bus L	University of Pennsylvania Journal of International Business Law
U Pa L Rev	University of Pennsylvania Law Review
U Pitt L Rev	University of Pittsburgh Law Review
US/USA	United States (of America)
Va J Int'l L	Virginia Journal of International Law
WITS	World Integrated Trade Solutions
Work Doc	Working Document
WTO	World Trade Organisation
Yale J World Pub Ord	Yale Journal of World Public Order
ZEuP	Zeitschrift für Europäisches Privatrecht

INTRODUCTION

The History of a Hague Judgments Convention

To this day, there is no global instrument that regulates both the exercise of international direct jurisdiction of courts and the recognition and enforcement of foreign judgments on a broad scale for civil and commercial matters. In technical terms, such an instrument is called a double instrument, or double convention, as it contains unified rules on both jurisdiction and the recognition and enforcement of foreign judgments.[1] This lack of a global double convention on jurisdiction and judgments means that as a rule, courts of every State in the world employ their own domestic rules of international (direct) jurisdiction[2] in order to determine whether they have the power to hear proceedings in civil and commercial matters with an international element, and to render a judgment against the defendant in these proceedings.[3] Moreover, as a rule, each State employs its own domestic rules on the recognition and enforcement of judgments in civil and commercial matters. Many States do not give effect to foreign judgments in civil and commercial matters (by way of recognition and enforcement) on their territory without an international instrument obliging them to do so.[4] Moreover, even if they do, foreign judgments normally face a series of obstacles before they can be recognised and enforced abroad.[5]

---

1 Arthur T von Mehren, 'Recognition and Enforcement of Foreign Judgments: A New Approach for the Hague Conference?' (1994) 57 Law & Contemp Probs 271, 282, 283.

2 See, e.g., Arthur T von Mehren and Donald T Trautman, 'Jurisdiction to Adjudicate: A Suggested Analysis' (1966) 79 Harv L Rev 1121, 1125; Trevor C Hartley, *International Commercial Litigation* (CUP 2020) 11; international (direct) jurisdiction is sometimes simply referred to as 'jurisdiction', or 'judicial jurisdiction', 'jurisdiction to adjudicate', or 'competence'.

3 There are international conventions that contain unified rules of jurisdiction for specific subject matters, see, e.g., the Convention on Choice of Court Agreements (adopted 30 June 2005, entered into force 1 October 2015) (2005 Hague Choice of Court Convention) 44 ILM 1294.

4 See, e.g., Ralf Michaels, 'Recognition and Enforcement of Foreign Judgments' in Rüdiger Wolfrum (ed), *Max Planck Encyclopedia of Public International Law* (2009), <https://scholarship.law.duke.edu/faculty_scholarship/2076/> accessed 3 April 2023 [10], [11]; for a full analysis, see below, Chapter 3.

5 One of these obstacles is the question of indirect jurisdiction; see also below, Chapter 3.

The appeal of creating a double instrument on jurisdiction and judgments is clear, therefore: unified, globally-applicable rules on jurisdiction would foster legal certainty and predictability in international civil and commercial proceedings for both claimants and defendants, as the same rules would apply in all States bound by the convention.[6] At the same time, the guaranteed recognition and enforcement of judgments rendered on the basis of these unified jurisdictional grounds would foster access to justice for judgment creditors, and would support cross-border trade and investment.[7] From 1992 onwards, the Hague Conference on Private International Law, an international organisation with its seat in the Netherlands, attempted to adopt a text for such a global double convention on jurisdiction and judgments for almost 10 years. This endeavour eventually failed, however, for reasons yet unknown. This book will provide the first comprehensive analysis of the totality of reasons for why the Hague Judgments Project failed.

The attempt to create a global double convention regulating both international direct jurisdiction and the recognition and enforcement of foreign judgments in civil and commercial matters is in fact even older than the Hague Conference on Private International Law itself. In 1874, the Dutch Government had already attempted to convene an international conference for the purpose of negotiating a multilateral convention on both jurisdiction and judgments.[8] This global judgments convention was meant to be the starting point for finding a uniform solution for the conflict of laws, and for establishing an international 'Judicial Union', a '*Union Judiciaire*', between States.[9] This attempt proved unsuccessful, however, due to a lack of political motivation on the invited governments' part.[10]

---

6 See Arthur T von Mehren, 'Enforcing Judgments Abroad: Reflections on the Design of Recognition Conventions' (1998) 24 Brook J Int'l L 17, 25.

7 Cf David Goddard, 'Rethinking the Hague Judgments Convention: A Pacific Perspective' (2001) 3 Yearbook of Private International Law 27, 29; see also below, Chapters 2 and 3.

8 'Mémoire', in *Actes de la Conférence de la Haye chargée de réglementer diverses matières de droit international privé (12–27 septembre 1893), Première partie* (Imprimerie Nationale 1893) 2, 6, 7; the States invited to participate in the conference were Austria, Belgium, France, Germany, Great Britain, Italy and the United States of America, see Kurt H Nadelmann, 'Ignored State Interests: The Federal Government and International Efforts to Unify Rules of Private Law' (1954) 102 U Pa L Rev 323, 323.

9 'Mémoire' (1893) (n 8).

10 Ibid 6; the United States, for example, had turned down the invitation due to difficulties arising from the US Constitution and the federal structure of the State, 'Papers relating to the foreign relations of the United States, transmitted to Congress, with the annual message of the President, December 7, 1874: No 509' <https://history.state.gov/historicaldocuments/frus1874/pg_794> accessed 16 October 2023, 794, 795; Nadelmann, 'Ignored State Interests' (n 8) 324. France had rejected the invitation because it thought the topic too sensitive to be treated at a multilateral conference,

Inspired by the work of the Italian scholar and politician Mancini[11] and the success of the Montevideo Conventions adopted by several Southern American States,[12] the Dutch government renewed its invitation to convene an international conference, and repeated its suggestion that 'a uniform solution of the conflict of laws' would be made complete by an international treaty on the recognition and enforcement of judgments.[13] Moreover, the Dutch government restated the view expressed in its memorandum from 1874 that the basis for a judgments convention should be the adoption of uniform rules on international direct jurisdiction (*'la compétence territoriale'*) of the courts in the Contracting States.[14] In response to the invitation from the Dutch government, 12 European States and Russia met in The Hague from 12 to 27 September 1893 as the first Hague Conference on Private International Law.[15] The Commission charged with discussing questions of

---

see Nadelmann, ibid; see also Kurt Nadelmann, 'The United States joins the Hague Conference on Private International Law: A "History" with Comments' (1965) 30 Law & Contemp Probs 291, 291.

11 In 1881, the Italian government, under the leadership of its then Foreign Minister Pasquale Stanislao Mancini, proposed to convene an international conference for the purpose of codifying rules of private international law, including the recognition and enforcement of foreign judgments; due to an outbreak of cholera in Northern Italy, the conference could not take place, however, see Nadelmann, 'Ignored State Interests' (n 8) 329; Mancini, 'Négociations Diplomatiques du Gouvernement Italien avec les Différentes Puissances Relativement à la Fixation par Traité de Certaines Règles de Droit International Privé et à l'Exécution des Jugements Etrangers' (1886) 13 J Dr Int'l Prive & Juris Comparée 35, 35; Heimo Schack, 'Hundert Jahre Haager Konferenz für IPR' (1993) 53 RabelsZ 224, 227.

12 In 1889, at the first South American Congress on Private International Law in Montevideo (Uruguay), Argentina, Bolivia, Brazil, Chile, Paraguay, Peru and Uruguay adopted eight multilateral conventions and one Protocol on various topics of private international law, see Margarita Argúas, 'The Montevideo Treaties of 1889 and 1940 and their Influence on the Unification of Private International Law in South America', in Maarten Bos (ed), *The Present State of International Law and Other Essays written in honour of the Centenary Celebration of the International Law Association 1873–1973* (Springer 1973) 345, 345, 346; Ana Delić, 'The Birth of Modern Private International Law: The Treaties of Montevideo (1889, amended 1940)' <https://opil.ouplaw.com/page/Treaties-Montevideo/the-birth-of-modern-private-international-law-the-treaties-of-montevideo-1889-amended-1940> accessed 3 April 2023. One of these conventions, the Treaty on International Civil Law of 12 February 1889, was the first convention to unify grounds of direct jurisdiction, see Georges A L Droz, 'Régards sur le droit international privé comparé: Cours général de droit international privé' (1991) 229 Recueil des Cours de l'Académie de Droit International 9, 69, 70.

13 'Mémoire' (1893) (n 8) 6, 7: 'la solution uniforme des conflits de droit civil.'

14 Ibid 6, 7.

15 The European States were Austria-Hungary, Belgium, Denmark, France, Germany, Italy, Luxembourg, the Netherlands, Portugal, Romania, Spain and Switzerland, see 'Liste des pays représentés à la Conférence de la Haye et de leurs délégués', in *Actes de la Conférence de la Haye* (n 8) 19–21.

jurisdiction and civil procedure in general decided unanimously, however, not to continue work on the subject of jurisdiction, as the legal systems of the States represented at the Conference were too different from one another, and scholarly opinions on how to approach the issue were too divergent as to be able to reach agreement on the matter during the time available at the conference.[16] As a result, no judgments convention was adopted at the first Diplomatic Session of the Hague Conference.[17]

Following the first Diplomatic Session, two more unsuccessful attempts were made under the auspices of the Hague Conference (which was to become a permanent international organisation in 1955)[18] to regulate at least the recognition and enforcement of foreign judgments in civil and commercial matters on a broad scale.[19] These projects did not try, however, to create rules on international direct jurisdiction. The recognition and enforcement of foreign judgments in civil and commercial matters was discussed by the Second Commission of the Fifth Session of the Hague Conference in 1925, but led only to the preparation of a draft convention text.[20] Moreover, this convention was only meant to be a model for concluding bilateral conventions; it was never meant to become a multilateral convention in its own right.[21] A further attempt to conclude a convention on the recognition and

16 'Annexe no 2 au procés-verbal no 6 – Rapport présenté au nom de la IVième Commission', in *Actes de la Conférence de la Haye* (n 8) 63; see also Georges A Droz, 'A Comment on the Role of the Hague Conference on Private International Law' (1994) 57 Law & Contemp Probs 3, 3.

17 Schack (n 11) 227–230.

18 Statute of the Hague Conference on Private International Law (adopted 31 October 1951, entered into force 15 July 1955) 220 UNTS 121 (Original Statute Hague Conference). The statute was amended during the Twentieth Session of the Hague Conference on 30 June 2005; the amended version of the Statute entered into force on 1 January 2007, see Statute of the Hague Conference on Private International Law (adopted 1 October 1951, entered into force 15 July 1955, as amended) (Statute Hague Conference).

19 In addition, one could mention the Convention on the jurisdiction of the selected forum in the case of international sales of goods (adopted 15 April 1958). However, this convention focusses only on jurisdiction and the recognition and enforcement of judgments regarding a forum selected by the parties to an international sales contract and has a very narrow scope, see Schack (n 11) 243, 244. It did not enter into force; see also Rolf Wagner, 'Das Haager Übereinkommen vom 30.6.2005 über Gerichtsstandsvereinbarungen' (2009) 73 RabelsZ 100, 102.

20 'Project d'une convention sur la reconnaissance et l'exécution de décisions judiciaires', in Conférence de la Haye de Droit International Privé, *Actes de la Cinquième Session, tenue du 12 octobre au 7 novembre 1925* (Imprimerie Nationale 1926) 344, 344, 345 (1925 Draft Hague Judgments Convention); according to its Article 4, the convention would have also applied to arbitral judgments and judicial settlements.

21 'Rapport de la Deuxième Commission', in Conférence de la Haye de Droit International Privé, *Actes de la Cinquième Session, tenue du 12 octobre au 7 novembre 1925* (Imprimerie Nationale 1926) 182, 183; Schack (n 11) 234.

enforcement of foreign judgments was made in the 1960s. In 1966, during an extraordinary session of the Hague Conference, its Member States adopted the Convention on the Recognition and Enforcement of Foreign Judgments in Civil and Commercial Matters.[22] The convention was supplemented by a Protocol, aimed at prohibiting the recognition and enforcement of judgments rendered on an exorbitant ground of international direct jurisdiction as defined in the Protocol.[23] This convention, however, proved to be ultimately unsuccessful. Although the convention technically entered into force, it only has five Contracting Parties as of January 2024,[24] and no bilateral Supplementary Agreements as required by its Article 21 seem to have been concluded by the Contracting Parties.

1. FROM THE ORIGINAL JUDGMENTS PROJECT (1992–2001) TO THE 2019 HAGUE JUDGMENTS CONVENTION

In 1992, it was the US who initiated a new attempt to create a convention regulating both jurisdiction and judgments under the auspices of the Hague Conference on Private International Law. In a letter to the then Secretary General of the Hague Conference, Georges Droz, the Legal Advisor to the US Department of State, Edwin D Williamson, suggested that the Hague Conference should

> resume work in the field of recognition and enforcement of judgments with a view to preparing a single convention to which Hague Conference Member

---

22 Convention on the Recognition and Enforcement of Foreign Judgments in Civil and Commercial Matters (adopted 1 February 1971, entered into force 20 August 1979) 1144 UNTS 249 (1971 Hague Judgments Convention); this convention was intended to serve as the basis for concluding bilateral 'Supplementary Agreements' between Contracting States based on Article 21 of the convention.

23 Supplementary Protocol to the Hague Convention on the Recognition and Enforcement of Foreign Judgments in Civil and Commercial Matters (adopted 1 February 1971; entered into force 20 August 1979), Article 4; exorbitant grounds of jurisdiction allow a court to hear proceedings and render a judgment against a defendant on the basis of only a week connection between this court (the forum) and the defendant (or the facts of the case), and are therefore normally regarded as an inappropriate exercise of jurisdiction, cf Arthur T von Mehren, 'Adjudicatory Jurisdiction: General Theories Compared and Evaluated' (1983) 63 BU L Rev 279, 283.

24 The Contracting Parties are Albania, Cyprus, Kuwait, Netherlands and Portugal, see Hague Conference on Private International Law, 'Convention of 1 February 1971 on the Recognition and Enforcement of Foreign Judgments in Civil and Commercial Matters: Status Table', <https://www.hcch.net/en/instruments/conventions/status-table/?cid=78> accessed 4 January 2024.

States and other countries might become parties and that would enter into force only between ratifying or acceding States that agree that it should enter into force as between them.[25]

Originally, the US envisaged the adoption of such a convention at the Eighteenth Diplomatic Session of the Hague Conference in 1996.[26] However, it took until the Eighteenth Session for the Hague Conference Member States to include 'the question of jurisdiction, and recognition and enforcement of foreign judgments in civil and commercial matters' in the agenda of the Hague Conference, with a view to adopt a convention during its Nineteenth Session.[27] This decision had been prepared by an informal meeting of a Working Group in 1992 (29–31 October) consisting of experts in private international law,[28] and two Special Commission meetings in 1994 (20–24 June) and 1996 (4–7 June).[29] After the topic of jurisdiction and judgments had been put on the agenda of the Hague Conference, five more meetings of the Special Commission took place (17–27 June 1997, 3–13 March 1998, 10–20 November 1998, 7–18 June 1999, and 25–30 October 1999).[30] During the last meeting of the Special Commission, after 86 plenary sessions,[31] a draft convention text (the October 1999 Preliminary Draft Convention)[32] was finalised

---

25 Edwin D Williamson (Legal Advisor, US Department of State), Letter to Georges Droz, Secretary General of the Hague Conference, May 5 1992 (on file with author), 1; the term 'single convention' in this context does not seem to designate a particular convention type (i.e., a convention regulating only the recognition and enforcement of foreign judgments) since the letter goes on to suggest to regulate both international direct jurisdiction and the recognition and enforcement of judgments at the same time, ibid, 2.

26 Ibid.

27 'Final Act of the Eighteenth Session', in Hague Conference on Private International Law, *Proceedings of the Eighteenth Session, 30 September to 19 October 1996, Tome I, Miscellaneous Matters* (SDU Publishers 1999) 29, 47.

28 Permanent Bureau, 'Conclusions of the Working Group Meeting on Enforcement of Judgments – Prel Doc No 19 of November 1992', in Hague Conference on Private International Law, *Proceedings of the Seventeenth Session, 10 to 29 May 1993, Tome I, Miscellaneous Matters* (SDU Publishers 1995) 257, 257 [1].

29 Peter Nygh and Fausto Pocar, 'Report of the Special Commission: Prel Doc No 11 of August 2000' (Nygh/Pocar Report), in Hague Conference on Private International Law, *Proceedings of the Twentieth Session, 14 to 30 June 2005, Tome II, Judgments* (Intersentia 2013) 207, 211, [2].

30 Ibid, [3].

31 Arthur T von Mehren, 'Drafting a Convention on International Jurisdiction and the Effects of Foreign Judgments Acceptable World-wide: Can the Hague Conference Project Succeed?' (2001) 49 Am J Comp L 191, 191.

32 Peter Nygh, Fausto Pocar, 'Preliminary Draft Convention adopted by the Special Commission: Prel Doc No 11 of August 2000' (October 1999 Preliminary Draft Convention), in *Proceedings of the Twentieth Session, Tome II* (n 29) 190.

which was supposed to be the basis for the multilateral negotiations during a Diplomatic Session on the Judgments Project.[33]

However, in a letter to Hans Van Loon, the then Secretary General of the Hague Conference, the then Legal Advisor to the US Department of State, Jeffrey D Kovar, informed the Hague Conference that the October 1999 Preliminary Draft Convention stood 'no chance of being accepted in the United States'.[34] Nevertheless, a Diplomatic Session was scheduled for 2001.[35] During this Nineteenth Diplomatic Session in June 2001, the Hague Conference Member States were unable to reach consensus on many of the provisions of the draft convention text.[36] Despite almost 10 years of preparatory work on the Judgments Project, and after an enormous amount of time, money and energy had been spent, the product of this Diplomatic Session, the 2001 Interim Text,[37] was regarded unsuitable to serve as a basis for further negotiations. In an effort to save some of the work that had been done, the Member States of the Hague Conference decided to narrow the scope of discussions and to focus only on certain core areas of jurisdiction in 2002.[38] Finally, in 2003, the decision was made to abandon the aim of creating a broad convention on jurisdiction and judgments for the time being, and to further narrow the scope of the project to exclusive choice-of-court agreements in business-to-business relationships.[39] These efforts ultimately resulted in the adoption of the Hague Choice of Court Convention in 2005, which entered

---

33 Nygh/Pocar Report (n 29) 211, [6].

34 Jeffrey D Kovar, Letter to Hans van Loon, 22 February 2000, regarding Preliminary Draft Hague Convention on Jurisdiction and the Enforcement of Civil Judgments, 3 <www.cptech.org/ecom/hague/kovar2loon22022000.pdf> accessed 3 April 2023.

35 The Diplomatic Session in 2001 was the first of two scheduled Diplomatic Sessions, see Permanent Bureau, 'Conclusions of the Special Commission on General Affairs and Policy of May 2000: Prel Doc No 10 of June 2000 for the attention of the Nineteenth Session' <https://assets.hcch.net/docs/a154cf31-1583-4602-90eb-6b251d2eb7a4.pdf> accessed 3 April 2023, 11. The second part of the Diplomatic Session did not take place.

36 Permanent Bureau and the Co-reporters, 'Summary of the Outcome of the Discussion in Commission II of the First Part of the Diplomatic Conference 6–20 June 2001: Interim Text', in *Proceedings of the Twentieth Session, Tome II* (n 29) 620–657 – a lack of consensus is indicated by square brackets around the relevant provisions.

37 Ibid.

38 Permanent Bureau, 'Commission I on General Affairs and Policy held on 22–24 April 2002' <https://www.hcch.net/en/governance/council-on-general-affairs/archive> accessed 3 April 2023, [3].

39 Permanent Bureau, 'Conclusions of the Special Commission of April 2003 on General Affairs and Policy of the Conference', <https://www.hcch.net/en/governance/council-on-general-affairs/archive> accessed 3 April 2023, 8; Permanent Bureau, 'Report of the Work of the Informal Working Group on the Judgments Project, in particular on the Preliminary Text Achieved at its Third Meeting: 25–28 March 2003' (Prel Doc No 22 of June 2003), in Hague Conference on Private International Law,

into force in October 2015.[40] This Convention guarantees that a court chosen by an exclusive choice-of-court agreement has jurisdiction to hear the proceedings, and that judgments rendered by such a court are recognised and enforced under the convention.[41]

Despite the significant political interest of the Hague Conference Member States in concluding a comprehensive convention that secured the recognition and enforcement of foreign judgments and unified grounds of international direct jurisdiction, which had been proven by the various attempts in the history of the Hague Conference to create such a convention, the 2005 Hague Convention on Choice of Court Agreements remains the only successful convention on jurisdiction *and* judgments in civil and commercial matters negotiated under the auspices of the Hague Conference for the time being.

In 2010, the Permanent Bureau (the secretariat of the Hague Conference)[42] suggested to resume work on the Judgments Project.[43] For this purpose, the Hague Conference set up a small group of private international law experts.[44] Originally, the Hague Conference considered whether work on both the recognition and enforcement of foreign judgments in civil and commercial matters *and* the question of international direct jurisdiction should be addressed at the same time.[45] Eventually, the decision was

---

Proceedings of the Twentieth Session, 14 to 30 June 2005, Tome III, Choice of Court (Intersentia 2010) 77 [3].

40 2005 Hague Choice of Court Convention (n 3); as of 4 January 2024, the 2005 Hague Choice of Court Convention had 33 Contracting Parties (Denmark, the other EU Member States, the EU, Singapore, Mexico, Montenegro, the United Kingdom and Ukraine), see Hague Conference on Private International Law, 'Convention of 30 June 2005 on Choice of Court Agreements: Status Table' <https://www.hcch.net/en/instruments/conventions/status-table/?cid=98> accessed 4 January 2024.

41 The Convention applies only to choice of court agreements in business-to-business relationships, see 2005 Hague Choice of Court Convention (n 3), art 2(1).

42 Statute Hague Conference (n 18), art 4(2), art 6(c).

43 Permanent Bureau, 'Process Paper on the Continuation of the Judgments Project – Document for the attention of the Working Group and the Experts' Group: August 2013', [1], [6]–[9] <https://assets.hcch.net/docs/79c4fd67-6f1e-4bf8-bf18-01e589862f45.pdf> accessed 3 April 2023; Council on General Affairs and Policy of the Conference (5–7 April 2011), 'Conclusions and Recommendations Adopted by the Council', [15] <www.hcch.net/en/governance/council-on-general-affairs/archive> accessed 3 April 2023; see also Paul Beaumont, 'The revived Judgments Project in The Hague' (2014) 4 NiPR 532, 535.

44 Council on General Affairs and Policy, 'Conclusions and Recommendations 2011' (n 43) [15].

45 Permanent Bureau, 'Background Note: Document for the attention of the Expert Group (meeting of 12–14 April 2012)', [35], [36]; [40]–[72] <https://assets.hcch.net/docs/d2355e5c-fd79-4366-9caa-8a434367ba84.pdf> accessed 3 March 2024; 'Process Paper on the Continuation of the Judgments Project: August 2013' (n 43) [1], [6]–[9].

made to divide further work on a new Hague instrument between these two topics.[46] An informal group of experts (the Experts' Group) was given the mandate to study 'the desirability and feasibility of making provisions in relation to matters of [international direct] jurisdiction.'[47] A second informal group of experts in private international law (the Working Group) was charged with making 'proposals for consideration by a Special Commission in relation to provisions for inclusion in a future instrument relating to recognition and enforcement of judgments, including jurisdictional filters [i.e., grounds of indirect jurisdiction[48]].'[49] From 2014 onward, only the Working Group continued its work on the recognition and enforcement of foreign judgments,[50] and the work of the Experts' Group on international direct jurisdiction was deferred

46 Permanent Bureau, 'Process Paper on the Continuation of the Judgments Project: August 2013' (n 43) ibid; see also Paul Beaumont, Lara Walker, 'Recognition and enforcement of judgments in civil and commercial matters in the Brussels I Recast and some lessons from it and the recent Hague Conventions for the Hague Judgments Project' (2015) 11 JPIL 31, 43.

47 Council on General Affairs and Policy of the Conference (17–20 April 2012), 'Conclusions and Recommendations adopted by the Council', <www.hcch.net/en/governance/council-on-general-affairs/archive> accessed 3 April 2023, [18]; the Experts' Group consisted of experts in private international law derived from 18 Hague Conference Members (Argentina, Australia, Belarus, Brazil, China (People's Republic of), Costa Rica, Cyprus, the European Union, France, Germany, Japan, Mexico, New Zealand, the Russian Federation, South Africa, Switzerland, the United Kingdom and the United States of America), and met under the chairmanship of Mr David Goddard QC, see Permanent Bureau, 'Ongoing work on International Litigation: Prel Doc No 3 of March 2013', Annex 2, i, fn 1 <https://assets.hcch.net/docs/d00eb333-41fc-4b92-8405-e7eb20039154.pdf#report2> accessed 3 April 2023.

48 Francisco Garcimartín, Geneviève Saumier, 'Judgments Convention: Revised Draft Explanatory Report – Preliminary Document No 1 of December 2018', <https://assets.hcch.net/docs/7d2ae3f7-e8c6-4ef3-807c-15f112aa483d.pdf> accessed 3 April 2023, [144].

49 Council on General Affairs and Policy, 'Conclusions and Recommendations 2012' (n 47) [17]; Permanent Bureau, 'Process Paper on the Continuation of the Judgments Project: August 2013' (n 43) [1], [6], [8]–[9]; the Working Group met back to back with the Experts' Group under the chairmanship of Mr David Goddard QC and consisted of experts in private international law derived from the same 18 Hague Conference Members which had sent experts to the Experts' Group meeting, see Permanent Bureau, 'Ongoing work on International Litigation: Prel Doc No 3 of March 2013' (n 47) Annex 1, i, fn 1.

50 According to Louise Ellen Teitz, 'Another Hague Judgments Convention: Bucking the Past to Provide for the Future' (2019) 29 Duke J Comp & Int'l L 491, 500, the decision to advance only work on the recognition and enforcement of foreign judgments, and not on international direct jurisdiction, was apparently due to strong reluctance from the United States of America to proceed with work on international direct jurisdiction against the background of the 'disastrous results' of the 2001 Diplomatic Conference.

to a later date.[51] Eventually, after four Special Commission meetings,[52] the Hague Conference adopted the Convention on the Recognition and Enforcement of Foreign Judgments in Civil or Commercial Matters (hereafter the 2019 Hague Judgments Convention) during its 22nd Session on 2 July 2019.[53] After the accession by the European Union and its ratification by Ukraine, the convention entered into force on 1 September 2023.[54]

Following the adoption of the 2019 Hague Judgments Convention, the Hague Conference resumed work on international direct jurisdiction in the context of the 'Hague Jurisdiction Project'.[55] For the time being, this project is focussing on the creation of an instrument that deals with parallel proceedings and conflicting judgments only.[56] The adoption of an instrument that would create unified provisions on international direct jurisdiction on a potentially global scale is still a possibility, however.

2. THE AIM OF THIS BOOK

This book provides the first comprehensive analysis of the various potential reasons for why the original Judgments Project did not lead to

---

51 Cf Permanent Bureau, 'Process Paper on the Continuation of the Judgments Project: August 2013' (n 43) [17], [20]; Permanent Bureau, 'Ongoing Work on Judgments: Choice of Court Convention and the Judgments Project – Prel Doc No 7A of January 2015', <https://assets.hcch.net/upload/wop/gap2015pd07a_en.pdf> accessed 3 April 2023, [6]–[9]; Beaumont/Walker, 'Hague Judgments Project' (n 46) 43.

52 The Special Commission met from 1 to 9 June 2016, 16 to 24 February 2017, 13 to 17 November 2017, and 24 to 29 May 2018, see Hague Conference on Private International Law, 'Meetings of the Special Commission' <https://www.hcch.net/en/publications-and-studies/details4/?pid=6644&dtid=61> accessed 3 April 2023.

53 Convention on the Recognition and Enforcement of Foreign Judgments in Civil or Commercial Matters (adopted 2 July 2019, entered into force 1 September 2023) (2019 Hague Judgments Convention).

54 2019 Hague Judgments Convention (n 53) art 28(1); as of 4 January 2024, the convention has 29 Contracting Parties (the EU, its Member States except Denmark, Ukraine and Uruguay), see Hague Conference on Private International Law, 'Convention of 2 July 2019 on the Recognition and Enforcement of Foreign Judgments in Civil or Commercial Matters: Status Table' <https://www.hcch.net/en/instruments/conventions/status-table/?cid=137> accessed 4 January 2024.

55 See Hague Conference on Private International Law, 'Jurisdiction Project' <https://www.hcch.net/en/projects/legislative-projects/jurisdiction-project> accessed 3 April 2023; Hague Conference on Private International Law, Council on General Affairs and Policy 2023 (March 2023) 'Conclusions & Decisions' <https://assets.hcch.net/docs/5f9999b9-09a3-44a7-863d-1dddd4f9c6b8.pdf> accessed 3 April 2023 [9].

56 Permanent Bureau of the Hague Conference on Private International Law, 'Working Group on Jurisdiction: Report – Prel Doc No 2 of February 2023 – Annex I: Report of the Chair of the Working Group on matters related to jurisdiction in transnational civil or commercial

the adoption of a convention text by the Hague Conference Members. Analysing the potential reasons for the failure of the Hague Judgments Project is important not only from a perspective of legal history and regime theory, but also in the context of the current Hague Jurisdiction Project of the Hague Conference, and other efforts which aim for the unification of rules on jurisdiction and judgments in civil and/or commercial matters.

If the original Judgments Project had been successful, it would have created a regime securing the mutual recognition and enforcement of foreign judgments in civil and commercial matters between the United States of America (hereafter: US) and the Member States of the European Community (hereafter: EC)[57] for the first time in history, and potentially between all other States adopting the convention. Moreover, the Hague Judgments Project would have created unified rules on international direct jurisdiction on a potentially global level. In this way, litigants in international civil and commercial proceedings would have been able to predict exactly in which State they could sue or be sued respectively. As a result, the Hague Judgments Project would have increased legal certainty and predictability in international civil and commercial litigation to a significant and unprecedented extent.

If the Hague Conference Member States do eventually decide to aim for the creation of an instrument that unifies grounds of jurisdiction on a global level in the context of the Hague Jurisdiction Project, then it will be vital to avoid the pitfalls that arose during the original Hague Judgments Project. As this book shows, it is not impossible to create rules on international direct jurisdiction that apply on a global level.[58] Rather, as the following analysis shows, unifying grounds of jurisdiction on a

litigation' <https://assets.hcch.net/docs/fd997e67-381e-47f1-9ff8-74c28e2faf68.pdf> accessed 3 April 2023 [4]; Paul Herrup, Ronald A Brand, 'A Hague Convention on Parallel Proceedings' (2022) 63 Harvard International Law Journal Online 1, 2.

57 The forerunner of the EC was the European Economic Community (EEC), founded by the Treaty of Rome in 1957, see Treaty Establishing the European Economic Community (adopted 25 March 1957, entered into force 1 January 1958) 298 UNTS 3 (EEC Treaty or Treaty of Rome). With the entry into force of the Maastricht Treaty in 1993, the European Economic Community became the EC and one of the three pillars of the European Union (EU), see Treaty on European Union (signed 7 February 1992, entered into force 1 November 1993) (Maastricht Treaty) 31 ILM 253, art A, art G. The reference to the EC in the following is slightly anachronistic when events before the entry into force of the Maastricht Treaty are discussed. The EU eventually replaced and succeeded the EC with the entry into force of the Treaty of Lisbon in 2009, see Treaty of Lisbon Amending the Treaty on European Union and the Treaty Establishing the European Community [2007] OJ C306/1, 10.

58 For a different view, see Herrup/Brand, 'A Hague Convention on Parallel Proceedings' (n 56) 1, 2.

global level is a real possibility if the correct approach to the negotiations, based on the correct convention type, is chosen. In order for the Hague Jurisdiction Project to lead to the adoption of an international instrument that unifies grounds of jurisdiction on a global level, it is vital that the Hague Conference draws the right lessons from the past.

This book combines traditional legal analysis with an analysis of the negotiations on the basis of project management, a discipline traditionally used in business and management studies. In this way, it is established that it is likely that a significant reason for the failure of the Judgments Project was that the Permanent Bureau did not employ its project management techniques with the same rigour as for preparing the work on other successful Hague conventions. Besides the officially available documents (in particular, the Working Documents submitted by the participants in the Judgments Project which contained drafting proposals for the provisions of the convention text, as well as reports, Preliminary Documents and the Proceedings of the Eighteenth, Nineteenth and Twentieth Diplomatic Session) which were produced in the context of the Hague Judgments Project, this book also analyses the preparatory documents that were prepared during the pre-negotiation stage (during the Special Commission meetings, June 1997–October 1999). In particular, the analysis relied on the official minutes that were taken during the Special Commission meetings which are not publicly available, but are on file with the author.[59] The author chose to rely on these official minutes on the Special Commission meetings instead of interviews with key participants in the Judgments Project (i.e., the members of staff of the Permanent Bureau, and the Hague Conference Member State experts or delegates working on the Project) since more than 30 years have passed since the beginning of the Judgments Project, and the official minutes seemed to be the more immediate source as they were produced directly during the meetings.

The project management approach was chosen because the Judgments Project was a project in the sense of project management literature, i.e., a temporary endeavour undertaken to create a unique result;[60] the Judgments Project intended to create a draft text for a new Hague

59 Unlike the minutes taken for the Diplomatic Session, the minutes produced on the Special Commission meetings are not verbatim records of the meetings but provide a summary of the discussions that took place among the participants in the Special Commission meetings (i.e., among the experts in private international law sent by the Hague Conference Member States as well as Observer States), and an account of the votes of the delegations on the proposals.

60 Project Management Institute (PMI), *A Guide to the Project Management Body of Knowledge (PMBOK Guide)* (6th edn, Project Management Institute, Inc 2017) 4; J Davidson Frame, *Managing Projects in Organizations* (1995 Jossey-Bass Inc) 2.

Judgments Convention that could have been adopted at a Diplomatic Conference at the end of the normally four-year long work cycle of the Hague Conference.[61] In general, project management techniques are used to manage undertakings so that they achieve their objectives within a set time frame, and within budget.[62] Since the Judgments Project did not lead to the adoption of a convention on jurisdiction and judgments as intended, applying these project management techniques on the Judgments Project seemed worthwhile from an ex-ante perspective. Moreover, as this book shows, the failure of the project was not rooted in the substance of the negotiations, but in the negotiation process. The book concludes that the Judgments Project did not lead to the adoption of a convention text in particular because the Permanent Bureau, the project managers of the Judgments Project, did not recommend a true mixed convention during the preparatory stages of the project as the only viable convention type with a real chance to successfully create a Hague Convention regulating both the recognition and enforcement of foreign judgments *and* the question of international direct jurisdiction. As a result, the pre-negotiation phase of the Judgments Project during the Special Commission meetings could not produce a draft convention text that could have served as a viable basis for official negotiations at a Diplomatic Conference.

The mixed convention concept had been recommended by the American scholar Arthur T von Mehren as a method to create a global convention on jurisdiction and judgments when the Judgments Project was initiated in 1992.[63] It has to be acknowledged that even if the Judgments Project had been prepared in the same way as other Hague Conventions, and if the Permanent Bureau had recommended the true mixed convention approach, the negotiations still may not have led to the adoption of a convention text during a Diplomatic Session. Thorough planning and management of the (pre-)negotiation phase of a multilateral conference is not a guarantee for the success of a project.[64] Multiple factors other than management and planning can contribute to the outcome of the immensely complex undertaking of multilateral international negotiations, such as, for example, the negotiation strategy, culture, communication

---

61 Eventually, the Diplomatic Conference was postponed and split into two parts, with the first part taking place in June 2001, see Permanent Bureau, 'Conclusions of the Special Commission on General Affairs and Policy of May 2000' (n 35) 11.

62 Frame, *Managing Projects in Organizations* (n 60) 6; see also PMI, *PMBOK Guide* (n 60) 1.

63 Von Mehren, 'New Approach' (n 1) 287.

64 Cf Frame, *Managing Projects in Organizations* (n 60) 22.

during the negotiations, personal conditions of the participants, or time.[65] However, as this book will show, without proper project management and planning of the pre-negotiation phase of a multilateral convention, official diplomatic negotiations will not be successful.[66]

For this reason, this book also gives further support to international relations theorists who have argued that effective negotiation management (for example by the negotiating agency) can be seen as a precondition for successful multilateral negotiations between States.[67] As this book shows, effective management of in particular the pre-negotiation phase of a multilateral conference is a condition for a successful outcome of multilateral negotiations. For this reason, this book adds to the existing literature on law-making by means of international treaties in general, and on law-making in private international law in particular. Besides this, the book also addresses the challenges and the opportunities in creating rules on international jurisdiction on a global level. Finally, this book also adds to the literature on law-making at the Hague Conference on Private International Law.[68]

3. AN OVERVIEW OF THE CONTENT

In order to determine why the 1992–2001 Hague Judgments Project failed, the following chapters address several sub-questions. Chapter 1 addresses the question of whether the Hague Conference on Private International Law was an appropriate forum to host the negotiations on a global judgments convention. Chapter 2 addresses the question of whether the Judgments Project failed because no feasibility studies were prepared on the part of

---

65 Christophe Dupont, Guy-Olivier Faure, 'The Negotiation Process', in Victor A Kremenyuk (ed), *International Negotiation: Analysis, Approaches, Issues* (2nd edn, Jossey-Bass 2002), 39, 40–59; even concerns of the negotiators about saving face can play a role, see ibid at 50, 51; see also William Zartman, 'Negotiating Cultures', in Peter Berton, Hiroshi Kimura, I William Zartman (eds), *International Negotiation: Actors, Structure/Process, Values* (Macmillan 1999) 1, 1–7.

66 Cf Frame (n 60) 22.

67 Kai Monheim 'The "Power of Process": How Negotiation Management Influences Multilateral Cooperation' (2016) 21 International Negotiation 345, 376.

68 See, e.g., Paul R Beaumont, Peter E McEleavy, *The Convention on International Child Abduction* (OUP 1999), Chapter 3; Paul R Beaumont, Peter E McEleavy, *Anton's Private International Law (Private International Law, A.E. Anton)* (3rd edn, W Green 2011), [3.16]–[3.17]; T Bradbrooke Smith, 'Achieving Results at International Meetings: Why the Hague Conference Succeeds', in Alegría Borras et al (eds), *E Pluribus Unum: Liber Amicorum Georges A L Droz* (Martinus Nijhoff Publishers 1996) 415.

the Permanent Bureau with regard to the strict double convention, and the mixed convention. Chapter 3 addresses the question of whether the Judgments Project failed because a Hague Judgments Convention would not have met the real needs of, in particular, the US and the Member States of the EC. Chapter 4, one of the key chapters, analyses whether the preparatory work done by the Permanent Bureau on the Hague Judgments Convention fell short of previously set standards for Hague Conference project management. In order to answer this question, the book analyses the preparatory work on the Judgments Project from the perspective of project management principles and draws a comparison to the preparatory work done for other successful Hague Conventions. Chapter 5 builds on Chapter 4 and analyses whether there was a lack of management of the formalised pre-negotiation phase during the Special Commission meetings from June 1997 until October 1999. Chapter 6 analyses whether the Diplomatic Session in June 2001 could not lead to the adoption of a convention text because there was no basis for consensus between the Hague Conference Member State, due to a lack of agreement on the convention type from the outset of negotiations. Chapter 7 addresses the question of whether the Judgments Project failed because the US, one of the key stakeholders in the project, voiced its concerns about the project too late in time. Chapter 8 addresses the question of whether the US eventually withdrew its support from the Judgments Project because it could not overcome the resistance of the EC and its Member States towards negotiating for a true mixed convention. The last chapter concludes that the Hague Conference must draw lessons from the failure of the original Judgments Project for future endeavours to unify grounds of international direct jurisdiction.

CHAPTER 1

THE CHOICE OF THE NEGOTIATING AGENCY

Law Making at the Hague Conference on Private International Law

1.1. INTRODUCTION

The first question that must be addressed in order to understand why the Hague Judgments Project failed is whether the Hague Conference on Private International Law was an appropriate forum to create a global judgments convention. As previously discussed, it was the Legal Advisor of the US Department of State who approached the Hague Conference with the idea of creating a global convention on jurisdiction and judgments.[69] The US chose the Hague Conference as a negotiating agency in particular because the US was interested in securing the recognition and enforcement of US judgments within the Member States of the EC (and the European Free Trade Association (EFTA)).[70] By means of this convention, the US had also hoped to reduce the risk to US litigants of being subject to civil proceedings in European courts on the basis of exorbitant, i.e., excessive, grounds of international direct jurisdiction.[71] In 1992, all of the Member States of the EC and most of the EFTA Member States were also Member

69 See above, Introduction at 1.

70 Letter Edwin D Williamson to Georges Droz (n 25) 1; Arthur T von Mehren, 'Recognition of United States Judgments Abroad and Foreign Judgments in the United States: Would an International Convention Be Useful?' (1993) 57 RabelsZ 449, 452, 455, 456, and fn 18.

71 'Exorbitant jurisdiction' is jurisdiction which is considered to be inappropriate by the State which has been addressed for recognition or enforcement of the judgment because jurisdiction was exercised on the basis of a weak connection between the forum and the defendant, or the forum and the facts of the case. See Joseph Halpern, 'Exorbitant Jurisdiction and the Brussels Convention: Toward a Theory of Restraint' (1983) 9 Yale J World Pub Ord 369, 378, 389; exorbitant jurisdiction is a relative term

States of the Hague Conference,[72] and so it was a suitable forum in which US interests in the project could be accommodated. However, negotiating under the auspices of the Hague Conference also offered distinct institutional features which made it a uniquely appropriate agency for creating a global judgments convention.

1.2. SUBJECT-MATTER EXPERTISE

The most obvious of these features was undoubtedly the subject-matter expertise of the Hague Conference. The two subject matters to be considered when creating a judgments convention (international jurisdiction and the recognition and enforcement of foreign judgments) belong to the area of private international law, and more specifically to international civil procedure law.[73] The very purpose of the Hague Conference is 'to work for the progressive unification of rules of private international law,'[74] and the organisation has a long history of treaty making in this area.[75] The travaux préparatoires, the preparatory documents on the conventions adopted under the auspices of the Hague Conference, are published in the 'Proceedings' of the Hague Conference, and contain a vast array of institutional knowledge.[76] Between 1955,

---

and which jurisdictional grounds exactly are considered to be exorbitant depends on the perspective of the state addressed for enforcement, cf Halpern, ibid, 375.

72 The 12 Member States of the European Economic Community were Belgium, Denmark, France, Germany, Greece, Ireland, Italy, Luxembourg, Netherlands, Portugal, Spain and the United Kingdom of Great Britain and Northern Ireland, see 'Country Profiles' <https://european-union.europa.eu/principles-countries-history/country-profiles_en> accessed 3 April 2023; Austria, Finland, Norway and Sweden were EFTA Member States, see Convention establishing the European Free Trade Association (signed 4 January 1960, entered into force 3 May 1960) 370 UNTS 5 (EFTA Convention), preamble; the other Hague Conference Member States in 1992 were Argentina, Australia, Canada, Chile, China (People's Republic of), Egypt, Hungary, Israel, Japan, Mexico, Netherlands, Poland, Romania, Suriname, Switzerland, Turkey, the United States of America and Venezuela, see Hague Conference on Private International Law, 'Statute of the Hague Conference on Private International Law: Status Table' <https://www.hcch.net/en/instruments/conventions/status-table/?cid=29> accessed 4 April 2023.

73 This term is used in German academic literature, see Alexander R Markus, *Internationales Zivilprozessrecht* (Stämpfli Verlag 2014) 3; Hartley, *International Commercial Litigation* (n 2) 4.

74 Original Statute Hague Conference (n 18) art 1; now Statute Hague Conference (n 18) art 1.

75 Peter E Pfund, 'Contributing to Progressive Development of Private International Law: The International Process and the United States Approach' (1994) 249 Recueil des Cours de l'Académie de Droit International 9, 22.

76 See, e.g., Hague Conference on Private International Law, *Proceedings of the Seventeenth Session, 10 to 29 May 1993, Tome II, Adoption* (SDU Publishers 1994).

when the Hague Conference became a permanent organisation,[77] and 1992, 31 multilateral conventions or protocols were negotiated and adopted under its auspices.[78] It can rightly be said, therefore, that the Hague Conference had long-established experience in producing multilateral treaties that addressed problems of private international law. Even if not all of the instruments negotiated under its roof had attracted large numbers of members,[79] some instruments were exceptionally successful. The two most successful Hague Conventions ever negotiated were the 1980 Hague Convention on International Child Abduction, and the 1993 Hague Convention on Intercountry Adoption.[80]

Moreover, the Hague Conference's experience in law making in private international law in general, and in the area of international civil procedure law in particular, was (and is) unique. None of the other potentially available fora for hosting negotiations concerning a global judgments convention (in particular, the International Institute for the Unification of Private Law (UNIDROIT) and the United Nations Commission on International Trade Law (UNCITRAL)) had relevant subject-matter experience that came close to that of the Hague Conference. Some of the projects of UNCITRAL had occasionally touched upon questions of international civil procedure, but only to a very limited extent.[81]

---

77 Original Statute Hague Conference (n 18).

78 'Conventions and other Instruments' <https://www.hcch.net/en/instruments/conventions> accessed 7 April 2023.

79 For an overview of the 31 conventions (or protocols) adopted under the auspices of the Hague Conference on Private International Law between 1951 and 1993, see Kurt Lipstein, 'One Hundred Years of Hague Conferences on Private International Law' (1993) 42 ICLQ 553, 650–653; only 23 of those instruments had entered into force, and not all were successful in terms of number of member states, see ibid.

80 As of 4 January 2024, there are 103 Contracting States to the 1980 Hague Convention on International Child Abduction (Convention on the Civil Aspects of International Child Abduction [adopted 25 October 1980, entered into force 1 December 1983] 343 UNTS 89), and 105 to the 1993 Hague Convention on Intercountry Adoption (Convention on Protection of Children and Co-operation in Respect of Intercountry Adoption [adopted 29 May 1993, entered into force 1 May 1995] [1993] 32 ILM 1134), see Hague Conference on Private International Law, 'Convention of 25 October 1980 on the Civil Aspects of International Child Abduction: Status Table' <www.hcch.net/en/instruments/conventions/status-table/?cid=24> and 'Convention of 29 May 1993 on Protection of Children and Co-operation in Respect of Intercountry Adoption: Status Table' <www.hcch.net/en/instruments/conventions/status-table/?cid=69> both accessed 4 January 2024.

81 The United Nations Convention on the Carriage of Goods by Sea (concluded 31 March 1978, entered into force 1 November 1992) 1695 UNTS 3 (Hamburg Rules) contains – besides substantive law provisions on the carriage of goods by sea – one provision on international jurisdiction and on parallel proceedings for proceedings relating to carriage of goods under the convention, see Hamburg Rules, art 21.

UNIDROIT only started to work on harmonising rules of international civil procedure in later years, and then only in a very narrow context.[82]

1.3. THE USE OF SPECIAL COMMISSION MEETINGS TO PREPARE A DIPLOMATIC CONFERENCE

Besides its subject-matter experience, law making at the Hague Conference was also characterised by other distinct features which made the Conference a uniquely appropriate forum for negotiating a global convention on jurisdiction and judgments. Traditionally, the work cycle of the Hague Conference lasted four years, with new conventions being adopted in every cycle at the end of a Diplomatic Session.[83] In between the Diplomatic Sessions, the Hague Conference Member States would meet as a Special Commission on various occasions in order to prepare a draft convention text that would then be used as a basis for negotiations during the Diplomatic Session.[84] The success of the Hague Conference in producing multilateral conventions has been attributed inter alia to the thorough preparation of its Diplomatic Sessions through these Special Commission meetings.[85] These Special Commission meetings can be described as a formalised pre-negotiation phase, or 'preliminary

---

82 The Convention on International Interests in Mobile Equipment (adopted 16 November 2001, entered into force 1 April 2004) 2307 UNTS 285) (Cape Town Convention) was negotiated under the auspices of UNIDROIT and contained some rules on international direct jurisdiction, see Cape Town Convention, ch XII. Later on, UNIDROIT, together with the American Law Institute (ALI), broadened its field of activities and also included projects on the harmonisation of transnational civil procedure law in its work programme, see ALI/UNIDROIT Principles of Transnational Civil Procedure (2004) 4 Unif L Rev 758–808. Besides principles (i.e., non-binding model rules) on transnational civil procedure in the broader sense the instrument also contains principles on international jurisdiction and the recognition and enforcement of foreign judgments, see ibid 762–64, 804–808.

83 Original Statute Hague Conference (n 18) art 3(6) (now Statute Hague Conference (n 18) art 4(6)); Beaumont/McEleavy, *Anton's Private International Law* (n 68) [3.13]. Exceptionally, also an Extraordinary Session could have been convened, see Original Statute Hague Conference (n 18) art 3(7) (now Statute Hague Conference (n 18) art 4(6)). An Extraordinary Diplomatic Session had only taken place twice in the history of the Hague Conference; the first Extraordinary Session took place on the enforcement of judgments in 1966, the second one took place in 1985 on the law applicable to sales contracts.

84 Original Statute Hague Conference (n 18) art 7; now Statute Hague Conference (n 18) art 8(1).

85 Beaumont/McEleavy, *Child Abduction* (n 68) 24, 25.

negotiations', as decisions taken during the Special Commission meetings are not binding for the governments of the Hague Conference Member States.[86] For this reason, the participants sent by the Hague Conference Member States are not called delegates, but are referred to as 'experts'.[87] These Special Commission meetings therefore often did not resemble traditional negotiations between States, but were characterised by open and comprehensive discussions by private international law experts.[88] The discussions during the Special Commission meetings mostly focused on the solution of substantive issues, while the drafting of the provisions for the draft convention was done by a committee.[89]

Moreover, all Hague Conference Member States had a right to participate in the meetings of the Special Commission (and also later in the Diplomatic Session).[90] Even if delegates of the Hague Conference Member States did not officially represent their governments during Special Commission meetings,[91] this early involvement ensured that all of the Member State delegations could participate equally in the process of creating a draft convention text that would serve as the basis for official negotiations during a Diplomatic Session.[92] The equal involvement of all Hague Conference Member States contributed to the fairness of the pre-negotiation phase, due to the equal opportunity for all Member States to contribute to its outcome.[93] From the outset, therefore, the pre-negotiation process was procedurally just.[94] This naturally enhanced the chances that the draft convention text elaborated during the pre-negotiation phase was a viable basis for the official negotiations during a Diplomatic Conference.[95]

86 Beaumont/McEleavy, *Child Abduction* (n 68) 24.
87 Ibid 25; Beaumont/McEleavy, *Anton's Private International Law* (n 68) [3.17].
88 Beaumont/McEleavy, *Child Abduction* (n 68) 25.
89 Beaumont/McEleavy, *Anton's Private International Law* (n 68) [3.15].
90 Cf Rules of Procedure for Plenary Meetings, art 1, reprinted in Hague Conference on Private International Law, *Proceedings of the Seventeenth Session, 10 to 29 May 1993, Tome I, Miscellaneous Matters* (SDU Publishers 1995) 20 (Original Rules of Procedure).
91 Beaumont/McEleavy, *Child Abduction* (n 68) 25.
92 Cf Hans van Loon, 'Report on Intercountry Adoption: Prel Doc No 1 of April 1990', in Hague Conference on Private International Law, *Proceedings of the Seventeenth Session, 10 to 29 May 1993, Tome II, Adoption* (SDU Publishers 1994) 11, 15 [2].
93 Cf I William Zartman, 'Negotiation as a Search for Justice', in I William Zartman, *Negotiation and Conflict Management: Essays on Theory and Practice* (Routledge 2008) 68, 71, 73; Cecilia Albin, Daniel Druckman, 'Procedures Matter: Justice and Effectiveness in International Trade Negotiations' (2014) 20(4) European Journal of International Relations 1014, 1017.
94 Albin, Druckman (n 93) 1017.
95 Cf Albin, Druckman (n 93) 1017, 1038.

Additionally, from its Tenth Session in 1964, the Hague Conference has had two official working languages, English and French,[96] and all relevant documents created in the process of drafting a new convention (in particular, Working Documents (drafting proposals) and Reports) were produced in both languages.[97] This may have enabled all of the Hague Conference Member States to contribute to the (pre-)negotiation process on a more or less equal footing,[98] as both languages were widely spoken on all continents. It was likely, therefore, that States participating in the Judgments Project could have sent a delegate to the meetings at the Hague Conference that was not only an expert in the subject matter, but was also able to participate actively in the (pre-)negotiation process.[99]

1.4. THE OPENNESS OF THE HAGUE CONFERENCE TOWARDS THIRD STATES

The processes employed by the Hague Conference in drafting a new convention text were also conducive for creating instruments that were

---

96 M H van Hoogstraten, J Offerhaus, 'Avis au Lecteur', in Conférence de la Haye de Droit International Privé, *Actes de la Dixième Session – 7 au 28 octobre 1964, Tome Premier* (Imprimerie Nationale 1965) 5, 6.

97 A side-effect of two official working languages, with all convention texts being equally authentic in both English and French, was that the resulting text was drafted in a 'neutral' language rather than being overly inspired by the legal system of the nation whose official language happened to be the working language, cf M H van Hoogstraten, 'La codification par traités en droit international privé dans le cadre de la Conférence de la Haye' (1967) 122 Recueil des Cours de l'Académie de Droit International 337, 348, 349; see also Beaumont/McEleavy, *Anton's Private International Law* (n 68) [3.15].

98 In recent years, also Spanish has been used as a working language, for example during the 14th Diplomatic Session (negotiation of the Convention on Intercountry Adoption), see Beaumont/McEleavy, *Anton's Private International Law* (n 68) [3.15], fn 56. During the Council on General Affairs and Policy of the Conference in March 2023, Spanish was adopted as the third working language of the Hague Conference from 1 July 2024, see Hague Conference on Private International Law, 'Conclusions & Decisions' (March 2023) <https://assets.hcch.net/docs/5f9999b9-09a3-44a7-863d-1dddd4f9c6b8.pdf> accessed 3 April 2023 [54].

99 Regarding the difficulties involved by negotiating legal texts in multilateral conferences in a language which is not the mother tongue of most delegates, and on difficulties regarding negotiating and drafting in general when delegates representing different legal systems are involved, see van Hoogstraten, 'La codification par traités en droit international privé dans le cadre de la Conférence de la Haye' (n 97) 345, 346–348; Fritz Schwind, 'Cours général de droit international privé' (1984) 187 Recueil des Cours de l'Académie de Droit International 9, 118.

attractive to non-Member States. Although the actual decision-making process (during the Special Commission meetings and the Diplomatic Session) was reserved for Hague Conference Members,[100] observers nevertheless could actively influence the work on new conventions. Observers were normally allowed to participate in discussions, and to submit working documents (i.e., drafting proposals) during the pre- and actual negotiation phase.[101] This openness of the (pre-)negotiation phase at the Hague Conference allowed the consideration of a topic from various viewpoints, thereby enhancing the chances that the convention text would be acceptable not only to Members of the Hague Conference, but also to third States.[102] For example, many non-Member States of the Hague Conference seem to have signed and ratified the 1993 Intercountry Adoption Convention[103] exactly because they were allowed to participate in the preparatory work and negotiations for the convention as observers.[104] As a rule, non-Member States of the Hague Conference were also allowed to join conventions negotiated under the auspices of the Hague Conference, as these conventions were normally 'open',[105] i.e., open to signature and accession by *all* States, not only by Member States of the Hague Conference.[106] Due to this, a judgments convention adopted under the auspices of the Hague Conference would have had the potential to become a truly global instrument.

---

[100] Hans van Loon, Andrea Schulz, 'The European Community and the Hague Conference on Private International Law', in Bernd Martenczuk, Servaas van Thiel (eds), *Justice, Liberty, Security: New Challenges for EU External Relations* (BUP 2008) 257, 258.

[101] Ibid (n 100) 257; Schulz, 'The Accession of the European Community to the Hague Conference on Private International Law' (2007) 56 Int'l & Comp L Q 931, 942; see also, e.g., Hague Conference on Private International Law, 'List of participants, Special Commission on international jurisdiction and the effects of foreign judgments in civil and commercial matters, 7–18 June 1999' (on file with author), listing Brunei Darussalam, Indonesia, Malaysia, New Zealand and the Russian Federation as observers.

[102] Pfund, 'Contributing to Progressive Development of Private International Law' (n 75) 28.

[103] 1993 Intercountry Adoption Convention (n 80).

[104] Cf Pfund, 'Contributing to Progressive Development of Private International Law' (n 75) 28; see Van Loon, 'Report on Intercountry Adoption: Prel Doc No 1 of April 1990' (n 92) 11, 15 [2].

[105] Van Loon, Schulz, 'The European Community and the Hague Conference on Private International Law' (n 100) 257, 258.

[106] See, e.g., 2005 Hague Choice of Court Convention (n 3) art 27(1), (3).

1.5. A REPUTATION FOR RESEARCH-BASED SUPPORT FOR THE (PRE-)NEGOTIATION PROCESS

A further important feature of choosing the Hague Conference as the agency to create a judgments convention was the research-based support provided by the Permanent Bureau, the secretariat of the organisation, for the creation of a new international convention,[107] and the leadership it thereby provided.[108] The first step in preparing a new Hague Convention was to assess the general feasibility of creating a Hague Convention on the identified subject-matter.[109] These studies were undertaken before a topic was added to the agenda of the Hague Conference, and these studies have therefore been called 'pre-initiation studies', or 'short feasibility studies'.[110] After the general feasibility of a convention project had been confirmed, more detailed preparatory work by the legal staff of the Hague Conference (its Secretaries) followed before a new topic was discussed by a Special Commission meeting.[111] This more detailed preparatory work normally consisted of a comparative legal study of the specific issues to be addressed.[112] Sometimes, this study was based on questionnaires which were sent to the governments of the Hague Conference Member States.[113] These studies or reports were then distributed to the governments of the Members of the Conference at the beginning of the preparatory work on a convention project.[114] The success of the negotiations on the 1980

---

[107] See Hans van Loon, 'The Global Horizon of Private International Law' (2016) Offprint of the Recueil des Cours 380, 30; Beaumont/McEleavy, *Child Abduction* (n 68) 23; Smith, 'Achieving Results at International Meetings' (n 68) 418, 419.

[108] Cf Smith, 'Achieving Results at International Meetings' (n 68) 417 fn 4.

[109] Beaumont/McEleavy, *Child Abduction* (n 68) 23; Beaumont/McEleavy, *Anton's Private International Law* (n 68) [3.16].

[110] UNGA, 'Review of the Multilateral Treaty-Making Process' UNGA 35th Session UN Doc A/35/312 (1980), [25].

[111] Smith, 'Achieving Results at International Meetings' (n 68) 418; Beaumont/McEleavy, *Anton's Private International Law* (n 68) [3.16].

[112] Smith, ibid, 415, 418, 419; Beaumont/McEleavy, ibid, [3.17].

[113] Smith, ibid, 415, 419; Beaumont/McEleavy, ibid.

[114] See, e.g., regarding the work on the 1961 Apostille Convention: Georges A L Droz, 'Mémoire sur la notification des actes judiciaires et extrajudiciaires à l'étranger: Doc Prél No 2 d'Octobre 1963', in Conférence de la Haye de Droit International Privé, *Actes et Documents de la Dixième Session – 7 au 28 octobre 1964, Tome III, Notification* (Imprimerie Nationale 1965) 11–20; Beaumont/McEleavy, *Child Abduction* (n 68) 16–18; Pfund, 'Contributing to Progressive Development of Private International Law' (n 75) 26, 27; Smith, 'Achieving Results at International Meetings' (n 68) 418, 419.

Hague Child Abduction Convention, for example, was attributed in part to the thorough preparation of the topic by means of these questionnaires and reports.[115] These documents highlighted the main issues of the subject matter and ensured that all participants had a clear overview of the problems to be addressed by the future convention, the legal issues involved, and the possible solutions to the identified problems.[116] The dissemination of this crucial information to the participants ensured the pre-negotiation phase was very efficient.[117]

1.6. STAFF OF THE PERMANENT BUREAU

For conducting the legal research on the topics on the agenda of the Hague Conference, and for preparing new convention projects in general, the Permanent Bureau could draw on the knowledge of its Secretaries, recruited from different geographic regions of the world.[118] According to the original Statute of the Hague Conference, '[t]he Permanent Bureau [...] shall be composed of a Secretary General and two Secretaries of different nationalities'.[119] During the Diplomatic Sessions, the Secretary directly responsible for the project was part of the 'Bureau', the 'steering committee'[120] tasked with assisting the chair in conducting the plenary sessions.[121] By ensuring that the Secretaries represented different geographic regions (and usually different legal systems), the Permanent Bureau could rely on diverse legal expertise when working on future conventions. In 1992, the year in which the Judgments Project was initiated, the Permanent Bureau consisted of the following members: Secretary General M. Georges A L Droz (France), M. M L Pelichet (Switzerland), Mr C A Dyer (US) and M. J H A van Loon (the Netherlands).[122]

---

115 Carol S Bruch, 'How to Draft a Successful Family Law Convention: Lessons from the Child Abduction Conventions', in Jaap Doek et al (eds), *Children on the Move: How to Implement Their Right to Family Life* (Kluwer Law International 1999) 47, 48.

116 Beaumont/McEleavy, *Child Abduction* (n 68) 17, 18.

117 Dupont/Faure, 'The Negotiation Process', in Kremenyuk (n 65) 53.

118 Georges A L Droz, 'La Conférence de La Haye de droit international privé en 1980: Évolution et Perspectives' (1980) 168 Recueil des Cours de l'Académie de Droit International 123, 135.

119 Original Statute Hague Conference (n 18) art 4(1); cf now Statute Hague Conference (n 18) art 5(1), (2).

120 Ronald A Walker, *Manual for UN Delegates* (EBSCO Publishing 2011) 62.

121 Beaumont/McEleavy, *Child Abduction* (n 68) 25.

122 Cf 'Secretariat of the Seventeenth Session', in Hague Conference on Private International Law, *Proceedings of the Seventeenth Session, 10 to 29 May 1993, Tome I, Miscellaneous Matters* (SDU Publishers 1995) 14, 14.

1.7. CONCLUSION

The Hague Conference was an appropriate forum to host the work for a global judgments convention. Not only did negotiating at the Hague Conference suit the needs of the US for cooperating with the Member States of the EC and EFTA, but the Hague Conference also offered vast institutional knowledge, distinct working methods and (pre-)negotiation processes which made it a uniquely suitable forum to work towards the creation of a global judgments convention. Its processes allowed for equal participation of potentially all Hague Conference Member States throughout the whole process of drafting a convention text as a basis for official multilateral negotiations during the final Diplomatic Session. Moreover, the thorough preparation of new convention projects by the Permanent Bureau, through feasibility studies and comparative legal research, ensured that new conventions were adopted on a regular basis during every session of the Hague Conference.[123]

[123] See Lipstein (n 79) 650–653.

CHAPTER 2

DID THE JUDGMENTS PROJECT FAIL BECAUSE NO COMPREHENSIVE FEASIBILITY STUDIES REGARDING THE CONVENTION TYPE WERE PREPARED?

Part of the preparation of previous convention projects by the Permanent Bureau of the Hague Conference consisted of studies which assessed the feasibility of these new projects before a topic was put on the agenda of the organisation.[124] These feasibility studies were then used by the Hague Conference Member States to decide whether the new topic should be included in the agenda of the Hague Conference for future work, i.e. whether a new Hague instrument should be created on this topic.[125] These studies used to analyse, for example, whether the subject matter of the future convention was a suitable one for harmonisation in the first place,[126] or whether the potentially available methods to achieve harmonisation of the law through a Hague convention in this area were feasible methods.[127] For the Hague Judgments Project, however, no comprehensive feasibility studies were prepared concerning the question which convention type should be pursued by the Hague Conference Member States.[128] Why such

124 These studies have been called 'short feasibility studies', or 'pre-initiation studies', see UNGA, 'Review of the Multilateral Treaty-Making Process' UNGA 35th Session UN Doc A/35/312 (1980), [25]; see also Chapter 1.

125 Adair Dyer, 'Report on International Child Abduction by One Parent: Prel Doc No 1 of August 1978', in Conférence de la Haye de droit international privé, *Actes et documents de la Quatorzième session – 6 au 25 octobre 1980, Tome III, Child Abduction* (Imprimerie Nationale 1982) 12, 12; Van Loon, 'Report on Intercountry Adoption: Prel Doc No 1 of April 1990' (n 92) 15, 17, [1]–[4].

126 See, e.g, Adair Dyer, 'Feasibility Study on the Law Applicable to Labour (Employment) Contracts', in *Actes et Documents de la Quinzième Session, Tome I*, ibid 114, 115, 116.

127 Ch N Fragistas, 'Rapport explicatif', in Conférence de la Haye, *Actes et Documents de la session extraordinaire – 13 au 26 avril 1966* (Imprimerie Nationale 1969) 360, 364, 365 ('Nature de la Convention').

128 See also below, Section 4.4.1.1.

feasibility studies would have been needed, and the effect of the lack of these studies on the Judgments Project will be analysed in the following.

2.1. THE NEED FOR A FEASIBILITY STUDY ON THE CONVENTION TYPE (THE SINGLE, DOUBLE AND MIXED CONVENTION)

The goal of the Hague Judgments Project was to create an international convention that would have secured the recognition and enforcement of judgments in civil and commercial matters between the future Contracting States. Conceptually, three convention types are available to achieve this goal: a single convention, a ('complete' or 'strict') double convention, and a mixed convention.[129]

A single convention (sometimes also referred to as '*traité simple*' or '*convention imparfaite*')[130] only secures the recognition and enforcement of foreign judgments, without regulating the question of direct jurisdiction (the question of *whether* domestic courts have the power to hear the proceedings and render a judgment against the defendant) at the same time.[131] Instead, a single convention regulates jurisdiction only indirectly, by means of what are called 'indirect grounds of jurisdiction'.[132] These unified grounds of indirect jurisdiction are a necessary component of a single convention, since they ensure that the exercise of jurisdiction over the defendant in the court of origin was appropriate, and has not been exercised in an excessive manner.[133] The check of indirect jurisdiction is therefore a universal requirement for the recognition and enforcement of foreign judgments.[134] If the Contracting States to a judgments convention have agreed on the appropriateness of

129 'Conclusions of the Working Group: Prel Doc No 19 of November 1992' (n 28) [3]–[6]; von Mehren, 'Enforcing Judgments Abroad' (n 6) 17–19, 29.

130 Fragistas, 'Rapport explicatif' (n 127) 364; 'Conclusions of the Working Group: Prel Doc No 19 of November 1992' (n 28) [2].

131 Von Mehren, 'Enforcing Judgments Abroad' (n 6) 18; Permanent Bureau, 'Some Reflections of the Permanent Bureau on a General Convention on Enforcement of Judgments: Prel Doc No 17 of May 1992', in Hague Conference on Private International Law (eds), *Proceedings of the Seventeenth Session, 10 to 29 May 1993, Tome I, First Part, Miscellaneous matters* (SDU Publishers 1995) 231, [11]–[14].

132 Permanent Bureau, 'Some Reflections: Prel Doc No 17 of May 1992' (n 131) [12], [14], [17], [19]; these indirect grounds of jurisdiction have been called 'jurisdictional filters' in the context of the 2019 Hague Judgments Convention, see Garcimartín/Saumier (n 48) [144].

133 Cf Arthur Lenhoff, 'International Law and Rules on International Jurisdiction' (1964) 50 Cornell Law Review 5, 23.

134 Cf Lenhoff, ibid.

certain grounds of indirect jurisdiction, they regard exercising jurisdiction over a defendant on a jurisdictional provision matching this indirect ground as appropriate. As a result, if a judgment has been rendered in one Contracting State based on a jurisdictional provision matching an indirect ground of jurisdiction in the convention text, then this judgment can be recognised and enforced in another Contracting State.[135] For example, for the 2019 Hague Judgments Convention (a single convention), States have agreed that it is appropriate for a court to exercise jurisdiction over and to render a judgment against a defendant if that defendant was habitually resident in the forum State (the State in which the court seized of the proceedings is located) at the time the proceedings were initiated.[136]

As opposed to a single convention, a double convention (sometimes also referred to as '*convention parfaite*')[137] regulates the question of international direct jurisdiction for proceedings within its scope directly by means of a 'green list'.[138] This green list consists of unified jurisdictional provisions on which the Contracting States have agreed that exercising jurisdiction on these bases over a defendant is appropriate. The double convention is able to regulate jurisdiction in an exhaustive or exclusive way when it does not allow its Contracting States to use domestic grounds of jurisdiction any longer if the convention applies.[139] In this case, Contracting States are allowed to exercise jurisdiction *only* on the basis of those grounds of jurisdiction that have been included in the green list.[140] For this reason, this type of double convention has also been called a 'strict double convention', and this term will be used in the following.[141]

135 Von Mehren, 'Enforcing Judgments Abroad' (n 6) 18; Ch N Fragistas, 'Rapport de la Commission spécial', in Conférence de la Haye, *Actes et Documents de la session extraordinaire – 13 au 26 avril 1966* (Imprimerie Nationale 1969) 27, 28.

136 2019 Hague Judgments Convention (n 53), art 5(1)(a).

137 Fragistas, 'Rapport explicatif' (n 127) 364.

138 Von Mehren, 'New Approach' (n 1) 282, 283 ('white list'); for the sake of political correctness, 'green list' will be used instead of the term 'white list'.

139 Von Mehren, 'Enforcing Judgments Abroad' (n 6) 19.

140 Von Mehren, 'New Approach' (n 1) 282, 283; von Mehren, 'Enforcing Judgments Abroad' (n 6), 19; an example for such a green list is Title II of the Convention on jurisdiction and the enforcement of judgments in civil and commercial matters (adopted 27 September 1968, entered into force 1 February 1973) (1968 Brussels Convention) [1972] OJ L299/32.

141 Catherine Kessedjian, 'International Jurisdiction and Foreign Judgments in Civil and Commercial Matters: Prel Doc No 7 of April 1997', in *Proceedings of the Twentieth Session, Tome II* (n 29) 13, [143], [154], [156], [157], [159], [179]; Arthur T von Mehren, 'Theory and Practice of Adjudicatory Authority' (2002) 295 Recueil de Cours de l'Académie International 9, 405; von Mehren, 'New Approach' (n 1) 282, 283 ('true *convention double*').

Furthermore, a strict double convention ensures that judgments that have been rendered on the basis of one of the jurisdictional provisions of the green list in one Contracting State are recognised and enforced in all the other Contracting States.[142] Examples for a strict double convention on a regional level are the 1968 Brussels Convention (in force for the EC Member States at the time the Judgments Project was initiated),[143] and its parallel instrument, the 1988 Lugano Convention.[144]

The third convention type available to create a judgments convention, the mixed convention, had been recommended by the US American scholar Arthur T von Mehren as the convention model which should be chosen as the basis for the work on the Judgments Project.[145] Unlike the strict double convention, a mixed convention does not aspire to regulate the exercise of international direct jurisdiction over defendants exhaustively.[146] Rather, the mixed-convention concept would have contained only some unified grounds of direct jurisdiction (by means of the green list), but it would have allowed its Contracting States to continue to exercise jurisdiction over defendants also on the basis of domestic jurisdictional provisions (the 'grey area').[147] This 'grey area' of domestic grounds of jurisdiction would have therefore existed in addition to the green list of jurisdictional provisions contained in the convention text.[148] If a Contracting State to the mixed convention had rendered a judgment against a defendant based on a jurisdictional provision appearing in the green list of the convention, then the recognition and enforcement of the

142 Von Mehren, 'New Approach' (n 1) 282, 283.

143 1968 Brussels Convention (n 140).

144 Convention on jurisdiction and the recognition and enforcement of judgments in civil and commercial matters (adopted 16 September 1988, entered into force 1 January 1992) SR 0.275.11 (1988 Lugano Convention); in 1992, the 1988 Lugano Convention had extended the rules of the 1968 Brussels Convention to the EFTA Member State Switzerland, see ibid, preamble.

145 Von Mehren, 'New Approach' (n 1) 272, 283–287; Von Mehren, 'Recognition of United States Judgments Abroad' (n 70) 458, 459. Hans Sperl had hinted at the idea of the possibility of creating an international convention regulating international direct jurisdiction in a non-exhaustive way in 1926, see Hans Sperl, *Eine internationale Zuständigkeitsordnung in bürgerlichen Rechtssachen* (Hölder-Pichler-Tempsky AG 1926) 15.

146 Von Mehren, 'Recognition of United States Judgments Abroad' (n 70) 458; von Mehren, 'New Approach' (n 1) 283.

147 Von Mehren, 'New Approach' (n 1) 283, 284.

148 Von Mehren, 'New Approach' (n 1) 283; Olivier Tell, 'Tentative Draft on the Jurisdiction and the Enforcement of Foreign Judgments: Can a Mixed Convention Work?', in John J Barceló, Kevin M Clermont (eds), *A Global Law of Jurisdiction and Judgments: Lessons from The Hague* (2002 Kluwer Law International) 37, 37–39.

resulting judgment was guaranteed.[149] If jurisdiction had been exercised on a domestic jurisdictional provision, the recognition and enforcement of the resulting judgment depended on the domestic law of the State addressed. Since a mixed convention creates some unified jurisdictional provisions by means of the green list, it is also a double convention (but not a strict one).[150]

Finally, another important aspect of regulating jurisdiction by means of an international convention was the opportunity to ban the use of certain grounds of jurisdiction that were considered to be excessive, or exorbitant.[151] Under the mixed-convention concept, it would have been possible to prohibit courts in Contracting States from exercising excessive jurisdiction over defendants for proceedings within the convention scope by means of a 'red list'.[152] Furthermore, it would have been possible to prohibit States from recognising and enforcing judgments rendered on the basis of an exorbitant jurisdictional provision (by including a 'red list of indirect grounds of jurisdiction' into the convention text).[153] In a strict double convention, technically such red lists of direct and indirect grounds were not needed because jurisdiction could only be exercised on the basis of the green list in the first place, and only judgments rendered on the basis of the green list would be recognised and enforced.[154]

Studying the feasibility of the different convention types and of the different levels of regulating jurisdiction and the recognition and enforcement of judgments would have been required for various reasons. Due to the challenges of creating unified grounds of jurisdiction on a global level, the feasibility of creating a strict double convention had been rejected in the past. This convention type had been regarded as unfeasible both during the first attempt to create a global double convention at the

149 Von Mehren, 'New Approach' (n 1) 283.

150 Von Mehren, 'Enforcing Judgments Abroad' (n 6) 19.

151 For a definition of this term, see above (n 71).

152 Von Mehren, New Approach' (n 1) 283, 287 ('black list'); for the sake of political correctness, the term 'red list' will be used hereafter; von Mehren, 'Enforcing Judgments Abroad' (n 6) 19 ('prohibited bases').

153 cf Article 4 of the Supplementary Protocol to the 1971 Hague Judgments Convention (n 23), which as a rule could have obliged States not to recognise and enforce judgments rendered on such a basis (see Articles 2 and 3 of the Protocol); see also Ralf Michaels, 'Some Fundamental Conceptions as Applied in Judgment Conventions', in Eckart Gottschalk et al (eds), *Conflict of Laws in a Globalized World: A Tribute to Arthur von Mehren* (CUP 2007) 38 ('excluded bases of indirect jurisdiction').

154 Von Mehren, 'Enforcing Judgments Abroad' (n 6) 23.

first session of the Hague Conference,[155] and during the preparatory work for the 1971 Hague Judgments Convention, the forerunner of the Hague Judgments Project.[156] In the 1960s, the view had been that the judicial and practical integration of the Member States of the Hague Conference would not allow for the creation of an exhaustive list of direct grounds of jurisdiction, which would have distributed the power of courts to hear proceedings in civil and commercial matters with a cross-border element among the Hague Conference Member States.[157] The number of Hague Conference Member States in 1962 (19)[158] had been considered too large, and the national legal systems of these Member States too different, so that reaching an agreement on an exhaustive list of direct grounds of jurisdiction seemed unrealistic.[159] By June 1994, the number of Hague Conference Member States had more than doubled to 41.[160] Harmonising different grounds of jurisdiction is further complicated by the fact that different stakeholders with different interests are involved in the process of international civil litigation. These stakeholders are in particular the forum State, the defendant, the claimant, and the State addressed for the recognition and enforcement of a foreign judgment. For creating rules of jurisdiction, the interests of these different stakeholders have to be balanced.[161]

From the perspective of the forum State (i.e., the State in which the court that has been seized by the claimant is located), regulating jurisdiction through a multilateral instrument concerns their ability to render judgments against a defendant (through their domestic courts), and to thereby settle these disputes by creating enforceable titles (i.e., enforceable decisions,

---

155 See above, Introduction at 1, and references at (n 10).

156 1971 Hague Judgments Convention (n 22).

157 Fragistas, 'Rapport de la Commission spécial', in *Actes et Documents de la session extraordinaire – 13 au 26 avril 1966* (n 127) 25.

158 The following were Member States of the Hague Conference in 1962: Austria, Belgium, Denmark, Egypt, Finland, Germany, Greece, Ireland, Italy, Japan, Luxembourg, the Netherlands, Norway, Portugal, Spain, Sweden, Switzerland, Turkey and the United Kingdom, see Hague Conference on Private International Law, 'Statue Hague Conference: Status Table' <https://www.hcch.net/en/instruments/conventions/status-table/?cid=29> accessed 3 April 2023.

159 Fragistas, 'Rapport explicatif' (n 127) 360, 364, 365.

160 The following States had joined the Hague Conference, adding even more diversity to the legal systems represented in this international organisation: Argentina, Australia, Canada, Chile, China (People's Republic of), Cyprus, Czech Republic, France, Hungary, Israel, Latvia, Mexico, Morocco, Poland, Romania, Slovakia, Slovenia, Suriname, Uruguay, the US and Venezuela, see 'Statue Hague Conference: Status Table' (n 158).

161 Von Mehren, 'Enforcing Judgments Abroad' (n 6) 25, 26.

judgments or orders for payment).[162] At the same time, if a State has jurisdiction over a dispute, this entails that it also has the ability to apply its own law to the dispute (depending on the domestic choice-of-law rules in force). Through applying its own law, the State with jurisdiction can foster important policies.[163] Essentially, from the point of view of the forum State, regulating jurisdiction directly concerns their sovereignty.[164] Defendants, and in particular defendants in international civil proceedings, have an interest in being sued in a forum that is geographically convenient for them,[165] and that the provision attributing jurisdiction is fair and just from their point of view.[166] From the point of view of the claimant, it is important that the jurisdictional rules in force in a State guarantee the availability of a forum so that claims can be enforced, i.e., that access to justice is guaranteed.[167] Finally, if a judgment is meant to be recognised and enforced abroad (for example because the judgment debtor does not have assets in the forum State), it is as a rule necessary that the exercise of jurisdiction over the defendant is acceptable also from the point of view of the State addressed for recognition and/or enforcement (this is the question of 'indirect jurisdiction').[168] In drafting the grounds of jurisdiction for a multilateral convention, not only would it have been necessary to balance these different interests, but different States would also put a varying emphasis on the interests of different stakeholders, which further complicated the drafting process.[169]

Not only was the attempt to unify grounds of jurisdiction challenging per se, but also the vehicle to achieve this unification, the convention type (i.e., the strict double convention and the mixed convention), would have required further studies, as the feasibility of both convention types had been rejected in the past. As discussed above in the Introduction, the feasibility of creating a double convention had been rejected during the first Diplomatic Session of the Hague Conference. During the preparatory work on the 1971 Hague Judgments Convention, the mixed convention

162 Hans Smit, 'Common and Civil Law Rules of in Personam Adjudicatory Authority: An Analysis of Underlying Policies' (1972) 21 ICLQ 335, 339.
163 See, e.g., Hartley, *International Commercial Litigation* (n 2) 15.
164 Herrup/Brand, 'A Hague Convention on Parallel Proceedings' (n 56) 3.
165 Von Mehren, 'Enforcing Judgments Abroad' (n 6) 25; Smit, 'Common and Civil Law Rules of in Personam Adjudicatory Authority' (n 162) 335.
166 Hartley, *International Commercial Litigation* (n 2) 14, 15.
167 Von Mehren, 'Enforcing Judgments Abroad' (n 6) 25.
168 Cf von Mehren, 'Enforcing Judgments Abroad' (n 6) 25; Hartley, *International Commercial Litigation* (n 2) 13, 14; see also below, Section 3.1.1.
169 Von Mehren, 'Can the Hague Conference Project Succeed?' (n 31) 194, 195, 201; see also below, Section 2.2.

concept had been discussed and rejected.[170] What is more, the mixed convention was a relatively novel convention concept, even if it had been briefly discussed by the Austrian legal scholar Hans Sperl in 1926.[171] These reasons would have warranted feasibility studies in the context of the preparations for the Hague Judgments Project. However, in reality, no comprehensive feasibility studies had been prepared by the Permanent Bureau, neither on the question of whether the unification of grounds of international direct jurisdiction was technically feasible in the first place, nor on whether the available methods to achieve the unification of jurisdiction and of rules on the recognition and enforcement of foreign judgments (the strict double convention and the mixed convention) were feasible methods.[172] The next question which must be addressed, therefore, in order to understand why the Hague Judgments Project failed, is whether the fact that no feasibility studies on the convention type had been prepared contributed to the failure of the project.

2.2. THE FEASIBILITY OF UNIFYING GROUNDS OF JURISDICTION

A study of the feasibility of unifying grounds of direct jurisdiction by means of an international instrument should have highlighted the general challenges discussed above, and analysed the particular legal and political circumstances affecting the regimes of international direct jurisdiction in the US and the Member States of the EC, the two most important actors during the Judgments Project.[173] To illustrate the difficulties of creating globally applicable rules of

---

170 During the Ninth Session, it was discussed whether a single convention could also provide for one ground of direct jurisdiction for choice of court, see Georges Droz, 'Mémoire sur la question de la reconnaissance et de l'exécution des jugements étrangers en matière patrimoniale – Document préliminaire No 1 de janvier 1962' in Conférence de la Haye, *Actes et Documents de la session extraordinaire – 13 au 26 avril 1966* (Imprimerie National 1969) 9, 14; if such a provision providing for direct jurisdiction on choice of court could have been agreed upon, then the 1971 Hague Judgments Convention (n 22) would have become the first mixed convention. At the time, however, it was felt that such a hybrid text would be unacceptable to some states, see Fragistas, 'Rapport de la Commission spécial' in *Actes et Documents de la session extraordinaire – 13 au 26 avril 1966* (n 127) 32, quoting the then Secretary General of the Hague Conference on Private International Law, Mr van Hoogstraten.

171 Sperl (n 145) 15.

172 See further discussion in Section 4.4.

173 A judgments convention without these two stakeholders as parties could not have been considered to be a successful convention, Andreas Bucher, 'Vers une convention mondiale sur la compétence et les jugements étrangers' (2000) 2 La Semaine Judiciaire 77, 77–79.

jurisdiction, the following will compare the rules underlying the jurisdictional concepts in the US and the EC Member States (as enshrined in the 1968 Brussels Convention) in more detail. The differences between these two stakeholders in terms of jurisdictional concepts were particularly wide,[174] and the particularities of each system would have made an agreement on common grounds of jurisdiction challenging. In the US, the limits of the exercise of jurisdiction over a defendant were prescribed by the Due Process clause of the US constitution.[175] In the case of the Member States of the EC, rules for international direct jurisdiction had already been unified by means of a multilateral convention, the 1968 Brussels Convention. Creating an exhaustive green list would have therefore required convergence between the constitutional approach of the US to regulating direct jurisdiction, and the supranational approach of the 1968 Brussels Convention.[176]

2.2.1. CONSTITUTIONAL LIMITS TO THE EXERCISE OF INTERNATIONAL DIRECT JURISDICTION IN THE UNITED STATES

In the US, the exercise of international direct jurisdiction over an 'out-of-state', i.e. a foreign defendant[177] (a defendant resident (or registered or incorporated, in case of corporate defendants) in another US state, or abroad) must meet the standards set by the Due Process Clause of the 14th Amendment of the US Constitution.[178] The 14th Amendment to the US Constitution requires that '[no state shall] deprive any person of life, liberty, or property, without due process of law'. According to the Due Process Clause, the exercise of state power over a person must meet the requirements of this clause. Since the exercise of jurisdiction is the exercise of state power, the reach of jurisdictional provisions cannot go further than allowed by the Due Process Clause. These limits to jurisdiction have been further defined by the case law of the US Supreme Court.[179] According to the US Supreme Court, the exercise of jurisdiction over an

174 Von Mehren, 'Can the Hague Conference Project Succeed?' (n 31) 195, 201.

175 Amendments to the Constitution of the United States of America, 5th Amendment, 14th Amendment.

176 Cf von Mehren, 'Can the Hague Conference Project Succeed?' (n 31) 201.

177 *Goodyear Dunlop Tires Operations, SA, et al v. Edgar D Brown et ux*, 564 US 915, 919 (2011); *Daimler AG v. Bauman et al* 571 US 117, 126 (2014).

178 *International Shoe v. State of Washington* 326 US 310, 316 (1945).

179 See, e.g., *International Shoe v. State of Washington* 326 US 310, 316 (1945); *Daimler AG v. Bauman et al* 571 US 117, 126 (2014).

out-of-state defendant (also called personal jurisdiction, or *in personam* jurisdiction in the US)[180] always requires a certain amount of contacts between the defendant and the forum state in order to meet these due-process requirements.[181] By requiring some contacts (i.e. connections) between the defendant and the forum under what has been called the 'minimum contacts' doctrine, the defendant is meant to be protected against having to defend him/herself in a forum that is inconvenient for them, i.e., the defendant is meant to be protected against unreasonable or unfair litigation.[182] Depending on the quality and quantity of the defendant's contacts, or connections, with the forum state, the court addressed can either exercise general jurisdiction[183] (the power to render a judgment against the out-of-state defendant regarding claims completely unrelated to the activities of the defendant in the forum state, also called 'all-purpose jurisdiction'),[184] or jurisdiction regarding specific contacts of the defendant with the forum, out of which the claim giving rise to the proceedings originated, or to which the claim related ('specific jurisdiction').[185] Specific jurisdiction can be exercised if the contacts of the defendant with the forum are 'continuous and systematic [and] give rise to the liabilities sued on'.[186] Also 'the commission of "single or occasional acts" in a state can be sufficient to render a corporation answerable in that state with respect to those acts, though not with respect to matters unrelated to the forum connections.'[187] General jurisdiction, on the other

[180] *International Shoe v. State of Washington* 326 US 310, 316 (1945); Hartley, *International Commercial Litigation* (n 2) 12; Patrick Borchers, 'Comparing Personal Jurisdiction' (1992) 40 Am J Comp L 121, 123.

[181] Ibid; *Helicopteros Nacionales v. Hall* 466 US 408, 414 (1984).

[182] *International Shoe v. State of Washington* 326 US 310, 316 (1945): 'due process requires only that, in order to subject a defendant to a judgment in personam, if he be not present within the territory of the forum, he have certain minimum contacts with it such that the maintenance of the suit does not offend "traditional notions of fair play and substantial justice"'; *World Wide Volkswagen v. Woodson* 444 US 286, 292 (1980).

[183] *Helicopteros Nacionales v. Hall* 466 US 408, 414 (1984); the term had been coined by von Mehren and Trautman, 'Jurisdiction to Adjudicate' (n 2) 1136 and is now used also outside the US legal system, see, e.g., Hartley, *International Commercial Litigation* (n 2) 16.

[184] *International Shoe v. State of Washington* 326 US 310, 318 (1945); *Helicopteros Nacionales v. Hall* 466 US 408, 414 (1984); *Goodyear Dunlop Tires Operations, SA, et al v. Edgar D Brown et ux*, 564 US 915, 919 (2011); *Daimler AG v. Bauman et al* 571 US 117, 121, 122 (2014).

[185] *Goodyear Dunlop Tires Operations, SA, et al v. Edgar D Brown et ux*, 564 US 915, 919 (2011).

[186] *International Shoe v. State of Washington* 326 US 310, 317 (1945); see also *Daimler AG v. Bauman et al*, 571 US 117, 121 (2014).

[187] *International Shoe v. State of Washington* 326 US 310, 318 (1945).

hand, can be exercised if the contacts of the out-of-state defendant with the forum are 'so substantial and of such a nature as to justify suit against [the defendant] on causes of action arising from dealings entirely distinct from those activities.'[188] It was very unlikely that the US Supreme Court could have accepted jurisdictional provisions created by a multilateral treaty that were not meeting the due-process requirements of the US Constitution.[189]

2.2.2. THE BRUSSELS CONVENTION'S APPROACH TO REGULATING INTERNATIONAL DIRECT JURISDICTION

For the Member States of the EC, the 1968 Brussels Convention had introduced supranational standards for exercising international jurisdiction over defendants domiciled in one of its Contracting States when it entered into force in 1973.[190] The 1968 Brussels Convention had been negotiated between the original six Member States of the EC (Belgium, France, Germany, Italy, Luxembourg and the Netherlands),[191] and it had 12 Member States in 1992 when the US approached the Hague Conference with the suggestion to create a new Hague Judgments Convention.[192] The 1988 Lugano Convention[193] had extended the rules of the 1968 Brussels Convention to Switzerland.[194] Moreover, in 1992, the EFTA Member States

---

188 Ibid.

189 Harold G Maier, 'A Hague Conference Judgments Convention and United States Courts: A Problem and a Possibility' (1998) 61 Alb L Rev 207, 209; Joachim Zekoll, 'The Role and Status of American Law in the Hague Judgments Project' (1998) 61 Alb L Rev 1283, 1286.

190 1968 Brussels Convention (n 140) art 2(1).

191 1968 Brussels Convention (n 140) preamble.

192 Besides the original six Contracting States, Denmark, Ireland, the United Kingdom, Greece, Spain and Portugal were also Contracting States to the Brussels Convention in 1992, see Fausto Pocar, 'Convention on jurisdiction and the recognition and enforcement of judgments in civil and commercial matters, signed in Lugano on 30 October 2007 – Explanatory Report' [2009] OJ 319/1 (Pocar Report), fn 3; all of these States were also Member States of the Hague Conference, see 'Statue Hague Conference – Status Table' (n 158).

193 1988 Lugano Convention (n 144); in 2010, the 1988 Lugano Convention was replaced by a revised version, the Convention on jurisdiction and the recognition and enforcement of judgments in civil and commercial matters (concluded 30 October 2007, entered into force 1 January 2010) SR 0.275.12 (2007 Lugano Convention).

194 1988 Lugano Convention (n 144) preamble; see also EDA, 'Convention concernant la compétence judiciaire et l'exécution des décisions en matière civile et commerciale faite à Lugano le 16 septembre 1988: Parties' <https://www.eda.admin.ch/dam/eda/

Austria, Finland, Norway and Sweden, which were also Member States of the Hague Conference, had already signed the Lugano Convention, and it was foreseeable that the Lugano Convention would enter into force for them eventually.[195] For disputes falling within their scope, the 1968 Brussels Convention and the 1988 Lugano Convention had created an exhaustive, unified regime of grounds of international direct jurisdiction for proceedings against defendants with a domicile in a Brussels/Lugano State,[196] coupled with a system to ensure the recognition and enforcement of civil and commercial judgments rendered in the Contracting States.[197] Since the Brussels Convention (and the Lugano Convention) regulated jurisdiction exhaustively for proceedings within its scope when the defendant was domiciled in a Contracting State, it was a strict double convention in this regard.[198] The Permanent Bureau acknowledged in one of its Preliminary Documents in 1992 that it would be very hard for the Contracting Parties to the Brussels Convention and the Lugano Convention to diverge from the jurisdictional standards set in these instruments: 'unless the new grounds of jurisdiction were to be framed very close to those of the Lugano Convention, one may expect some reluctance on the part of (some of) the Lugano countries to accept such grounds.'[199] Apparently, there was some concern among the Contracting Parties to the Brussels Convention and Lugano Convention (the Brussels/Lugano States) that these conventions could be devalued if a global Hague Convention employed connecting factors for exercising jurisdiction over defendants that differed from the ones used by these instruments.[200] Oddly, these reasonable concerns by the Permanent Bureau were not repeated when the majority of governmental

---

fr/documents/aussenpolitik/voelkerrecht/autres-conventions/lugano1/Lugano-1-parties_fr.pdf> accessed 7 April 2023; 1988 Lugano Convention (n 144) preamble.

195 1988 Lugano Convention: Parties (n 144), and Convention establishing the European Free Trade Association (signed 4 January 1960, entered into force 3 May 1960) 370 UNTS 5 (EFTA Convention), preamble; 'Statue Hague Conference: Status Table' (n 158).

196 1968 Brussels Convention (n 140)/1988 Lugano Convention (n 144), art 2(1), (2), art 3(1), (2); Paul Jenard, 'Report on the Convention on jurisdiction and the enforcement of judgments in civil and commercial matters' [1979] OJ C59/1 (Jenard Report) 13; some jurisdictional provisions also applied for defendants with a domicile in third States, see below, Section 3.2.2.

197 Ibid Title I, Title III.

198 1968 Brussels Convention (n 140)/1988 Lugano Convention (n 144) art 2(1), art 3(1); art 26(1), art 31.

199 Permanent Bureau, 'Some Reflections: Prel Doc No 17 of May 1992' (n 131) 239 [16], see also [12]; see also below, Section 4.4.1.1.

200 Cf Paul R Beaumont, 'A United Kingdom Perspective on the Proposed Hague Judgments Convention' (1998) 24 Brook J Int'l L 75, 93.

experts expressed a preference for negotiating a double convention during the Special Commission meeting in June 1994.[201]

2.2.2.1. *General and Specific Jurisdiction: The Brussels Convention Approach and the United States Constitutional Approach Compared*

Big differences of opinion existed between the US and the Brussels/Lugano States regarding the question of whether general jurisdiction should be exercised on the basis of continuous and systematic business contacts of an out-of-state defendant with the forum, a jurisdictional standard employed in the US.[202] Other countries, and especially countries with a civil law tradition, regarded the exercise of this type of jurisdiction over foreign defendants as exorbitant in its reach and refused to recognise and enforce judgments rendered on this basis.[203] Moreover, in the US, general jurisdiction could be exercised over an out-of-state defendant (i.e., a non-resident defendant) on the basis that they were served with a claim form while being temporarily present in the forum state (also called 'tag jurisdiction', or 'transient jurisdiction').[204] This too was considered

201 See Permanent Bureau of the Hague Conference on Private International Law, 'Conclusions of the Special Commission of June 1994 on the Question of the Recognition and Enforcement of Foreign Judgments in Civil and Commercial Matters: Prel Doc No 2 of December 1995 for the attention of the Special Commission of June 1996 on the question of the recognition and enforcement of foreign judgments in civil and commercial matters' <https://assets.hcch.net/docs/4a144f70-bab3-4d18-85bc-646b24d7c640.pdf> accessed 3 April 2023, [6].

202 *International Shoe v. State of Washington* 326 US 310, 318 (1945): 'there have been instances in which the continuous corporate operations within a state were thought *so substantial* and of *such a nature* as to justify suit against it on causes of action arising from dealings entirely distinct from those activities' (emphasis added); Kevin M Clermont, 'Jurisdictional Salvation and the Hague Treaty' (1999–2000) 85 Cornell L Rev 89, 114, 115; in 2011, the US Supreme Court narrowed the reach of general doing business jurisdiction by requiring that the contacts of the defendant with the forum state should be such as to make the defendant essentially 'at home' in the forum state, see *Goodyear Dunlop Tires Operations, SA, et al v. Edgar D Brown et ux*, 564 US 915, 919 (2011); a foreign corporation is in particular 'at home' at its place of incorporation, or its principal place of business, see *Daimler AG v. Bauman et al*, 571 US 117, 137 (2014).

203 See, e.g., Bucher, 'Vers une convention mondiale' (n 173) 77, 79.

204 *Burnham v. Superior Court of California* 495 US 604 (1990); Hartley, *International Commercial Litigation* (n 2) 184; Arthur T von Mehren, 'Recognition and Enforcement of Foreign Judgments – General Theory and the Role of Jurisdictional Requirements' (1980) 167 Recueil des Cours de l'Académie de Droit International 9, 53; personal jurisdiction could also be exercised over an out-of-state defendant on the basis of

exorbitant, or inappropriate, from the point of view of most of the other Member States of the Hague Conference, and in particular of those following a civil law tradition.[205] Under the 1968 Brussels Convention, general jurisdiction could only be exercised in the State of the defendant's domicile.[206]

Moreover, there were differences between the US and Brussels Convention's approaches to specific, or special, jurisdiction (i.e., jurisdiction where the power to exercise jurisdiction of a court depended on the specific claim).[207] According to the 1968 Brussels Convention, specific jurisdiction in contractual matters could be exercised over a defendant with a domicile in one of the other Contracting States where the place of performance of the obligation in question was located.[208] According to the case law of the European Court of Justice (hereafter ECJ),[209] the 'obligation in question' referred to the obligation on which the claim was based, 'namely the contractual obligation of the grantor [defendant] which corresponded to the contractual right relied upon by the grantee [claimant] in support of the application.'[210] In addition, the place where this obligation was to be performed had to be determined by the applicable law designated by the forum State.[211]

From a US point of view, such a mechanical way of determining jurisdiction over an out-of-state defendant was very difficult to accept. Rather, the exercise of specific jurisdiction over a foreign defendant at the place of performance of a contract was only acceptable if the defendant had certain minimum contacts with the place of performance of the contract, making the exercise of jurisdiction fair and reasonable in the specific case.[212] In later judgments, the US Supreme Court held that in cases where specific jurisdiction was to be exercised on the basis of a single contract

consent, see Eugene F Scoles, Peter Hay, *Conflict of Laws* (2nd edn, West Publishing Co 1992) 267, 275–285, 332–334.

205 See, e.g., Bucher, 'Vers une convention mondiale' (n 173) 79.

206 1968 Brussels Convention (n 140)/1988 Lugano Convention (n 144) art 2(1).

207 Von Mehren, Trautman, 'Jurisdiction to Adjudicate' (n 2) 1136; Borchers (n 180) 133.

208 1968 Brussels Convention (n 140)/1988 Lugano Convention (n 144) art 4(1), art 5(1).

209 Now Court of Justice of the European Union (CJEU), Treaty on European Union (Consolidated version 2016) [2016] OJ C 202/13, art 13(1), art 19; Treaty on the Functioning of the European Union (Consolidated Version 2016) (TFEU) [2016] OJ C202/47, art 251.

210 Case 14/76 *De Bloos v. Bouyer* EU:C:1976:134, [1976] ECR 01497, [15].

211 Case 12-76 *Industrie Tessili Italiana Como v. Dunlop AG* EU:C:1976:133, [1976] ECR 01473, [13].

212 *International Shoe v. State of Washington* 326 US 310, 317 (1945) (regarding a corporate defendant); *World Wide Volkswagen v. Woodson*; Ronald A Brand, 'Due Process, Jurisdiction, and a Hague Judgments Project' (1998) 60 U Pitt L Rev 661, 680; Bucher, 'Vers une convention mondiale' (n 173) 84.

that the defendant must have shown some intent to avail him-or herself of the protection of the laws in a State by conducting activities within the forum State.[213] In *Burger King*, the US Supreme Court clarified that it had 'long ago rejected the notion that personal jurisdiction might turn on "mechanical" tests [...] or on "conceptualistic ... theories of the place of contracting or of performance".'[214] Rather, in order to determine whether the exercise of jurisdiction in contractual matters was appropriate, the US Supreme Court would apply

> a 'highly realistic' approach that recognizes that a 'contract' is 'ordinarily but an intermediate step serving to tie up prior business negotiations with future consequences which themselves are the real object of the business transaction.' [...] It is these factors, prior negotiations and contemplated future consequences, along with the terms of the contract and the parties' actual course of dealing that must be evaluated in determining whether the defendant purposefully established minimum contacts within the forum.[215]

Furthermore, another type of jurisdiction admitted by the 1968 Brussels Convention was difficult to reconcile with US due-process standards. The 1968 Brussels Convention allowed the exercise of direct jurisdiction over a defendant domiciled in another Contracting State for matters relating to tort or delict at the place where a harmful event occurred.[216] According to the interpretation by the ECJ, 'the place where the harmful event occurred' encompassed both the place where the harmful event leading to the damage occurred, and the place where the actual harm occurred.[217] Exercising jurisdiction at the place where the actual harm occurred could have violated US due-process standards if the harm had manifested in a State in which the defendant had not exercised any activity. In this case, the exercise of jurisdiction was unforeseeable for the defendant and therefore unreasonable, thereby violating due-process standards.[218]

---

213 *Lakeside Bridge & Steel Co v. Mountain State Construction Co, Inc* (7th Cir 1979) 597 F2d 596.

214 *Burger King v. Rudzewicz* 471 US 462, 478 (1985).

215 Ibid 479.

216 1968 Brussels Convention (n 140)/1988 Lugano Convention (n 144) art 5(3).

217 Case C-21/76 *Bier v Mines de Potasse d'Alsace* EU:C:1976:166, [1976] ECR 1976-01735, [24].

218 In *Worldwide Volkswagen v. Woodson* 444 US 286, 299 (1980), the US Supreme Court decided that the sole fact that a car which had been sold by the defendant to the claimants in New York caught fire in Oklahoma due to a construction fault was not enough to establish minimum contacts between the defendant and the forum in Oklahoma.

2.2.2.2. *Further Particularities of United States Law on International Direct Jurisdiction*

Efforts to converge the US approach to international direct jurisdiction and the Brussels/Lugano Convention approach were made even more complicated by the fact that the US rules on jurisdiction were contained in a large body of case law generated by the US Supreme Court. In the 1980s and the 1990s, American scholars had struggled to develop clear doctrines for the exercise of international direct jurisdiction from this body of case law.[219] This was due inter alia to the fact that in some cases, the opinions of the judges were equally divided, and no plurality opinion could be established on certain questions relating to international direct jurisdiction. One example concerned the standards for exercising specific jurisdiction in product liability cases. In *Asahi*, the US Supreme Court denied jurisdiction of the Florida courts over Asahi, a company domiciled in Japan.[220] The cross-defendant Asahi manufactured tyre valves and sold them to tyre manufacturers all over the world, inter alia to a company based in Taiwan (Cheng Shin rubber).[221] Cheng Shin in turn sold some of these tyres with the valves produced by Asahi to companies in the US which were manufacturing motorcycles. One of these motorcycles had an accident in Florida, allegedly because the tyre valve was faulty.[222] The victim brought proceedings against Cheng Shin, which in turn filed a cross-complaint against Asahi in Florida.[223] While the original claim against Cheng Shin was settled, the dispute regarding the jurisdiction of the Florida courts over Asahi led to a decision by the US Supreme Court.[224] Eight judges of the Court agreed that the Florida courts did not have jurisdiction in the case. They disagreed, however, on the reasons for declining jurisdiction.

Four judges were of the opinion that jurisdiction should be declined due to a lack of minimum contacts between Asahi and the forum. Although it might have been foreseeable to Asahi that its valves might be swept into the state of Florida by the stream of commerce, mere foreseeability of this result was not sufficient to establish minimum contacts between Asahi and

---

219 Friedrich K Juenger, 'A Shoe Unfit for Globetrotting' (1995) 28 UC Davis L Rev 1027, 1040; Clermont, 'Jurisdictional Salvation and the Hague Treaty' (n 202) 84: '[t]he United States' law of territorial jurisdiction is a mess'.

220 *Asahi Metal Industry Co v. Superior Court* 480 US 102, 102, 116 (1987).

221 Ibid 106.

222 Ibid 105, 106.

223 Ibid 106.

224 Ibid 106, 108.

the forum state.[225] Rather, in order to establish such minimum contacts, it was required to show that Asahi had an intent to serve the Florida market, and to avail itself purposefully of the privilege to do business in Florida.[226] The other four judges were of the opinion that the mere placement of the valves into the stream of commerce should have been enough to establish minimum contacts between Asahi and Florida. Asahi could have reasonably foreseen that its valves could end up in Florida, and that potential lawsuits might result from the sale of its products there.[227] Furthermore, since the valves were marketed in Florida, these sales were also protected by Florida laws.[228] Therefore the defendant would have benefitted indirectly from the protection of the laws of Florida, and it would have indirectly availed itself of the privilege of doing business in Florida.[229] Nevertheless, these judges thought that it would be unreasonable all the same to make Asahi defend itself in a State far away from its home forum in Japan.[230]

These divided plurality opinions made it difficult to assess the limits of international direct jurisdiction according to US law. Furthermore, the case law of the US Supreme Court also employed terminology whose exact meaning depended on the single case and did not lend itself to the drafting of generally applicable rules. As explained above, in order to validly exercise international direct jurisdiction over an out-of-state defendant, it was necessary for the defendant to have what is called 'minimum contacts' with the forum 'such that the maintenance of the suit [does] not offend "traditional notions of fair play and substantial justice"'.[231] Both of these prongs of jurisdictional analysis were quite vague and could not be cast easily into legal provisions. The purpose of both prongs was to ensure justice for the defendant in the specific case, which made it difficult to develop generally applicable standards. This state of US law on international direct jurisdiction with unclear doctrines and vague terminology created an additional obstacle to the process of creating unified grounds of international direct jurisdiction through a multilateral convention.[232]

---

225 Ibid 103, 104.

226 Ibid 112.

227 Ibid.

228 Ibid.

229 Ibid.

230 Ibid 116.

231 *International Shoe v. State of Washington* 326 US 310, 316 (1945).

232 Juenger, 'A Shoe Unfit for Globetrotting' (n 219) 1040: '[t]he difficulty of presenting our confused jurisdictional law to the outside world is bound to impede the negotiation of recognition treaties and conventions with foreign nations'. This confused state of the US law on jurisdiction might already have hindered the negotiations of a bilateral

2.3. THE CONTENT OF A FEASIBILITY STUDY CONCERNING THE CREATION OF A STRICT DOUBLE CONVENTION AND A MIXED CONVENTION

In addition to analysing the general challenges of creating global rules of jurisdiction between the Hague Conference Member States, the Permanent Bureau should have studied the feasibility of the two convention types available for creating a convention on jurisdiction and judgments: the strict double convention, and the mixed convention.[233]

2.3.1. THE CONTENT OF A FEASIBILITY STUDY FOR A STRICT DOUBLE CONVENTION

A study concerning the feasibility of creating a strict double convention should have discussed three issues in particular. First, the question of whether the exhaustive regulation of international direct jurisdiction was feasible on a global level in general, and between the US and the Contracting States to the 1968 Brussels Convention and the 1988 Lugano Convention in particular should have been discussed.[234] Second, a feasibility study should have discussed whether it was possible to require the recognition and enforcement of every judgment rendered on the basis of a unified jurisdictional provision contained in the green list of the convention. That means that the question should have been addressed whether complete symmetry between the unified grounds of direct and indirect jurisdiction, as required by a strict double convention like the 1968 Brussels Convention, was possible in a global double convention.[235] Finally, the Permanent Bureau should have analysed whether a global double convention could become workable without a global court (or a functional equivalent) comparable to the European Court of Justice which was able to interpret the provisions of a strict double convention in order to ensure access to justice.[236]

---

judgments convention between the US and the United Kingdom in the 1970s (the Convention on the reciprocal recognition and enforcement of judgments in civil matters (ad referendum text, initialed at London, October 26, 1976) (1977) 16 ILM 71–87), ibid.

233 For a definition of these terms, see Section 2.1.

234 Section 2.3.1.1.

235 Section 2.3.1.2.

236 Section 2.3.1.3.

2.3.1.1. *The Potential to Reach Agreement on an Exhaustive List of International Direct Jurisdiction, in Particular between the United States and the Member States of the European Community*

As discussed previously, regulating international direct jurisdiction in general is challenging as the question of jurisdiction directly concerns the sovereignty and regulatory power of the Contracting States. Moreover, creating unified grounds of jurisdiction requires balancing the interests of the different stakeholders involved in the process of international civil litigation, as discussed above.[237] These general difficulties were acerbated through the need to accommodate the particular requirements of the US Constitution, and the interests of the Brussels/Lugano States in the negotiation process.[238] These general challenges in regulating jurisdiction were acerbated further by the specific requirements of a strict double convention. A strict double convention allows its Contracting States to exercise jurisdiction only on the basis of the jurisdictional provisions of the green list.[239] This exhaustive regulation of jurisdiction means that for proceedings within the convention's scope, all the national grounds of direct jurisdiction are superseded by the unified grounds of international direct jurisdiction in the green list of the strict double convention.[240] Superseding all existing domestic rules of international direct jurisdiction was a sensitive undertaking, as creating an exhaustive green list could have potentially resulted in a loss of power of a State to create enforceable titles in civil proceedings with a cross-border element for certain claims, if the unified grounds of jurisdiction in the green list differed from domestic grounds of jurisdiction. Moreover, this could have entailed the risk that States would no longer be able to grant access to a forum to their nationals, or to other claimants wishing to sue within their territory.[241] As a result, claimants could lose the ability to enforce debts, and this in turn even could have resulted in the bankruptcy of the judgment creditor, with detrimental effects for the economy of a State.[242]

For these reasons, since a strict double convention regulates jurisdiction exhaustively, the green list had to be broad enough to ensure access to justice

---

237 Section 2.2.

238 Cf von Mehren, 'Can the Hague Conference Project Succeed?' (n 31) 201.

239 Von Mehren, 'New Approach' (n 1) 282, 283; von Mehren, 'Enforcing Judgments Abroad' (n 6) 19.

240 1968 Brussels Convention (n 140) art 2(1), (2), art 3(1), (2); Pocar Report (n 192) 35.

241 Cf Smit, 'Common and Civil Law Rules of in Personam Adjudicatory Authority' (n 162) 352.

242 Cf ibid.

(i.e., the availability of a forum) for all potential proceedings within the convention's scope. In particular, a vital component of a global convention on jurisdiction and judgments in civil and commercial matters was a provision granting jurisdiction in contractual matters. For one, a globally unified rule on jurisdiction in contractual matters is desirable in order to provide for a more convenient forum for the claimant than the defendant's home forum.[243] What is more, without a jurisdictional provision for contractual claims, the exhaustive regulation of jurisdiction could even amount to a denial of justice if the home forum of the defendant was far from the claimant's State of residence.[244] Moreover, it was also possible that the defendant in a contractual dispute was domiciled in a non-Contracting State. Without a provision on contract jurisdiction, the claimant located in a Contracting State could have been forced to sue in a non-Contracting State even though the contract was performed in the territory of a Contracting State of the judgments convention.[245] Contract jurisdiction was therefore one of the most important jurisdictional provisions in a strict double convention.[246] As shown above, creating a globally acceptable rule for specific jurisdiction in contractual matters would have been very difficult to attain, however, due to the different jurisdictional standards applicable in the US and the EC Member States.[247] A feasibility study should have addressed this point.

243 A globally unified rule on jurisdiction in contractual matters is desirable in order to provide for a more convenient forum for the claimant than the defendant's home forum (which could be far away from the claimant's home forum), see Georges A L Droz, 'Preliminary Draft of the Convention on Jurisdiction and Foreign Judgments in Civil and Commercial Matters: Provisions of Jurisdiction', in John J Barceló, Kevin M Clermont (eds), *A Global Law of Jurisdiction and Judgments: Lessons from The Hague* (Kluwer Law International 2002) 15, 18.

244 Martha Weser, 'Bases of Judicial Jurisdiction in the Common Market Countries' (1961) 10 *Am J Comp L* 331, 332; cf also Earl Johnson Jr, 'Thinking About Access: A Preliminary Typology of Possible Strategies', in Mauro Capelletti, Bryant Garth (eds), *Access to Justice Volume III: Emerging Issues and Perspectives* (Sijthoff and Noordhoff/Dottore A Giuffrè 1979) 3, 10; I H Jacobs, 'Access to Justice in England', in Mauro Capelletti, Bryant Garth (eds), *Access to Justice Volume I: A World Survey, Book I* (Sijthoff and Noordhoff/Dottore A Giuffrè 1978) 417, 437; Special Commission June 1997, 'Report of Meeting No 14' (on file with author).

245 Weser, ibid.

246 See, e.g., Droz, 'Preliminary Draft of the Convention on Jurisdiction and Foreign Judgments' (n 243), 18: '[a] Preliminary Draft of an international convention on jurisdiction in civil and commercial matters could not "politically" abstain from formulating rules applicable to contracts'; Weser, 'Bases of Judicial Jurisdiction' (n 244) 331, 332; Hélene Gaudemet-Tallon, 'De quelques raisons de la difficulté d'une entente au niveau mondial sur les regles de competence judiciaire internationale directe', in James A R Nafziger, Symeon Symeonides (eds), *Law and Justice in a Multistate World: Essays in Honour of Arthur T von Mehren* (Transnational Publishers Inc 2002) 55, 67.

247 Section 2.2.2.1.

2.3.1.2. *Synchronising Direct and Indirect Grounds of Jurisdiction in a Strict Double Convention*

The process of creating unified jurisdiction rules on a global level was further complicated by the fact that a strict double convention as a rule required from its Contracting States not only to exercise jurisdiction over defendants based on the provisions of the green list, but also to recognise and enforce judgments that had been rendered on these bases.[248] Therefore, not only did the interests of the forum State, the claimants and the defendants have to be accommodated in the process of negotiating a strict double convention, but also those of the States in which the judgments should be recognised and enforced. The US had raised concerns from the beginning of the Judgments Project that the total symmetry between the grounds of direct and indirect jurisdiction as achieved by the 1968 Brussels Convention might not be achievable in the context of a global convention. A Working Document submitted by the US during the Special Commission on General Affairs and Policy of the Conference in June 1992 already noted that 'the one-to-one linkage that [the] Brussels [Convention] establishes between jurisdiction to adjudicate and recognition and enforcement gives rise to difficulty when one thinks in terms of a broad international community.'[249] A feasibility study on creating a strict double convention therefore should have addressed the question of whether it was possible in a global double convention to 'mirror' the list of direct grounds of jurisdiction completely in the (green) list of indirect grounds of jurisdiction.[250] This means that the question of whether States would be prepared to recognise and enforce judgments rendered on the basis of every single jurisdictional provision included in the green list, as was the case for the 1968 Brussels Convention, should have been addressed.[251] The fact that States were prepared to regard

---

248 1968 Brussels Convention (n 140) Title III.

249 Hague Conference on Private International Law, 'Special Commission on general affairs and policy of the Conference (1–4 June 1992), Work Doc No 1 – distributed 1 June 1992' (on file with author), 3; see also 'Intervention Mr von Mehren', in Arthur T von Mehren, Konstantinos Kerameus, 'The Scope of Recognition of Judgments', in Andreas F Lowenfeld, Linda J Silberman (eds), *The Hague Convention on Jurisdiction and Judgments: Records of the Conference Held at New York University School of Law on the Proposed Convention – April 30–May 1, 1999* (Juris Publishing Inc 2001) 59, 64.

250 Cf Arthur T von Mehren, 'Jurisdictional Requirements: To What Extent Should the State of Origin's Interpretation of Convention Rules Control for Recognition and Enforcement Purposes?', in Lowenfeld, Silberman (n 249) Annex-29.

251 Under the regime of the 1968 Brussels Convention, all judgments rendered on the basis of a unified ground of international direct jurisdiction are ensured recognition

a provision of direct jurisdiction as appropriate for exercising jurisdiction did not necessarily entail that States would also be prepared to recognise and enforce a judgment rendered on this basis in a foreign court, as different policy considerations regarding grounds of direct and indirect jurisdiction can apply in practice.[252] Equally, when States regarded a connecting factor as appropriate as a ground for indirect jurisdiction (i.e., for recognising and enforcing a judgment rendered on this basis in another State), this did not necessarily entail that States would also be prepared to exercise international direct jurisdiction on such a basis.[253] For example, under domestic law, English courts could exercise jurisdiction over a defendant domiciled abroad on the basis that either a contract was breached[254] or a tort had been committed in England.[255] For the purposes of recognition and enforcement, however, English common law would not recognise a judgment rendered in a foreign State if a contract was breached or a tort had been committed there.[256] A feasibility study could have shown, therefore, that an attempt to create completely synchronised green lists of direct and indirect jurisdiction could be very difficult to achieve due to a possible 'double standard' concerning jurisdiction.[257]

2.3.1.3. *Technical Challenges: The Need for a Common Court*

Finally, a feasibility study by the Permanent Bureau should have addressed the question of whether a strict double convention regulating the exercise of international direct jurisdiction exhaustively for proceedings within

---

and enforcement according to the convention, see 1968 Brussels Convention (n 140) art 26(1), art 31(1). This symmetry was not complete, however, since the 1968 Brussels Convention also applied to the recognition and enforcement of judgments rendered in its Contracting States on the basis of domestic law against defendants domiciled in a third State, see Michaels, 'Some Fundamental Conceptions as Applied in Judgment Conventions' (n 153) 48, 59, 60; von Mehren, 'Enforcing Judgments Abroad' (n 6) 20, 21.

252 Von Mehren, 'Recognition and Enforcement of Foreign Judgments – General Theory' (n 204) 56, 57, 61, 62; Michaels, 'Some Fundamental Conceptions as Applied in Judgment Conventions' (n 153) 38, 39, 61; Hartley, *International Commercial Litigation* (n 2) 466.

253 Michaels, 'Some Fundamental Conceptions as Applied in Judgment Conventions' (n 153) ibid 39; Jones Day, 'Comparative Study of Jurisdictional Gaps and Their Effect on the Judgments Project (July 1, 2015)' 1, 3 <https://assets.hcch.net/docs/7ebd2982-351a-4ca7-b6b3-356c8cdc1778.pdf> accessed 16 October 2023.

254 See Civil Procedure Rules, Rule 6.36; Practice Direction 6B 3.1(7).

255 Ibid 3.1(9).

256 Hartley, *International Commercial Litigation* (n 2) 444, 446; see also below, Section 3.1.1.

257 Hartley, ibid 444; this situation also has been described with the term 'jurisdictional gap', see Jones Day (n 253) 1.

the convention's scope was viable without a global court (or a functional equivalent) in order to ensure access to justice for litigants.[258] Even if a complete list of direct grounds of jurisdiction could have been created, such a list might not have been able to ensure that a forum was indeed available in all cases. Rather, the closed, exhaustive nature of the jurisdictional regime of a strict double convention could have created what has been called 'negativer Kompetenzkonflikt' (hereafter 'negative conflict of jurisdiction'[259]) in German academic literature.[260] For example, the only available forum against a defendant according to the convention text might have been his/her domicile or habitual residence in a Contracting State. If the defendant had moved away from the Contracting State of his/her original domicile/place of habitual residence, and relocated to an unknown place, a lack of international direct jurisdiction would result. This negative conflict of jurisdiction could have been resolved only by interpreting the convention text in an extensive way that stretched the ordinary meaning of a term, for example by granting jurisdiction to the State of the *last known domicile* of the defendant, when the convention text only granted jurisdiction to the State of *domicile* of the defendant.[261] Such interpretation could not have been achieved by domestic courts, as this would have threatened the uniform application of the convention in the Contracting States.[262] In general, it can never be guaranteed that a judgments convention which regulates jurisdiction exhaustively ensures access to justice in all cases within the convention's scope, even if the drafters took all care to avoid negative conflicts of competence.[263] The risk of such a negative conflict of

258 Von Mehren, 'Can the Hague Conference Project Succeed?' (n 31) 198.

259 Peter Schlosser, 'Report on the Convention on the Association of the Kingdom of Denmark, Ireland and the United Kingdom of Great Britain and Northern Ireland to the Convention on jurisdiction and the enforcement of judgments in civil and commercial matters and to the Protocol on its interpretation by the Court of Justice' [1979] OJ C59/71 (Schlosser Report) [78].

260 Arthur von Bülow, 'Vereinheitlichtes Internationales Zivilprozessrecht in der Europäischen Wirtschaftsgemeinschaft: Der Entwurf eines Abkommens über die internationale Zuständigkeit, die Anerkennung und die Vollstreckung gerichtlicher Entscheidungen' 29 RabelsZ (1965) 473, 508; Schlosser Report (n 259) [78] (German version); cf also Die Regierungen des Königreichs Belgien, der Bundesrepublik Deutschland, der Französischen Republik, der Italienischen Republik, des Großherzogtums Luxemburg und des Königreichs der Niederlande, 'Gemeinsame Erklärung' [1972] OJ L299/45.

261 Cf Case C-292/10 *G v. Cornelius de Visser* EU:C:2012:142, [42].

262 Cf Rupert H Graveson, 'The International Unification of Law' (1968) 16 Am J Comp L 4, 12.

263 Von Bülow, 'Vereinheitlichtes Internationales Zivilprozessrecht in der Europäischen Wirtschaftsgemeinschaft' (n 260) 508.

competence arising in practice might not be very high, but it had been regarded as sufficient by the drafters of the 1968 Brussels Convention; inter alia for this reason, they had advocated for giving the ECJ jurisdiction to interpret the exhaustive jurisdictional regime of the Brussels Convention.[264]

2.3.1.4. *Preliminary Result*

A feasibility study would have shown that a strict double convention was very challenging to attain on a global level. Regulating international jurisdiction was very difficult in general, due to the need to balance the interests of the different stakeholders involved in international civil and commercial litigation, as well as the need to converge US due process standards and the jurisdictional standards of the Brussels/Lugano States. These difficulties were heightened by the requirement of the strict double convention for Contracting States to not only make the jurisdictional provisions on the green list available in their domestic law, but to recognise and enforce every judgment rendered on the basis of a jurisdictional provision on the green list. For these reasons, achieving an agreement between States with different legal traditions in multilateral negotiations on a broad green list as required for the strict double convention seemed unlikely. Moreover, the strict double convention would have been very restrictive to the sovereignty of States since they would have lost the ability to regulate the exercise of jurisdiction over defendants for proceedings within the convention's scope. Finally, since there was no global court that could have interpreted the provisions of the green list, creating a strict double convention would have raised access to justice concerns.

2.3.2. THE CONTENT OF A FEASIBILITY STUDY FOR A TRUE MIXED CONVENTION

Besides the feasibility of a strict double convention, the Permanent Bureau should have studied the feasibility of a mixed convention, the convention type proposed by the US at the outset of the project.[265] A study of the

---

[264] Von Bülow, ibid; 'Gemeinsame Erklärung' (n 260); the need for having a common court able to ensure access to justice within the closed jurisdictional system of a strict double convention was demonstrated by Case C-292/10 *G v. Cornelius de Visser* EU:C:2012:142, [42].

[265] Letter Edwin D Williamson to Georges Droz (n 25); Permanent Bureau, 'Some Reflections: Prel Doc No 17 of May 1992' (n 131) 235, [14], [15]; 'Conclusions of the Working Group: Prel Doc No 19 of November 1992' (n 28) 257, 259.

feasibility of the mixed-convention approach would have shown that this convention type was the only one that had a chance of successfully creating a global regime of common rules on both the recognition and enforcement of foreign judgments *and* international direct jurisdiction in civil and commercial matters.

2.3.2.1. Less Need for the Convergence of National Standards of International Direct Jurisdiction

Creating a mixed convention would have required less convergence of different national standards of international direct jurisdiction. Rather, jurisdictional provisions would only have been included in the green list of a mixed convention if States reached consensus that exercising jurisdiction over defendants on these bases would be appropriate.[266] This means that the green list most likely would have been rather narrow.[267] Moreover, a mixed convention would have put less pressure on the negotiation process, since there was no need to ensure access to justice for all potential proceedings within the convention's scope. Contracting States to a mixed convention could have continued to use national grounds of jurisdiction (the 'grey area') in addition to the unified grounds of jurisdiction in the green list in order to provide a forum for potential claimants.[268] For example, in order to create a workable mixed convention, the Contracting States did not have to agree on a jurisdictional provision for contractual

266 Von Mehren, 'New Approach' (n 1) 287; von Mehren, 'Enforcing Judgments Abroad' (n 6) 27; von Mehren, 'The Case for a Convention-mixte Approach to Jurisdiction to Adjudicate and Recognition and Enforcement of Foreign Judgments' (1997) 61 RabelsZ 86, 92; Peter Nygh, 'Arthur's Baby: The Hague Negotiations For a World-Wide Judgments Convention', in Nafziger, Symeonides (eds), *Law and Justice in a Multistate World* (n 246) 151, 154, 155. Including a ground of direct jurisdiction into the green list of a mixed convention would have at the same time entailed in general that States also would be prepared to recognise and enforce judgments that had been rendered on this basis, see 'Conclusions of the Working Group: Prel Doc No 19 of November 1992' (n 28) [6], and von Mehren, 'Enforcing Judgments Abroad' (n 6) 19.

267 Nygh, 'Arthur's Baby' (n 266) 155; see also Ronald A Brand, 'Current Problems, Common Ground, and First Principles: Restructuring the Preliminary Draft Convention Text', in John J Barceló, Kevin M Clermont (eds), *A Global Law of Jurisdiction and Judgments: Lessons from The Hague* (Kluwer Law International 2002) 75, 77; 'Work Doc No 33: Proposal by the delegation of United States of America', in *Proceedings of the Twentieth Session, Tome II* (n 29) 405; Jeffrey D Kovar, Letter to Hans van Loon (n 34) 5.

268 Cf von Mehren, 'New Approach' (n 1) 287.

matters.[269] Unlike a strict double convention, a mixed convention without a provision on contract jurisdiction was still a workable convention since a forum for contractual disputes could still be ensured by domestic law.

The mixed-convention approach was also easier to attain for other reasons. It did not – unlike the strict double convention - infringe extensively upon the power of States to regulate the exercise of international direct jurisdiction. A mixed convention only requires that its Contracting States make the jurisdictional provisions of the green list available in their legal systems.[270] These jurisdictional provisions in the green list would not, however (unlike under the double-convention approach), supersede existing domestic grounds of jurisdiction.[271] Rather, the green list would have created an additional set of available grounds of jurisdiction in addition to the domestic grounds in the grey area (sometimes also referred to as the 'status quo'[272]).[273] Obviously, the recognition and enforcement would only be guaranteed for those judgments that had been rendered on the basis of a jurisdictional provision in the green list.[274] Under the mixed convention concept, only the red list (which was an optional addition) would have restricted the power of Contracting States to regulate jurisdiction directly by prohibiting the use of certain exorbitant grounds of jurisdiction.[275]

2.3.2.2. Less Need for Symmetry between Grounds of Direct and Indirect Jurisdiction; Less Potential for Negative Conflicts of Jurisdiction

Finally, a mixed convention might have been easier to attain than the strict double convention also because it did not require complete symmetry between direct and indirect grounds of jurisdiction. In general, States would include grounds of jurisdiction in the green list of a mixed convention

269 See above, Section 2.3.1.1.

270 'Conclusions of the Working Group: Prel Doc No 19 of November 1992' (n 28) [6]; von Mehren, 'New Approach' (n 1) 285.

271 'Conclusions of the Working Group: Prel Doc No 19 of November 1992' (n 28) [6].

272 Nygh, 'Arthur's Baby' (n 266) 155.

273 Letter Edwin D Williamson to Georges Droz (n 25); 'Conclusions of the Working Group: Prel Doc No 19 of November 1992' (n 28) [6]; von Mehren, 'Recognition of United States Judgments Abroad' (n 70) 458; von Mehren, 'New Approach' (n 1) 283; Tell, 'Can a Mixed Convention Work?' (n 148) 37–39.

274 'Conclusions of the Working Group: Prel Doc No 19 of November 1992' (n 28) [6]; von Mehren, 'Recognition of United States Judgments Abroad' (n 70) 458.

275 Von Mehren, 'Recognition of United States Judgments Abroad' (n 70) 458; von Mehren, 'New Approach' (n 1) 283 ('black list'); 'Conclusions of the Working Group: Prel Doc No 19 of November 1992' (n 28) [6].

if they fulfilled two conditions: first, all States agreed that the exercise of international direct jurisdiction over defendants based on these connecting factors was 'clearly appropriate',[276] and second, all States agreed that it was also reasonable to recognise and enforce a judgment rendered on these bases.[277] Those provisions on direct and indirect jurisdiction on which States could not reach consensus regarding their appropriateness in either of these categories would have remained in the grey area.[278] Besides this list of synchronised, or mirrored, grounds of 'accepted' provisions of indirect and direct jurisdiction,[279] a mixed convention offered an additional option: it allowed the existence of indirect grounds of jurisdiction which did not have a counterpart in the green list of direct grounds of jurisdiction. This means that the green lists of direct and indirect grounds of jurisdiction could be asymmetrical, and this specific type of mixed convention has been called an 'asymmetric mixed convention'.[280] Under this concept, a mixed convention could have contained a green list of direct grounds of jurisdiction that was narrower than the green list of indirect grounds of jurisdiction.[281] States could have agreed to not only recognise and enforce judgments rendered on the basis of a direct ground of jurisdiction contained in the green list, but also to recognise those judgments that were rendered based on a domestic ground of jurisdiction, if this domestic rule would have matched an indirect ground of jurisdiction.[282]

This option could have increased the number of judgments that could potentially circulate under the convention. Such an asymmetric regulation of direct and indirect jurisdiction could have made it even less difficult for

276 Von Mehren, 'New Approach' (n 1) 287; in order to determine which jurisdictional grounds are 'clearly appropriate', the Special Commission meetings should have employed a decision-making process on the basis of consensus, see ibid; von Mehren, 'Enforcing Judgments Abroad' (n 6) 27; von Mehren, 'The Case for a Convention-mixte Approach' (n 266) 92; Nygh, 'Arthur's Baby' (n 266) 154, 155.

277 Cf von Mehren, 'Recognition of United States Judgments Abroad' (n 70) 457; see also 'Conclusions of the Working Group: Prel Doc No 19 of November 1992' (n 28) [6]; von Mehren/Kerameus, 'The Scope of Recognition of Judgments' (n 249) 64.

278 'Conclusions of the Working Group: Prel Doc No 19 of November 1992' (n 28) [6]; von Mehren, 'New Approach' (n 1) 287; von Mehren, 'Recognition of United States Judgments Abroad' (n 70) 458.

279 Von Mehren, 'New Approach' (n 1) 285.

280 Michaels, 'Some Fundamental Conceptions as Applied in Judgment Conventions' (n 153) 59–62; von Mehren, 'Enforcing Judgments Abroad' (n 6) fn 16; von Mehren, 'Jurisdictional Requirements' (n 250) A-39, A-40; see also von Mehren, 'Can the Hague Conference Project Succeed?' (n 31) 198, 199.

281 Von Mehren, 'New Approach' (n 1) 287.

282 Von Mehren/Kerameus, 'The Scope of Recognition of Judgments' (n 249) 64.

States to agree on common jurisdictional solutions for proceedings within the convention's scope.[283] The American scholar and member of the US delegation to the Judgments Project, Arthur T von Mehren, introduced the concept of an asymmetric mixed convention into the academic discussions about the Hague Judgments Convention only in 1999 when the project had already been underway for some time.[284] However, the concept of an asymmetric mixed convention was not completely novel. The preparatory work for the 1971 Hague Judgments Convention showed that the Permanent Bureau had already worked with the concept of creating asymmetric lists of direct and indirect grounds of jurisdiction. For the preparatory work on the 1971 Convention on the Recognition and Enforcement of Foreign Judgments in Civil and Commercial Matters, the concept of an asymmetric mixed convention had been discussed (albeit not under the name 'mixed convention').[285] At the time, this concept had been rejected since it was felt that such a 'hybrid' convention type would decrease the chances of the convention being accepted by certain States.[286] Since this convention type could have fostered agreement between States, however, the asymmetric mixed convention could, or rather, *should* have been expressly considered as a possible method for creating a judgments convention. The Permanent Bureau, and as a result also the Special Commission, had however 'not explored the modalities that the mixed convention format allow[ed].'[287] In the Report on the Special Commission meeting in June 1997, the then Secretary General, Catherine Kessedjian, had hinted at an asymmetric mixed convention.[288] This analysis of a mixed convention was hidden in

---

283 Von Mehren, 'Jurisdictional Requirements' (n 250) Annex A-44.

284 Cf von Mehren, 'Enforcing Judgments Abroad' (n 6) fn 16; Von Mehren, 'Jurisdictional Requirements' (n 250) Annex-39, A-40; see also von Mehren, 'Can the Hague Conference Project Succeed?' (n 31) 198, 199; in the original US proposal for a mixed convention, this special kind of a mixed convention had not been mentioned (see 'Conclusions of the Working Group: Prel Doc No 19 of November 1992' (n 28) [6]).

285 Fragistas, 'Rapport de la Commission spécial' (n 127) 32, quoting the then Secretary General of the Hague Conference on Private International Law, Mr van Hoogstraten. See also above (n 170).

286 Fragistas, 'Rapport de la Commission spécial' (n 127) ibid.

287 Von Mehren, 'Jurisdictional Requirements' (n 250) Annex A-43.

288 'Moreover, it is also conceivable that, within the framework of a mixed convention, providing the exorbitant fora have been eliminated, the effects of judgments rendered under a jurisdiction not covered by the convention might form the subject of provisions in the Convention rather than leaving the matter for national law to decide', see Catherine Kessedjian, 'Synthesis of the Work of the Special Commission of June 1997 on International Jurisdiction and the Effects of Foreign Judgments in Civil and Commercial Matters: Prel Doc No 8 of November 1997 for the attention of the

a footnote,[289] however, and did not explain the concept of an asymmetric mixed convention in a straightforward way. This might have contributed to the fact that this concept had not been considered at the Special Commission meetings.

The mixed convention concept also offered more flexibility for dealing with exorbitant grounds of jurisdiction. By means of a red list of *indirect* grounds of jurisdiction, the mixed-convention concept could have given States the option to ban the recognition and enforcement of judgments that had been rendered based on an exorbitant ground of direct jurisdiction, but without prohibiting the use of exorbitant bases in the domestic law of its Contracting States through a red list of *direct* grounds of jurisdiction.[290] This option could have made a convention text even more acceptable to some Hague Conference Member States, as it would have been able to solve some of the controversies regarding which connecting factors are appropriate for exercising jurisdiction over defendants. For example, it had been regarded as vital by US legal practice to be able to exercise general jurisdiction over defendants who continually did business in a US state (under the concept of 'general doing business jurisdiction').[291] For the EC Member States, exercising general jurisdiction based on business contacts was inappropriate.[292] By including general doing-business jurisdiction in the red list of unacceptable indirect grounds of jurisdiction, a mixed convention would have prevented the recognition and enforcement of such a judgment abroad. At the same time, US courts could have continued to exercise jurisdiction on this basis, as its use would not have been prohibited by the convention.[293] A mixed convention would have provided for more

Special Commission of March 1998 on the question of jurisdiction, recognition and enforcement of foreign judgments in civil an commercial matters', in *Proceedings of the Twentieth Session, Tome II* (n 29) 81, 81 fn 1.

289 Ibid.

290 Von Mehren, 'Recognition of United States Judgments Abroad' (n 70) 457, 458 ('at the minimum, the other Contracting States would always be required to deny recognition to judgments resulting from such assertions [of exorbitant jurisdiction]'); this variety had also been explored in later years by Michaels, 'Some Fundamental Conceptions as Applied in Judgment Conventions' (n 153) 38.

291 See, e.g., Kevin M Clermont, 'An Introduction to the Hague Convention', in John J Barceló, Kevin M Clermont (eds), *A Global Law of Jurisdiction and Judgments: Lessons from The Hague* (Kluwer Law International 2002) 3, 12.

292 Wolfgang Wurmnest, 'Recognition and Enforcement of U.S. Money Judgments in Germany' (2005) 23 Berkeley J Int'l L 175, 178 fn 18.

293 Michaels, 'Some Fundamental Conceptions as Applied in Judgment Conventions' (n 153) 61; for an alternative approach to achieve a compromise, see Linda Silberman, 'Can the Hague Judgments Project Succeed? A Perspective from the United States', in

flexibility in dealing with exorbitant grounds of direct jurisdiction than a complete double convention, thereby making it easier for States to reach agreement on a final convention text.[294]

The viability of a mixed convention also did not depend on the existence of a common court in the same way as a strict double convention, since it did not regulate the exercise of international direct jurisdiction exhaustively.[295] Rather, it allowed Contracting States to make use of their national grounds of jurisdiction (within the limits of the red list).[296] As a result, it was less likely under a mixed convention than a double convention that negative conflicts of jurisdiction, i.e., situations where no forum was available to hear proceedings, would arise. Even if a situation occurred where neither the green list of the mixed convention nor the domestic grounds of jurisdiction provided for a forum, States would still be free under a mixed convention to either extensively interpret their own domestic rules or to create new jurisdictional provisions in the grey area in order to avert negative conflicts of jurisdiction for similar situations in the future.[297]

2.4. THE MIXED CONVENTION AS THE METHOD OF CHOICE

For these reasons, a mixed convention would have been more attainable than a strict double convention. The mixed convention required less need for convergence from its Contracting States in terms of direct and indirect grounds of jurisdiction, and it was less restrictive on their sovereignty due to the possibility to continue to use and create jurisdictional provisions in the grey area. The existence of this grey area would have also been able to alleviate access to justice concerns. The mixed convention was therefore a feasible method for creating a convention containing rules on both jurisdiction and judgments.

John J Barceló, Kevin M Clermont (eds), *A Global Law of Jurisdiction and Judgments: Lessons from The Hague* (Kluwer Law International 2002) 159, 175–178.

294 Michaels, 'Some Fundamental Conceptions as Applied in Judgment Conventions' (n 153) 61.

295 Von Mehren, 'Would an International Convention Be Useful?' (n 70) 458.

296 Von Mehren ibid.

297 Cf von Mehren ibid.

2.5. REALITY: USING THE 1968 BRUSSELS CONVENTION AS A MODEL

In reality, the challenges in unifying grounds of international direct jurisdiction exhaustively on a global level were not assessed properly. Moreover, no comprehensive study was prepared by the Permanent Bureau regarding the feasibility of a strict double convention, or a mixed convention, neither in the preparatory stages before the Judgments Project was put officially on the agenda during the Eighteenth Diplomatic Session, nor during the Special Commission meetings from 1997–1999. Instead of independently assessing the feasibility of a strict double convention, the Permanent Bureau relied on the 1968 Brussels Convention for guidance on the feasibility of creating a global double convention.[298] The 1968 Brussels Convention was a strict double convention, as it regulated the question of international direct jurisdiction for proceedings within its scope exhaustively.[299] In addition, it ensured the recognition and enforcement of resulting judgments.[300] On a regional level, this convention had successfully created a harmonised regime for jurisdiction and judgments between the EC Member States.

However, the 1968 Brussels Convention was an unsuitable model for creating a global double convention.[301] The creation of this Convention had not required the same level of compromise on the part of the States involved in its drafting as would have been required from the Member States of the Hague Conference. Agreeing on common rules for exercising jurisdiction against defendants domiciled in a Member State of the EC had been comparatively easy as the drafting process had only involved the six original Member States of the EC. These six States (Belgium, France, Germany, Italy, Luxembourg and the Netherlands) furthermore all

298 See in particular Kessedjian, 'Prel Doc No 7 of April 1997' (n 141) 13–69; Permanent Bureau, 'Examples of Treaty Provisions on International Jurisdiction: Information Document, Enforcement of Judgments, June 1997' (on file with author); Peter D Trooboff, 'Ten (and Probably More) Difficulties in Negotiating a Worldwide Convention on International Jurisdiction and Enforcement of Judgments: Some Initial Lessons' in John J Barceló, Kevin M Clermont (eds), *A Global Law of Jurisdiction and Judgments: Lessons from The Hague* (Kluwer Law International 2002) 263, 265.

299 1968 Brussels Convention (n 140) art 2(1), 3(1).

300 1968 Brussels Convention (n 140) art 26(1), art 31; von Mehren, 'New Approach' (n 1) 282, 283.

301 Von Mehren, 'Can the Hague Conference Project Succeed?' (n 31) 196, 197.

belonged to the civil-law tradition.[302] In addition, the creation of the 1968 Brussels Convention had been prepared by an extensive comparative study of the differences and, maybe more importantly, the communalities of the rules on international direct jurisdiction between the six prospective Contracting States.[303] This comparative study had inter alia concluded that the communalities between the six States would be large enough to allow for the creation of a unified jurisdictional regime, allowing for a convention text to be agreed upon.[304]

What is more, the Member States of the EC had been highly motivated to reach an agreement on an exhaustive list of direct grounds of jurisdiction in order to enable the free movement of judgments, which in turn was seen as a necessary tool to support a common market and the free movement of goods, services, labour and capital within the EC.[305] In fact, the Member States of the EC had no choice but to agree on an exhaustive list of unified grounds of international direct jurisdiction. Creating this list was an indispensable precondition for the free movement of judgments in civil and commercial matters, as full free movement of judgments could only be assured by a total alignment of the grounds of direct jurisdiction with the accepted grounds of indirect jurisdiction (i.e., the green list of indirect grounds of jurisdiction was required to completely match the green list of direct grounds of jurisdiction).[306] In this way, recognition and enforcement was guaranteed for all judgments rendered on the basis

302 Cf Jenard Report (n 196) 3–6; C G J Morse, 'International Shoe v. Brussels and Lugano: Principles and Pitfalls in the Law of Personal Jurisdiction' (1995) 28 UC Davis L Rev 999, 1013.

303 Marta Weser, 'Les conflits de juridictions dans le cadre du Marché Commun. Difficultés et remèdes' (1959) RCDIP 613–649; (1960) RCDIP 21–41; 151–172; 314–333; 533–556; (1961) RCDIP 105–129.

304 Marta Weser, 'Les conflits de juridictions dans le cadre du Marché Commun. Difficultés et remèdes (suite et fin)' (1961) RCDIP 105, 126 [294]: '[n]ous avons longuement étudié les avantages incontestables [...] d'un traité multilatéral qui, en plus de l'assimilation, unifierait les règles de compétence de ces six pays [...] nous pouvons affirmer qu'une telle solution ne demanderait de concessions substantielles à *aucun* des États membres. En effet, la similitude des principes généraux qui régissent la compétence des tribunaux dans les six pays du Marché commun est véritablement frappante'.

305 EEC Treaty (Treaty of Rome) (n 57) art 220; 1968 Brussels Convention (n 140) preamble; von Bülow, 'Vereinheitlichtes Internationales Zivilprozessrecht in der Europäischen Wirtschaftsgemeinschaft' (n 260) 474, 475.

306 Fragistas, 'Rapport de la Commission spécial' (n 127) 25; see also Weser, 'Les conflits de juridictions dans le cadre du Marché Commun' (n 304) 127 [297].

of jurisdictional provision of the green list within the scope of the 1968 Brussels Convention.[307]

This full synchronisation of direct and indirect grounds of jurisdiction, which was necessary for supporting a common market of the EC, was unnecessary for a global judgments convention. The aim of a Hague Judgments Convention was not to create a common market between the Hague Conference Member States, but merely to improve international civil cooperation between States with regard to the recognition and enforcement of foreign judgments, and to improve access to justice for litigants and judgment creditors as compared to the status quo. The 1968 Brussels Convention was therefore also an unsuitable role model regarding the possible extent of synchronisation between direct and indirect grounds of jurisdiction. The 1968 Brussels Convention aimed at the unification of rules of international direct jurisdiction (for proceedings in which the defendant was domiciled in a Contracting State) not only for the sake of fostering legal certainty, but also (or mainly) for the sake of fostering the EC's common market. Had the Permanent Bureau conducted an independent study of the feasibility of a strict double convention, it should have rejected the suitability of this convention type for creating a global convention on jurisdiction and judgments.

Since the feasibility of exhaustively regulating international direct jurisdiction had not been studied before the drafting phase of the convention began, the difficulties of converging different concepts of international direct jurisdiction only began to show in the Special Commission phase from June 1997 onwards. For example, according to one of the participants of the Special Commission meetings on the Judgments Project, finding an appropriate connecting factor for jurisdiction in contractual matters had proven to be one of the most difficult questions to resolve in drafting a convention text.[308] The development of the draft convention texts that had been prepared by the Special Commission meetings in November 1998,[309] June 1999 and October 1999, as well as the draft convention text negotiated

---

307 Fragistas, ibid; see also Weser, ibid; for the 1968 Brussels Convention, there is not an express green list of indirect grounds of jurisdiction; rather, the convention guarantees the recognition and enforcement of all judgments rendered in proceedings within its scope; in proceedings against defendants domiciled in a Contracting State, domestic courts can only exercise jurisdiction on the basis of one of the jurisdictional provisions enshrined in the 1968 Brussels Convention (n 140), see art 2(1), art 3(1); jurisdiction over defendants domiciled in a non-Contracting State is as a rule left to the domestic rules of the Contracting State concerned, see 1968 Brussels Convention (n 140), art 4(1).

308 Bucher, 'Vers une convention mondiale' (n 173) 84.

309 'Work Doc 144 – November 1998 – Proposal by the Drafting Committee' (November 1998 Draft), in Lowenfeld, Silberman (n 249) Appendix C-1–C-17.

by the Diplomatic Conference in 2001, provide evidence for the enormous difficulty of converging in particular the US and the Brussels/Lugano Convention's approaches to specific jurisdiction in contractual matters.[310] The November 1998 Draft contained two variants for a provision on contract jurisdiction, with Variant 1 reflecting the US activity-based approach to contractual jurisdiction,[311] and with Variant 2 having its origin in the Brussels Convention approach to contractual jurisdiction, as interpreted by the ECJ.[312] The draft provisions of the June 1999 Draft[313] and the October 1999 Preliminary Draft Convention[314] on contract jurisdiction only followed the Brussels approach to contractual jurisdiction.[315] The provision reflecting the

---

310 See also Bucher, 'Vers une convention mondiale' (n 173) 84.

311 November 1998 Draft (n 309), Variant 1 of art 6 (Contracts) read: '[a] plaintiff may bring a claim, in matters relating to contracts, in the courts of Contracting State [sic] if 1. The plaintiff's habitual residence or seat is located in that State; and 2. the defendant engaged in activity in that State that constituted a significant step a. in the creation of the contract obligation on which the claim is based, such as solicitation of business, or b. in the defendant's preparation to perform the obligation on which the claim is based, or c. in the place of performance of the obligation on which the claim is based'.

312 November 1998 Draft (n 309), Variant 2 of art 6 (Contracts) read: '1. A plaintiff may bring a claim, in matters relating to contracts, in the Contracting State in which the obligation in question was to be performed under the terms of the contract, provided that a significant part thereof was in fact performed. If the claim is based on several obligations, the principal obligation shall be determinative. 2. The preceding paragraph shall not apply where the obligation in question is to pay for goods or services'; November 1998 Draft, Variant 2 of art 6, number 1, first sentence partly codifies a decision of the European Court of Justice (ECJ) in Case C-14/76 *De Bloos v. Bouyer* EU:C:1976:134, [1976] ECR 01497, [15] – [16]; the second sentence of November 1998 Draft, Variant 2 of art 6, number 1 codifies the decision of the ECJ in Case C-266/85 *Hassan Shenavai v. Klaus Kreischer* EU:C:1987:11, [1987] ECR 00239, [19].

313 June 1999 Draft, in Lowenfeld, Silberman (n 249) Appendix C-19–C-37.

314 October 1999 Preliminary Draft Convention (n 32) 190.

315 June 1999 Draft (n 313) art 6 and October 1999 Preliminary Draft Convention (n 32), art 6 read: '[a] plaintiff may bring an action in contract in a Contracting State a) in matters relating to the supply of goods, in the courts for the place where the goods were supplied in whole or in part; b) in matters relating to the provision of services, in the courts for the place where the services where provided in whole or in part; c) in matters relating both to the supply of goods and the provision of services, in the courts for the place where performance of the principal obligation took place in whole or in part'. This provision reflected the European approach to international direct jurisdiction, as the proposal was strongly based on the provision on contract jurisdiction in the proposal for a Community instrument replacing the 1968 Brussels Convention, see Commission of the European Communities, 'Proposal for a Council Regulation (EC) on jurisdiction and the recognition and enforcement of judgments in civil and commercial matters: COM (1999) 348 final', 32, art 5(1)(b), first and second indent <http://aei.pitt.edu/47831/1/COM_(99)_348_final.pdf> accessed 16 October 2023; this provision was later adopted in Council Regulation (EC) No 44/2001 of 22 December 2000 on jurisdiction and the recognition and enforcement of judgments in civil and commercial matters [2001]

US approach to jurisdiction in contractual matters was removed from the draft convention text in June 1999. The US concept of contractual jurisdiction only re-entered the convention text during the Diplomatic Session in June 2001, after the Hague Conference Member States had decided that the Session would proceed on the basis of consensus rather than majority voting.[316] The 2001 Interim Text contained two options for jurisdiction in contractual matters,[317] with Alternative A reflecting the US approach to contractual jurisdiction,[318] and Alternative B reflecting the approach of the Brussels regime.[319] Eventually, no consensus could be reached on a provision on contract jurisdiction during the Diplomatic Session of June 2001.[320]

OJ L12/1 (Brussels I Regulation), art 5(1)(a) and (b), which as a rule granted jurisdiction in contractual matters to the State where the goods were supplied for matters relating to the supply of goods, or to the State where the services were provided for matters relating to the provision of services.

316 Permanent Bureau, 'Conclusions of the Special Commission on GAP of May 2000' (n 35) 12.

317 2001 Interim Text (n 36), art 6.

318 Alternative A (which was placed into square brackets) reads:

'1. [Subject to the provisions of arts 7 and 8,] [...] a plaintiff may bring an action in contract in the courts of the State – a) in which the defendant has conducted frequent [and] [or] [...] significant activity; [or b) into which the defendant has directed frequent [and] [or] significant activity;] [...] provided that the claim is based on a contract directly related to that activity [and the overall connection of the defendant to that State makes it reasonable that the defendant be subject to suit in that State].
[...]
[Variant 1 [...] 2. For the purposes of the preceding paragraph, 'activity' means one or more of the following – a) [regular and substantial] promotion of the commercial or professional ventures of the defendant for the conclusion of contracts of this kind; b) the defendant's regular or extended presence for the purpose of negotiating contracts of this kind, provided that the contract in question was performed at least in part in that State. [...] c) the performance of a contract by supplying goods or services, as a whole or to a significant part].
[Variant 2 [...] 2. For the purpose of the preceding paragraph, 'activity' includes, inter alia, the promotion, negotiation, and performance of a contract. [3. The preceding paragraphs do not apply to situations where the defendant has taken reasonable steps to avoid entering into or performing an obligation in that State.] [...]].'

319 Alternative B (which was also placed into square brackets) corresponded with the draft provision on contract jurisdiction of the October 1999 Preliminary Draft Convention, see 2001 Interim Text (n 36) 625, fn 42; it was strongly based on 'COM (1999) 348 final' (n 315), 32, art 5(1)(b), first and second indent, see (n 315); 2001 Interim Text, Alternative B (c), which attributed jurisdiction to the State in which the performance of the principal obligation took place in whole or in part in matters relating to both the supply of goods and the provision of services, was based on case law of the ECJ in Case C-266/85 *Hassan Shenavai v. Klaus Kreischer* EU:C:1987:11, [1987] ECR 00239, [19], interpreting the provision on contract jurisdiction of the 1968 Brussels Convention (n 140).

320 2001 Interim Text (n 36) fn 33.

Regarding the need for a common court to avoid negative conflicts of jurisdiction, it is not clear whether the lack of an international court affected discussions during the Special Commission meetings in a negative way. Nevertheless, the possibility that a strict double convention could lead to a denial of justice due to the unavailability of a forum posed a big challenge to a least some Hague Conference Member States. In a comment on the October 1999 Preliminary Draft Convention,[321] the expert for Japan proposed to allow States to use exorbitant grounds of jurisdiction in case no other forum would be available according to the convention text.[322] The question of a denial of access to justice was not just a theoretical problem, therefore, but a practical problem which could have prevented States from ratifying the convention text, even if it is unclear how the lack of analysis of this question influenced the negotiation process.

2.6. CONCLUSION

If the Permanent Bureau had prepared comprehensive studies on the feasibility of unifying grounds of jurisdiction on a global level, and of the available methods for concluding a global convention on jurisdiction and judgments, it should have recommended the mixed convention as the only viable method with a reasonable chance for concluding a global judgments convention in general, and between the US and the EC in particular.[323] From a theoretical perspective, the mixed convention was the only model that would have allowed future Contracting States to maintain a sufficient amount of flexibility in regulating the exercise of jurisdiction, while enhancing legal certainty and predictability at the same time. Moreover, the mixed convention would have been able to improve access to justice by ensuring the recognition and enforcement of those judgments that had been rendered based on a jurisdictional provision on the green list, or on a domestic ground of jurisdiction matching one of the approved grounds of indirect jurisdiction (under an asymmetric mixed convention).

---

321 The October 1999 Preliminary Draft Convention allowed for the exercise of international jurisdiction on the basis of national law. Access-to-justice concerns should have applied with less force to the 1999 Draft Convention than to a true double convention, therefore.

322 Masato Dogauchi, 'The Draft Convention on Jurisdiction and Foreign Judgments in Civil and Commercial Matters – A View from the Far East – The Hague Draft Convention from the Perspective of Japan', UIA Seminar Edinburgh, April 20–21, 2000 <www.cptech.org/ecom/jurisdiction/Dogauchi.pdf> accessed 3 April 2023, [6].

323 Von Mehren, 'Can the Hague Conference Project Succeed?' (n 31) 201.

In reality, however, the Special Commission meetings charged with creating a draft convention text began their work by attempting to create a strict double convention from 1997 onwards. For guidance, the Special Commission meetings relied on the structure of the 1968 Brussels Convention. Some of the negative effects of not having studied the feasibility of a strict double convention and of a mixed convention have been discussed above. A full analysis of the effects of the lack of preparation of feasibility studies will be provided in Chapters 4 and 5.

CHAPTER 3

DID THE JUDGMENTS PROJECT FAIL DUE TO A LACK OF INTEREST FROM THE MEMBER STATES OF THE EUROPEAN COMMUNITY AND THE UNITED STATES?

Another question which needs to be considered in order to understand why the Judgments Project failed is whether or not the project addressed any real interests or needs of the Hague Conference Member States in general, and of the two main stakeholders in the Judgments Project, the US and the EC Member States, in particular. As discussed above, creating a global double convention that would unify grounds of international direct jurisdiction and secure the recognition and enforcement of judgments in civil and commercial matters had a strong theoretical appeal.[324] In particular, unified grounds of jurisdiction would have enhanced legal certainty and predictability in international civil and commercial proceedings as compared to the status quo, and the guaranteed recognition and enforcement of judgments would have fostered access to justice for litigants, and supported trade relations between States.[325] However, if these theoretical interests had not matched any real national interests or needs of, in particular, the US and the EC Member States, the two key stakeholders in the project, this could have contributed to the fact that the Judgments Project did not lead to the adoption of a convention text.[326]

---

324 See above, Introduction at 1.

325 Ibid.

326 Cf Cecilia Albin, 'Justice, Fairness and Negotiation: Theory and Reality', in Berton, *International Negotiation* (n 65) 257, 257.

3.1. UNITED STATES INTERESTS IN THE JUDGMENTS PROJECT IN 1992

3.1.1. SECURING THE RECOGNITION AND ENFORCEMENT OF UNITED STATES JUDGMENTS IN THE EUROPEAN COMMUNITY

It was the US who proposed to put negotiations on a general convention on the recognition and enforcement of foreign judgments in civil and commercial matters on the agenda of the Hague Conference in 1992.[327] The proposal by the US, contained in a letter to the Secretary General of the Hague Conference, Georges Droz, referred to a *global* judgments convention, involving the participation of 'many regions of the world including Eastern-Europe, North-America, Central and South America and the Far East'.[328] However, this letter expressly highlighted the interest of the US in negotiating with the Member States of the EC (including the Member States of the European Free Trade Area (EFTA)) under the roof of the Hague Conference on Private International Law.[329] In 1992, no treaty on the mutual recognition and enforcement of foreign judgments in civil or commercial matters between the US and the then 12 EC Member States,[330] or the then seven EFTA States (Austria, Finland, Iceland, Liechtenstein, Norway, Sweden and Switzerland)[331] existed.[332] By concluding a multilateral convention, the US had hoped to improve the recognisability

327 Letter Edwin D Williamson to Georges Droz (n 25).

328 Ibid.

329 Ibid 1; see also von Mehren, 'Recognition of United States Judgments Abroad' (n 70) 455, 456, fn 18; Peter H Pfund, 'The Project of the Hague Conference on Private International Law to Prepare a Convention on Jurisdiction and the Recognition/Enforcement of Judgments in Civil and Commercial Matters' (1998–1999) 24 Brook J Int'l L 7, 10, 11.

330 Cf European Union, 'Countries', <https://europa.eu/european-union/about-eu/countries/member-countries_en> accessed 5 April 2023.

331 Cf EFTA Secretariat, 'The EFTA Convention: The Free Trade Association of Iceland, Liechtenstein, Norway and Switzerland (2017) <www.efta.int/sites/default/files/publications/fact-sheets/EFTA-Convention-guide/EFTA-Convention-brochure.pdf> accessed 4 April 2023, 8. Both Iceland and Liechtenstein were not Member States of the Hague Conference at the time (Liechtenstein still is not), and did not participate in the Judgments Project as observers, see 'List of participants in the Special Commission meetings', in *Proceedings of the Twentieth Session, Tome II* (n 29) 76–79; 'Members of the Second Commission', ibid 386–390.

332 Letter Edwin D Williamson to Georges Droz (n 25); Volker Behr, 'Enforcement of United States Money Judgments in Germany' (1994) 13 JL & Com 211, 213; in fact, the

and enforceability of US judgments in civil and commercial matters within Europe.[333] The common opinion of US legal scholars and of the US Department of State at the time was that US judgments faced difficulties in terms of their ability to be recognised and enforced in Europe.[334]

US law, on the other hand, was seen as being quite receptive to the recognition and enforcement of foreign judgments.[335] This receptive nature of US law was based on the decision of the US Supreme Court in *Hilton v. Guyot* of 1895, according to which foreign judgments should in general be recognised and enforced for the sake of international comity between States, i.e., out of respect for the foreign sovereign nation.[336] In later years, after the decision of the US Supreme Court in *Eerie Railroad*,[337] recognising and enforcing foreign judgments became mainly a matter for the law of the separate US states.[338] Nevertheless, the theory of international comity continued to be the guiding principle.[339] As a result, foreign judgments in civil and commercial matters normally were recognised and enforced in the respective US states (subject to the checks which are normally required before a foreign judgment can be recognised and enforced like the question of jurisdiction of the court or origin, checks of procedural fairness or of the consistency with the public policy of the State addressed).[340]

The theory of international comity, which favoured the recognition and enforcement of foreign judgments, had no real bearing on the recognition

US had not entered into treaty relations concerning the recognition and enforcement of judgments in civil and commercial matters with any State, see, e.g., David Luther Woodward, 'Reciprocal Recognition and Enforcement of Civil Judgments in the United States, the United Kingdom and the European Economic Community' (1982) 8 NCJ Int'l L & Com Reg 299, 299.

333 Letter Edwin D Williamson to Georges Droz (n 25); Matthew H Adler, 'If We Build It, Will They Come? -The Need for a Multilateral Convention on the Recognition and Enforcement of Civil Monetary Judgments' (1994–1995) 26 Law & Pol'y Int'l Bus 79, 80, 81, 95; see also Brandon B Danford, 'The Enforcement of Foreign Money Judgments in the United States and Europe: How Can We Achieve a Comprehensive Treaty?' (2004) 23 Rev Litig 381, 402.

334 Adler ibid 81; von Mehren, 'New Approach' (n 1) 277, 278.

335 Von Mehren ibid.

336 *Hilton v. Guyot* 159 US 113, 164, 165 (1895).

337 *Eerie Railroad Co v. Tomkins* 304 US 64 (1938); 58 S Ct 817; 82 L Ed 1188.

338 Ronald A Brand, 'Enforcement of Judgments in the United States and Europe' (1994) 13 JL & Com 193, 196, 200.

339 Ibid 196.

340 Cf Uniform Foreign Money-Judgments Recognition Act (1962), sec 3; Ronald A Brand, 'Enforcement of Foreign Money-Judgments in the United States: In Search of Uniformity and International Acceptance' (1991) 67 Notre Dame Law Review 253, 262–280; von Mehren, 'New Approach' (n 1) 277.

and enforcement of foreign judgments in the civil law jurisdictions of the European States.[341] Rather, European civil law courts recognised and enforced a foreign judgment if a domestic statute or a treaty obligation obliged them to.[342] As a result, two of the Member States of the EC did not recognise and/or enforce US judgments at all due to a lack of treaty obligation (nor did three of those EFTA States which were also Member States of the Hague Conference). Denmark did not (and still does not) recognise and enforce foreign judgments without a treaty obligation or a 'royal administrative order'.[343] In the case of the Netherlands, foreign judgments could be recognised, but not be declared enforceable in the absence of a treaty obligation.[344] Among the EFTA States, neither Norway nor Sweden recognised and enforced foreign judgments without a treaty obligation.[345] Equally, Austria required a guarantee of the reciprocal enforcement of foreign judgment by either treaty or law.[346]

---

341 Dieter Martiny, 'Recognition and Enforcement of Foreign Money Judgments in the Federal Republic of Germany' (1987) 35 Am J Comp L 721, 727, 728 (for Germany); von Mehren, 'New Approach' (n 1) 278; Scott H Fairley, 'In Search of a Level Playing Field: The Hague Project on Jurisdiction and the Recognition and Enforcement of Foreign Judgments', in Chi Carmody, Yuji Iwasawa, Sylvia Rhodes (eds), *Trilateral Perspectives on International Legal Issues: Conflict and Coherence* (Cadmus-Port City Press Division 2003) 57, 68, 69.

342 For Germany, see Code of Civil Procedure, art 328; Martiny ibid 727; in general, see Committee on Foreign and Comparative Law: Association of the Bar of the City of New York, 'Survey on Foreign Recognition of US Money Judgments' (31 July 2001) <www.cptech.org/ecom/jurisdiction/CFCL.rtf> accessed 4 April 2023, 3.

343 Morten M Fogt, 'Denmark', in Jürgen Basedow et al (eds), *Encyclopedia of Private International Law, Volume 3* (Edward Elgar Publishing 2017) 2019, 2035; see also Behr (n 332) 217.

344 See Dutch Code of Civil Procedure, art 431; Marielle Koppenol-Laforce, Freek Vermeulen, 'Comparative Study of "Residual Jurisdiction" in Civil and Commercial Disputes in the EU – National Report for: Netherlands', [26] (on file with author); see also René Verschuur, 'Recognition and Enforcement of Foreign Judgments in the Netherlands' in Gerhard Walter, Samuel Baumgartner (eds), *Recognition and Enforcement of Foreign Judgments Outside the Scope of the Brussels and Lugano Conventions* (Kluwer Law International 2000) 403, 409.

345 Robert E Lutz, *A Lawyers Handbook for Enforcing Foreign Judgments in the United States and Abroad* (CUP 2007) 432; Liechtenstein and Iceland also do not recognise and enforce foreign judgments without a treaty obligation, for Iceland, see Lutz ibid 432; for Liechtenstein, see Rudolf Graupner, 'Some Recent Aspects of the Recognition and Enforcement of Foreign Judgments in Western Europe' (1963) 12 ICLQ 367, 371 fn 14, Gesetz vom 24. November 1971 über das Exekutions- und Rechtssicherungsverfahren (Exekutionsordnung; EO), art 52.

346 Graupner ibid 371 fn 14, see also Gesetz vom 27. Mai 1896, über das Exekutions- und Sicherungsverfahren (Exekutionsordnung – EO), art 406 <https://www.ris.bka.

The European States which would recognise and enforce foreign judgments without a treaty obligation had other particular requirements for the recognition and enforcement of foreign judgments that could hinder access to justice for holders of a US judgment. The Federal Republic of Germany and Spain, for example, both required the reciprocal treatment of their judgments in the State where the foreign judgments originated (the State of origin).[347] According to the relevant Belgian law, a review of the merits of the foreign judgment was required,[348] allowing the foreign court to review the findings of the facts, and the application of the foreign law to the facts, which could be as time-consuming as having to re-litigate the matter.[349] In Italy, separate recognition proceedings were required.[350]

Another obstacle for the recognition and enforcement of foreign judgments in Europe (and generally in all States that recognise and enforce foreign judgments)[351] was the question of indirect jurisdiction.[352]

---

gv.at/GeltendeFassung/Bundesnormen/10001700/EO%2c%20Fassung%20vom%20 12.04.2020.pdf> accessed 28 February 2024; see also Rolf Wagner, 'Die Bemühungen der Haager Konferenz für Internationales Privatrecht um ein Übereinkommen über die gerichtliche Zuständigkeit und ausländische Entscheidungen in Zivil- und Handelssachen – Ein Sachstandsbericht nach dem 1. Teil der Diplomatischen Konferenz' (2001) 6 IPRax 533, 534.

347 For Germany, see German Code of Civil Procedure, art 328(1)(1); Behr (n 332) 221–223; even though Germany seldom denied recognition of US judgments due to lack of reciprocity since German judgments were generally recognised and enforced in the US, the reciprocity requirement nevertheless was a potential obstacle to the recognition and enforcement of US judgments, see Behr ibid 223; Rolf A Schütze, 'The Recognition and Enforcement of American Civil Judgments Containing Punitive Damages in the Federal Republic of Germany' (1990) 11 U Pa J Int'l Bus L 581, 602. For Spain, see Civil Procedure Code, arts 952 and 953, and Eduardo Albors, 'Spain', in Charles Platto (ed), *Enforcement of Foreign Judgments Worldwide* (Graham & Trotman and International Bar Association 1989) 164, 165.

348 Belgian Judicial Code (Code Judiciaire), art 570 (now revised); Daphne Fevery, 'La reconnaissance et l'exécution des décisions judiciaires étrangères en Belgique en dehors du champ d'application des Conventions de Bruxelles et de Lugano', in Walter/Baumgartner (n 344) 75, 95.

349 Friedrich K Juenger, 'The Recognition of Money Judgments in Civil and Commercial Matters' (1988) 26 Am J Comp L 1, 28, 29.

350 Italian Civil Procedure Code (Codice di procedura civile 1942), art 797 [repealed by the Reform of the Italian System of Private and Procedural International Law Act of 31 May 1995 (legge 218/95)], see Michele Angelo Lupoi, 'Recognition and Enforcement of Foreign Judgments Outside the Scope of Application of the Brussels and Lugano Conventions: Italy', in Walter/Baumgartner (n 344) 347; Gianni Nunziante, 'Italy', in Platto (n 347) 157–159; Behr (n 332) 217 fn 25.

351 Fragistas, 'Rapport de la Commission spécial', in *Actes et Documents de la session extraordinaire – 13 au 26 avril 1966* (n 127) 29; Lenhoff (n 133) 23.

352 Ibid.

This concerned the requirement that the court of origin must have had jurisdiction to render the judgment in the original proceedings. The standard for indirect jurisdiction is determined by the State addressed for recognition and enforcement ('the State addressed').[353] All of the 10 Member States of the EC that would recognise and enforce foreign judgments without a treaty obligation (France, Germany, Greece, Ireland, Italy, Luxembourg, Portugal, Spain, and the United Kingdom of Great Britain and Northern Ireland (UK)) required a check of the jurisdiction of the court of origin as a condition for the recognition and enforcement of a foreign judgment,[354] and so did the EFTA State Switzerland.[355] Some of these countries were quite liberal regarding the required jurisdictional standards. Belgian courts, for example, would check the jurisdiction of the court of origin only with respect to whether the foreign court had assumed jurisdiction solely on the basis of the claimant's nationality.[356] Portuguese courts would only check whether the jurisdiction of the foreign court resulted from a fraudulent evasion of the law (*fraude a la loi*), or whether Portuguese courts would have had exclusive jurisdiction in the matter.[357]

353 Von Mehren, 'Recognition and Enforcement of Foreign Judgments – General Theory' (n 204) 55–57; Lenhoff (n 133) 23.

354 For Germany, see German Code of Civil Procedure, arts 12–40, 170; Michael Eberstein, 'Federal Republic of Germany', in Platto (n 347) 142, 147. For Greece, see Nikolaos K Klamaris, 'Enforcement of Court Orders and Judgments: Greece', in Walter/Baumgartner (n 344) 275, 294. For Ireland, see William Binchy, 'Ireland' in Jürgen Basedow et al (eds), *Encyclopedia of Private International Law, Volume 3* (Edward Elgar Publishing 2017) 2183, 2186. For Italy, see Italian Civil Procedure Code (Codice di procedura civile 1942), art 797(1) [repealed by the Reform of the Italian System of Private and Procedural International Law Act of 31 May 1995 (legge 218/95)], see Lupoi (n 350) 347. For Luxembourg, see Thierry Hoscheit, 'Luxembourg', in Walter/Baumgartner (n 344) 380. For Spain, see Albors (n 347) 166; in England/Wales and Northern Ireland, US judgments would be recognised and enforced according to the rules of the common law, see Jeremy Carver and Christopher Napier, 'United Kingdom', in Platto (n 347) 195; according to these common law rules, the foreign court must have had jurisdiction according to the English rules, see Carver/Napier ibid 199; in Scotland, the foreign court must have exercised jurisdiction validly from the point of view of Scottish private international law, see ibid 200, 201. French law seemed to have been quite liberal regarding its standards of indirect jurisdiction: unless the French courts were deemed to have exclusive jurisdiction, the jurisdiction of the foreign court was to be recognised if the proceedings had a 'characteristic connection with the state where the judge was seized with the matter and if the choice of jurisdiction was not fraudulent', see Cour de Cassation, *Simitch*, 6 February 1986, as translated by Robert Byrd, Christian Bouckaert, 'France', in Platto (n 347) 172 but see 71, 72.

355 1987 Swiss Code on Private International Law, art 25(a), art 26.

356 Belgian Judicial Code, art 570, and Christine Sartini Vandenkerckhove, 'Belgium', in Platto (n 347) 131, 137, 138.

357 Carlos Manuel Fereira Da Silvi, 'Portugal', in Walter/Baumgartner (n 344) 465, 474, 475.

The jurisdictional requirements in Germany were also quite liberal, with the result that judgments were seldom denied recognition because of a lack of jurisdiction.[358] Courts in the Netherlands, finally, although they would not enforce a foreign judgment without a treaty obligation, would recognise a foreign judgment if the foreign court had exercised jurisdiction on the basis of a jurisdictional standard internationally regarded as appropriate.[359]

In other European States, the jurisdictional requirements were more restrictive. Spain, for example, required inter alia a sufficient link between the foreign court and the proceedings in order for the judgment to be recognised in Spain.[360] As the US due-process standard required a sufficient connection between the forum and the defendant for exercising jurisdiction, this requirement could potentially hinder the recognition and enforcement in Spain of US judgments.[361] In Luxembourg, a foreign judgment could only be recognised and enforced if the jurisdiction of the foreign court existed both according to the relevant rules of the law of Luxembourg and the law of the State of origin.[362] The standards of indirect jurisdiction in Ireland were also quite restrictive. For example, in the late 1980s, Irish courts were apparently not prepared to recognise or enforce a judgment rendered on the basis of the defendant's domicile in the state of origin.[363] Moreover, Irish courts would not recognise and enforce a judgment for damages for breach of contract if the contract had been concluded abroad and therefore had to be performed abroad.[364] French courts, despite their generally liberal approach to indirect jurisdiction, nevertheless would not recognise and enforce a US judgment (or foreign judgments in general) rendered against a French national as a rule.[365] A French court would deny recognition and enforcement of a foreign judgment if a court other than the one rendering the judgment had exclusive jurisdiction according to French law.[366] Article 15 of the French Code Civil had been interpreted as

---

358 Eberstein (n 354) 147.
359 See Paul M Storm, 'Europe', in Platto (n 347) 116, 117.
360 Albors (n 347) 166: although the Spanish Civil Procedure Code in force at the time did not expressly provide for a jurisdictional review, the Spanish Supreme Court nevertheless held that inter alia a sufficient link between the foreign court and the proceedings was required in order for the judgment to be recognised in Spain.
361 Albors (n 347) 166; 'Survey on Foreign Recognition of US Money Judgments' (n 342) 7.
362 Hoscheit (n 354) 380.
363 William Binchy, *Irish Conflicts of Law* (Butterworth (Ireland) Ltd 1988) 596, 597.
364 Ibid 597.
365 'Survey on Foreign Recognition of US Money Judgments' (n 342) 6.
366 Byrd, Bouckaert (n 354) 172, 173.

providing a French defendant the right to be sued in France in international civil litigation, thereby attributing exclusive jurisdiction to French courts (unless the defendant waived the protection of Article 15 Code Civil[367]).[368] The rules of indirect jurisdiction in England and Wales, finally, were also slightly restrictive. Jurisdiction of a foreign country was regarded as proper if the judgment debtor had been resident in the forum,[369] or if he had been temporarily present in the foreign country at the time the proceedings were instituted.[370] If the defendant was a foreign corporation (a corporation not incorporated in the forum State), jurisdiction was recognised if exercised in the State where the defendant had carried on business (including through a representative) for more than a minimal period of time, and at or from a fixed place of business.[371] Otherwise, foreign judgments would only be recognised if the judgment debtor had in some way submitted to the jurisdiction of the foreign court.[372] As a result of these requirements, a US judgment which was to be enforced in Europe in the early 1990s faced a patchwork of diverse legal regimes. Moreover, the national regimes of Denmark, the Netherlands, Austria, Norway and Sweden were barring the enforcement of a foreign judgment altogether without a treaty obligation, thereby making re-litigation necessary.[373]

As a result, recognising and enforcing a US judgment in Europe in the early 1990s was a complex, time-consuming and costly process.[374] This lack of a coherent regime for the mutual recognition and enforcement of judgments between the US and Europe proved to be particularly problematic from the point of view of the US with regard to the Member States of the EC, as the Community was its most important trading partner at the time,[375] with a huge potential for cross-border disputes. Furthermore,

367 Article 15 Code Civil reads '[u]n Français pourra être traduit devant un tribunal de France, pour des obligations par lui contractées en pays étranger, même avec un étranger' ('A French national may be brought before a French court for obligations contracted by him in a foreign country, even with a foreigner' [translation provided by the author]).

368 Byrd, Bouckaert (n 354) 173.

369 Carver, Napier (n 354) 200.

370 *Adams v. Cape Industries* [1990] Ch 433; Hartley, *International Commercial Litigation* (n 2) 437.

371 *Adams v. Cape Industries* [1990] Ch 433.

372 Carver, Napier (n 354) 199; cf also 'Survey on Foreign Recognition of US Money Judgments' (n 342) 5.

373 See above, (n 343–346).

374 Cf 'Survey on Foreign Recognition of US Money Judgments' (n 342) 27.

375 See, e.g., Robert C Shelburne, Gregory K Schoepfle, 'The European Community 1992 program and US workers' (1990) Monthly Lab Rev 22, 22.

the EC was also the most important trading bloc in the world at that time: in 1992, the EC Member States accounted for 17.9% of total global exports (followed by the US, with a share of 13.6%, and Japan with a share of 10.1% of total world exports).[376] In terms of imports, the EC accounted for 18.9% of global imports in 1992, with the US and Japan as the second and third largest importers worldwide (with the US accounting for 15.8%, and Japan for 6.7%).[377]

3.1.2. PROTECTING UNITED STATES CITIZENS AGAINST EXORBITANT GROUNDS OF JURISDICTION

Besides ensuring the recognition and enforcement of US judgments in particular in the Member States of the EC, the US was also interested in protecting its citizens against exorbitant grounds of international direct jurisdiction which existed in the domestic law of the European Member States of the Hague Conference.[378] Many of these exorbitant grounds of jurisdiction made it possible for claimants to bring suits against US citizens in Europe even if there was no strong factual connection between the forum state and the US defendant. The most notorious of these exorbitant grounds was Article 14 of the French Code Civil, which allowed a French national to sue a defendant who was domiciled in another State before a French court on the mere basis of the business contacts of the defendant with the French claimant.[379] The 1968 Brussels Convention intensified

---

376 See European Commission, *External and intra-EU trade: Statistical yearbook – Data 1958–2006* (eurostat Statistical books 2008) <https://ec.europa.eu/eurostat/documents/3217494/5729733/KS-GI-11-001-EN.PDF/9e06d19b-bdce-49e0-a766-65fbbfc78081> accessed 4 April 2023, 14.

377 Ibid 16.

378 Hans Smit, 'International Control of International Litigation: Who Benefits?' (1994) 57 Law & Contemp Probs 25, 26, 27; von Mehren, 'Recognition of United States Judgments Abroad' (n 70) 452, fn 9; von Mehren, 'New Approach' (n 1) 279; Adler (n 333) 79, 91; Toshiyuki Kono, 'Some considerations on International Jurisdiction and the Draft Convention on Jurisdiction and Foreign Judgments in Civil and Commercial Matters from a Japanese Perspective', in Carmody/Iwasawa/Rhodes (eds), *Trilateral Perspectives* (n 341) 157, 163; see also Russel J Weintraub, 'How Substantial is Our Need for a Judgments-Recognition Convention and What Should We Bargain Away to Get It?' (1998–1999) 24 Brook J Int'l L 167, 172, who doubted the need for protection against exorbitant grounds of jurisdiction, with further references.

379 See, e.g., Pierre Raoul-Duval, Marie Stoyanov, 'Comparative Study of "Residual Jurisdiction" in Civil and Commercial Disputes in the EU – National Report for: France', 2, 7 (on file with author).

the discriminatory effects of these exorbitant grounds of jurisdiction.[380] For one, it enabled the use of these exorbitant bases against all defendants without a domicile in one of the Brussels Convention Contracting States.[381] What is more, the 1968 Brussels Convention also allowed any person domiciled in a Contracting State, irrespective of his or her nationality, to make use of the rules of jurisdiction in force in their State of domicile, including exorbitant grounds of jurisdiction.[382] Finally, the 1968 Brussels Convention also obliged all its Contracting States to recognise and enforce judgments rendered on such an exorbitant basis, enabling access to assets of the judgment debtor located in all the States party to the 1968 Brussels Convention.[383] On 1 January 1992, this regime had been extended to Switzerland by means of the 1988 Lugano Convention.[384] This discriminatory treatment of defendants without a domicile in a Brussels/ Lugano State was perceived as very problematic by legal scholars in the US,[385] and by the US legislator. In fact, the issue had been considered as so problematic that the US had undertaken treaty negotiations with the United Kingdom in order to protect US citizens from the enforcement of judgments rendered on an exorbitant basis at least in the UK.[386] The result of these negotiations, the draft Convention on the Recognition and Enforcement of Judgments in Civil Matters of October 1976 (hereafter 1976 UK-US draft convention),[387] had also been intended to serve as a prototype for further

---

380 1968 Brussels Convention (n 140).

381 Ibid art 4(1).

382 Ibid art 4(2).

383 Ibid art 26, 31; Smit (n 378) 25, 26.

384 1988 Lugano Convention: Parties (n 194).

385 See Smit (n 378) 26, 27; von Mehren, 'Recognition of United States Judgments Abroad' (n 70) 452, fn 9; 454; Adler (n 333) 79, 91.

386 Back then, the 1968 Brussels Convention (n 140) in its art 59 allowed its Contracting States to conclude international treaties with third States, permitting the Contracting States to commit to an exception to the general duty to recognise and enforce judgments rendered in other Contracting States (if the judgment was rendered solely on the basis of an exorbitant ground of jurisdiction); see also Brand, 'In Search of Uniformity' (n 340) 297; Smit (n 378) 25, 27.

387 Convention on the reciprocal recognition and enforcement of judgments in civil matters [ad referendum text, initialed at London, October 26, 1976] [1977] 16 ILM 71–87 (1976 UK-US draft Convention); in 1978, an agreement ad referendum regarding modifications of the 1976 UK-US draft Convention was negotiated, see von Mehren, 'New Approach' (n 1) 274; the main US negotiators of these texts were Arthur T von Mehren and the late Ambassador Richard D Kearney, see von Mehren ibid fn 10.

bilateral treaties with other EC Member States for this purpose.[388] The negotiations on this bilateral treaty had failed, however, in particular due to the resistance by the UK insurance industry and by UK manufacturers who were concerned about being subject to product-liability lawsuits in the US, with the resulting judgments being enforceable in the UK.[389] Consequently, the US chose to resort to multilateral negotiations under the auspices of the Hague Conference on Private International Law.[390]

3.1.3. OVERCOMING THE PUBLIC POLICY DEFENCE?

Another main reason why US judgments were not readily recognised and enforced by foreign States was that US courts could issue damages awards that did not compensate the claimant for a sustained loss, but which had the additional purpose to punish the defendant, or to deter others from similar behaviour (like 'punitive damages awards' and 'multiple damages awards').[391] In many foreign jurisdictions (such as Germany or Japan), the recognition and enforcement of an award of punitive damages potentially raised public policy concerns.[392] A judgments convention could have overcome these obstacles only to a certain extent.[393] It was unlikely that negotiating States would have changed their notions of public policy in the negotiation process, as this would have required a State to change fundamental principles of its national law. Nevertheless, a judgments convention could have provided clear rules for the treatment of multiple or punitive damage awards,[394] thereby speeding up the recognition and enforcement process. For example, a judgments

388 Smit (n 378) 26, 27; cf also Peter Herzog, 'Common Market Convention on Jurisdiction and the Enforcement of Judgments: An Interim Update' (1976–1977) 17 Va J Int'l L 417, 426, fn 45.

389 Von Mehren, 'New Approach' (n 1) 274; Peter M North, 'The Draft U.K./U.S. Judgments Convention: A British Viewpoint' (1979) 1 Nw J Int'l L & Bus 219, 223, 238.

390 Von Mehren, 'New Approach' (n 1) 274, 280.

391 'Survey on Foreign Recognition of US Money Judgments' (n 342) 10; Behr (n 332) 225, 226.

392 For Germany, see Schütze (n 347) 598–602; Behr (n 332) 225, 226; for Japan, see the case *Bryant v. Mansei Kogyo Co*, as reported in Takonobu Takehara, 'Japan', in Charles Platto, William G Horton (eds), *Enforcement of Foreign Judgments Worldwide* (2nd edn, Springer 1993) 54, 58; Inae Yang, 'International Enforcement of Punitive Damages Awards' (2014) 9 J Comp L 353, 365; Kevin M Clermont, 'A Global View of Jurisdiction and Judgments: Views from the United States and Japan' (2004) 37 Cornell Int'l LJ 1, 12; see also Arthur Anyuan Yuan, 'Enforcing and Collecting Money Judgments in China from a US Judgment's Creditor's Perspective' (2004) 36 Geo Wash Int'l L Rev 757, 779, 780.

393 Cf Bucher, 'Vers une convention mondiale' (n 173) 79.

394 Cf von Mehren, 'Recognition of United States Judgments Abroad' (n 70) 458.

convention could have secured the partial enforcement of such a judgment, to the extent that the judgment did actually compensate for a sustained loss or for harm suffered.[395]

3.2. INTERESTS OF THE MEMBER STATES OF THE EUROPEAN COMMUNITY IN THE JUDGMENTS PROJECT

3.2.1. IMPROVING TRADE RELATIONSHIPS WITH THE UNITED STATES?

In theory, the interest of the Member States of the EC in fostering their trade relations with the US by means of a judgments convention should have been high. In the early 1990s, the US was the most important actor behind the EC in terms of global imports and exports.[396] In reality, however, the interest of the 12 EC Member States to conclude a judgments convention with the US was lower than the interest of the US in concluding a judgments convention with the EC Member States. Intra-Community trade far outweighed the extra-Community trade with the US. For example, in 1992, the main trading partners of Germany (the leading exporter of goods and services worldwide in 1990)[397] in terms of exports were France, Italy, the Netherlands, the United Kingdom, and Belgium and Luxembourg.[398] These six countries were also Germany's main trading partners in terms of imports.[399] To illustrate, since 1996, trade within the EU had continued to account for approximately 70 per cent of the trading bloc's total merchandise exports.[400] These trade relations had

---

395 Cf 2005 Hague Choice of Court Convention (n 3) art 11(1); 2019 Hague Judgments Convention (n 53) art 10.

396 In 1990, the 12 EC Member States accounted for 18.3% of exports worldwide, while the US accounted for 13.2%, Japan accounted for 10.1%, followed by Canada with 4.2%. In terms of imports, the 12 EC Member States accounted for 19.2% of imports worldwide in 1990, the US for 16.1%, Japan for 7.4%, and Canada for 4.2%, see European Commission, *External and intra-EU trade* (n 376) 14; Statistisches Bundesamt, 'Export, Import, Globalisierung – Deutscher Außenhandel und Welthandel, 1990–2008' (Destatis 2010), 38.

397 Statistisches Bundesamt ibid 37.

398 WITS, 'Trade Summary for Germany 1992', <http://wits.worldbank.org/CountryProfile/en/Country/DEU/Year/1992/SummaryText> accessed 4 April 2023.

399 Ibid.

400 WTO, *International Trade Statistics 2015*, 27 <https://www.wto.org/english/res_e/statis_e/its2015_e/its15_toc_e.htm> accessed 4 April 2023.

been supported by the 1968 Brussels Convention since its entry into force in 1972, and were not in need of another international regime fostering the recognition and enforcement of judgments. Furthermore, although no coherent framework between the US and the EC Member States existed, European judgments were normally also readily enforced by the courts in the US.[401] Therefore, the recognition and enforcement of foreign judgments in civil and commercial matters was basically a non-issue for the EC Member States in 1992. The recognition and enforcement of civil and commercial judgments between the main trading partners of the EC were secured either by means of the 1968 Brussels Convention, by bilateral conventions,[402] or, with respect to the US, by the liberal recognition and enforcement practice of the US states.[403] Merely guaranteeing the recognition and enforcement of foreign judgments in the US was therefore not regarded as being a sufficiently attractive prospect for the EC Member States (or the Lugano States).[404]

However, even if European judgments were normally recognised and enforced by US courts, a coherent framework with common rules for recognition and enforcement which was valid in all US states did not exist.[405] In terms of legal certainty, predictability, and effective and speedy enforcement of a European judgment in the US, there was therefore room for improvement. As mentioned above, the recognition and enforcement of foreign judgments had been a matter of state law since the decision in *Eerie Railroad*.[406] As a result, originally every US state had its own regime on the recognition and enforcement of foreign judgments. The National Conference of Commissioners on Uniform State Laws had tried to harmonise the rules for the recognition and enforcement by creating a model law, the 'Uniform Money-Judgments Recognition Act', hoping that the separate states would adopt its rules.[407] In 1994, only 22 out of

---

401 Von Mehren, 'New Approach' (n 1) 277, 278; Adler (n 333) 81.

402 See, e.g., the Convention Between Canada and the United Kingdom of Great Britain and Northern Ireland Providing for the Reciprocal Recognition and Enforcement of Judgments in Civil and Commercial Matters, as published in the 1985 Canada-United Kingdom Civil and Commercial Judgments Convention Act (RSC, 1985, c C-30), Schedule 2.

403 Bucher, 'Vers une convention mondiale' (n 173) 79; cf also Behr (n 332) 213.

404 Bucher ibid.

405 Brand, 'In Search of Uniformity' (n 340) 262–265.

406 *Eerie Railroad Co v. Tomkins* 304 US 64 (1938).

407 National Conference of Commissioners on Uniform State Law, 'Uniform Money-Judgments Recognition Act' (adopted 1962), Preparatory Note; see now also the Foreign-Country Money Judgments Recognition Act (2005).

50 US states had adopted the Uniform Money-Judgments Recognition Act, however.[408] The law on the recognition and enforcement of foreign judgments in the remaining states remained regulated by the common law. As a result, a European judgment faced a regime of different sets of rules on the recognition and enforcement of foreign judgments in the US.[409] And while the intra-Community trade outweighed the trade of the EC Member States with the US, trade relationships with the US were nevertheless not insignificant. In terms of extra-Community-trade, the US was the most important trading partner for the EC trading bloc.[410] The interest in fostering these trade relationships by means of a judgments regime might have existed in particular from the point of view of Germany and the United Kingdom, which were the US' main trading partners within the Community at the time.[411]

3.2.2. ENHANCING LEGAL CERTAINTY AND PREDICTABILITY

While the Member States of the EC did not have a huge (perceived) interest in securing the recognition and enforcement of their judgments in the US, they were very interested in enhancing legal certainty for EC-domiciled defendants and claimants. Indeed, the EC Member States felt that the effort to create a global judgments convention would only be justifiable if legal certainty regarding international direct jurisdiction could be improved for European litigants on the international plane, and especially with respect to proceedings in the US.[412] In particular, the EC (and EFTA) Member States were very interested in protecting EC-/EFTA-domiciled defendants against the exercise of exorbitant

408 Brand, 'Enforcement of Judgments in the United States and Europe' (n 338) 207, 197.

409 Brand, 'In Search of Uniformity' (n 340) 262–265; von Mehren, 'Recognition of United States Judgments Abroad' (n 70) 453.

410 See, e.g., Shelburne, Schoepfle (n 375) 22.

411 WITS, 'United States Trade Summary 1992' <https://wits.worldbank.org/CountryProfile/en/Country/USA/Year/1992/SummaryText> accessed 4 April 2023.

412 Permanent Bureau, 'Conclusions of the Special Commission of June 1994 on the Question of the Recognition and Enforcement of Foreign Judgments in Civil and Commercial Matters: Prel Doc No 2 of December 1995' (n 201), 'Annex: Extract of the Conclusions of the Special Commission of June 1995 on general affairs and policy of the Conference', 3; Bucher, 'Vers une convention mondiale' (n 173) 79; Gaudemet-Tallon (n 246), 63.

jurisdiction by US courts.[413] International general jurisdiction (i.e., jurisdiction over the defendant for all claims on the basis of the relationship between the forum and the defendant)[414] exercised by US courts on the basis of the defendant's doing business in a US state, as well as 'tag jurisdiction' (jurisdiction exercised on the basis that the claim had been served on the defendant while he/she was present in the forum State, even if that presence was only temporary),[415] had always been a point of concern for European States.[416] These concerns were increased by the fact that jury trials in civil proceedings in US courts were known to render damage awards considered excessive from a civil-law perspective.[417] During the Special Commission meeting on General Affairs and Policy in June 1995, the French Expert, on behalf of the Council of Ministers of the EU,[418] expressly noted that it would be 'vital' that an EU-domiciled defendant would be 'protected against any obligation whereby foreign judgments imposing punitive or excessive damages on them were enforced'.[419]

Moreover, the EC Member States had also expressed an interest in enhancing legal certainty in general through unifying grounds of international direct jurisdiction during the Special Commission meeting in June 1995:[420]

> On behalf of the Member States of the European Union, the French expert (France holding the Presidency of the European Union from 1 January till 30 June 1995) explained the position of the Council of Ministers of the European Union [...] In the light of the global tendency towards international private contacts and trade, a universal convention might be beneficial to the Member States of the European Union [...] It would be desirable for the future

413 See, e.g., Bucher, 'Vers une convention mondiale' (n 173) 79; Wagner, 'Gerichtsstandsvereinbarungen' (n 19) 103.
414 *Daimler AG v. Bauman* 571 US 1, 2 (2014); von Mehren, Trautman, 'Jurisdiction to Adjudicate' (n 2) 1136.
415 *Burnham v. Superior Court of California*, 495 US 604 (1990).
416 'Survey on Foreign Recognition of US Money Judgments' (n 342) 4; Wurmnest (n 292) 178 fn 18.
417 Trooboff, 'Ten (and Probably More) Difficulties' (n 298) 267; Brand, 'In Search of Uniformity' (n 340) 294, 295; Behr (n 332) 225, 226; 'Survey on Foreign Recognition of US Money Judgments' (n 342) 10–12; see also above, Section 3.1.3.
418 The Council of Ministers represented the EC Member States, see Treaty establishing the European Community (Maastricht Consolidated Version) [1992] OJ C224/6, art 146(1); see now TEU (n 209) art 16(2).
419 'Conclusions of the Special Commission on general affairs and policy 1995' (n 412) 3.
420 Ibid.

> universal system to be based on a double convention, which would need to include both rules for the enforcement of decisions and also rules on direct jurisdiction; the future Convention could contain a list of generally accepted grounds of jurisdiction and a list of prohibited grounds.

In the same intervention, the French expert also declared that this new regime should leave 'intact the regional system of the Brussels and Lugano Conventions in the relations between States Parties to these Conventions'.[421] Although the rules for international direct jurisdiction were unified regarding defendants domiciled in a Brussels/Lugano State,[422] there was a real gap regarding international direct jurisdiction within the Brussels/Lugano regime concerning jurisdiction over defendants *without* a domicile in an aforementioned State. As a rule, the Brussels/Lugano States continued to apply their domestic, non-unified grounds of international direct jurisdiction over defendants without a domicile in one of these States.[423] Since these rules were not unified, claimants in different EC and EFTA Member States were not guaranteed access to justice in the same way. A unification of jurisdictional provisions on a global level for defendants with a domicile in a third State could have therefore created a level playing field for claimants within the EC and EFTA Member States.

3.3. CONCLUSION

As was shown in this chapter, both the US and the EC had real interests in a Hague Judgments Convention with rules on both the recognition and enforcement of foreign judgments and international direct jurisdiction in general. The US had hoped that a Hague Judgments Convention would redress the imbalance in terms of recognition and enforcement of judgments between the US and the EC (and EFTA) Member States. At the same time, the US had hoped to achieve some protection for US citizens

---

421 Ibid.

422 1968 Brussels Convention (n 140)/1988 Lugano Convention (n 144) art 2(1), art 3(1); Brussels I Regulation (n 315), art 2(1), art 3(1). Only exceptionally did the jurisdictional provisions of these instruments also apply to defendants who were not domiciled in the territory of the States to which these instruments applied, see, e.g., 1968 Brussels Convention (amended version as published in [1990] OJ 189/2)/1988 Lugano Convention (n 144) art 13(2); see also the parallel provisions of the Brussels I Regulation, art 15(2).

423 1968 Brussels Convention (n 140)/1988 Lugano Convention (n 144) art 4(1); Brussels I Regulation (n 315), art 4(1).

against exorbitant grounds of jurisdiction found in Europe. The EC Member States, on the other hand, were particularly interested in enhancing legal certainty for litigants through unified grounds of jurisdiction, something which had been achieved on a regional level already by means of the 1968 Brussels Convention. In addition, the European States had an interest in protecting European defendants against exorbitant grounds of jurisdiction in the US. Moreover, even though the US was normally quite receptive to foreign judgments, European judgments could have nevertheless benefitted from a more streamlined regime of recognition and enforcement that a Hague Judgments Convention could have provided. Finally, a Hague Judgments Convention could have protected European judgment debtors against the enforcement of US judgments that awarded punitive or excessive damages.[424] A Hague Judgments Convention could have addressed real needs of both the US and the EC Member States, and it cannot be concluded therefore that it failed due to a lack of interest of the States concerned.

---

424 Cf 2005 Hague Choice of Court Convention (n 3) art 11(1); 2019 Hague Judgments Convention (n 53) art 10.

CHAPTER 4

DID THE JUDGMENTS PROJECT FAIL DUE TO A LACK OF PROJECT MANAGEMENT BY THE PERMANENT BUREAU?

4.1. INTRODUCTION

As discussed in Chapter 2, the Permanent Bureau deviated from its established practices by not preparing feasibility studies on each of the possible types of convention in order to create a convention on jurisdiction and judgments in the context of the Hague Judgments Project. A closer analysis of the preparatory work the Permanent Bureau undertook for successful past convention projects (the 1980 Hague Convention on International Child Abduction[425] and the 1993 Hague Convention on Intercountry Adoption[426]) shows that for the Hague Judgments Project, the Permanent Bureau also departed from past usage in other ways. When looking into the preparatory work on the 1980 Hague Child Abduction Convention and the 1993 Hague Intercountry Adoption Convention, a specific pattern of preparation can be identified.[427] The Permanent Bureau not only prepared feasibility studies before a new topic was added to the agenda of the Hague Conference. Additionally, it conducted research on the needs or problems of the Hague Conference Member States, and on the possible solutions which could be employed by a new private international law instrument.[428] Furthermore, the Permanent Bureau used to partake in detailed planning for a new Hague Convention once potential solutions

[425] 1980 Hague Child Abduction Convention (n 80).

[426] 1993 Hague Intercountry Adoption Convention (n 80).

[427] See Beaumont/McEleavy, *Child Abduction* (n 68) 16.

[428] Permanent Bureau, 'Note on legal kidnapping', in Conférence de la Haye de Droit International Privé, *Actes et Documents de la Treizième Session – 4 au 23 octobre 1976, Tome I, Miscellaneous Matters* (Imprimerie Nationale 1978) 121–124 (hereafter Droz, 'Note'); Hans van Loon, 'Note on the desirability of preparing a new Convention on

of private international law for addressing the relevant problems or needs had been identified. This preliminary work on new Hague instruments, intentionally or unintentionally, followed established patterns used in the discipline of project management. Project management is a method originating from business and management studies which is used to plan, manage and control the different life cycles of a project in order to achieve the project objectives within a certain pre-defined time limit.[429] In fact, the preparatory work undertaken by the Permanent Bureau for these two conventions can be viewed as a good-practice guide for applying techniques of project management, and in particular of the project-management sub-discipline project planning.[430] By applying project management techniques, the Permanent Bureau (as the project managers) enabled the Hague Conference Member States, the customers of the project,[431] to develop a draft convention text during the relevant Special Commission meetings (the pre-negotiation phase) concerning these two Conventions. These draft convention texts, the 'project deliverables',[432] were then used as a basis for the official multilateral negotiations by the Hague Conference Member States during a Diplomatic Conference.

From a project management perspective, good project planning begins by developing a concept for the project.[433] In general, developing a concept requires researching two questions: first, why the project is needed (i.e., which problems are to be addressed by the project), and second, what solutions can be used to address these needs or problems. This initial phase of project planning is called 'the concept phase', addressing the 'why' and the 'what' of a project.[434] In the case of Hague Conference project management, after a basic concept for a new project had been developed, this basic

---

international co-operation in respect of intercountry adoption: Prel Doc No 9 of December 1987 for the attention of the Special Commission of January 1988', in Hague Conference on Private International Law, *Proceedings of the Sixteenth Session, 3 to 20 October 1988, Tome I, Miscellaneous Matters* (SDU Publishers 1991) 165 (hereafter van Loon, 'Note').

429 Frame, *Managing Projects in Organizations* (n 60) 6; Project Management Institute, *PMBOK Guide* (n 60) 1, 4, 5.

430 Cf Pfund, 'Contributing to Progressive Development of Private International Law' (n 75) 109; cf also Bruch, 'How to Draft a Successful Family Law Convention' (n 115) 48.

431 Frame, *Managing Projects in Organizations* (n 60) 44.

432 Association for Project Management, *Introduction to Project Planning* (Association for Project Management 2008) 15.

433 Ibid 3, 12–14.

434 Ibid 12: '[t]he concept phase is the first phase in the project life cycle. During this phase, the need, the opportunity or problem is confirmed, the overall feasibility of the project is considered and a preferred solution is identified'.

concept was then approved by the Hague Conference Member States, and the project entered into its next phase, the phase of detailed planning (also called the 'definition phase', addressing the question of 'how').[435] During this phase of detailed planning, possible solutions were developed further.[436] After a strategic concept for creating a new convention had been developed by the Permanent Bureau during these first two phases, the Hague Conference Member States could then begin to work on the draft convention text during the Special Commission meetings.[437] These meetings were manned by experts in private international law who were engaged by the Members of the Hague Conference. In terms of project management, this phase was 'the implementation phase', as the strategy which had been developed during the concept phase, and which had been refined in the definition phase, was now implemented.[438] After a draft convention text, the 'project deliverable',[439] had been developed by the Special Commission meetings, it was then sent to the plenary meeting of the Hague Conference Member States, the Diplomatic Session.[440] There, the text was used as a basis for the official diplomatic negotiations among the Hague Conference Member States.[441] This penultimate phase of a project life cycle is called the 'handover phase'.[442]

In general, the work of the project managers does not stop after the definition phase. Rather, good project management requires the project managers to monitor and manage the plan that has been developed during the concept and definition phases throughout the whole process of developing a project, and to make adjustments if necessary.[443] The Permanent Bureau had always performed its project management duties

---

435 Ibid 14, 15: '[d]uring the definition phase the preferred solution is further evaluated and optimised – often an iterative process. This phase requires a transition to strategic planning […]. The plan defines how the project should be implemented and provides the basis for monitoring and control'.

436 Ibid.

437 Original Statute Hague Conference (n 18) art 7; see also Statute Hague Conference (n 18) art 8(1).

438 Association for Project Management (n 432) 15.

439 Ibid.

440 The Diplomatic Sessions, or Ordinary Sessions of the Hague Conference, should take place every four years, see Statute Hague Conference (n 18) art 4(6).

441 Statute Hague Conference (n 18) art 8(1).

442 Association for Project Management (n 432) 15: '[d]uring the handover phase, the project deliverables are handed over to the client and /or the users'; the final phase of a project life cycle is the closeout phase, in which 'project matters are finalised, final project reviews are carried out, project information is archived and the project team is redeployed', see ibid 16.

443 Association for Project Management (n 432) 15.

by means of a permanent physical presence in the meeting room of the Special Commission meetings and the Diplomatic Session.[444] This physical presence (known as the 'Bureau'[445]) enabled the lawyers of the Permanent Bureau, supported by its administration staff, to monitor and assist the discussions and the drafting process during the Special Commission meetings, and the negotiation process at the Diplomatic Conference. The Bureau also included the 'Officers of the Special Commission',[446] i.e., the Chairman of the meetings, the Vice-Chairmen, Reporter(s), and – depending on whether the stage of drafting the convention text had been reached – the Chairman of the drafting committee.[447] The role of the Bureau was to steer the meetings and to enable progress in the discussions.[448] In project-management terms, the 'Bureau' was the steering committee responsible for ensuring that the plan developed in the concept phase, and redefined during the phase of detailed planning, was implemented.[449]

In order to illustrate how project management by the Permanent Bureau normally looked, the following two parts will analyse in more detail the project management steps undertaken by the Permanent Bureau for preparing the Special Commission meetings on the 1980 Hague Convention on International Child Abduction and the 1993 Hague Convention on Intercountry Adoption. Following this, the project management techniques employed for these two projects will be compared to the preparatory work on the Judgments Project.

4.2. HAGUE CONFERENCE PROJECT MANAGEMENT FOR THE WORK ON THE 1980 HAGUE CONVENTION ON INTERNATIONAL CHILD ABDUCTION

The Permanent Bureau began to prepare work on the 1980 Hague Convention on International Child Abduction once the Canadian expert

444 Beaumont/McEleavy, *Child Abduction* (n 68) 25.

445 Ibid 25.

446 Cf Permanent Bureau, 'Conclusions of the Special Commission of June 1994 on the Question of the Recognition and Enforcement of Foreign Judgments in Civil and Commercial Matters: Prel Doc No 2 of December 1995' (n 201) 7, 8.

447 Cf Special Commission on the question of jurisdiction, recognition and enforcement of foreign judgments (17–27 June 1997), 'Report of Meeting No 1', 1 (on file with author).

448 Beaumont/McEleavy, *Child Abduction* (n 68) 25.

449 Cf Thomas G Lechler, Martin Cohen, 'Exploring the role of steering committees in realizing value from project management' (2009) 40 PMJ 42, 42.

T Bradbrooke Smith had made the Permanent Bureau aware in 1976 that States might be interested in the conclusion of a convention that could address the problems raised by international child abduction.[450] First, Georges A L Droz, the then Deputy Secretary General, conducted a preliminary study on the topic of international child abduction ('Note on Legal Kidnapping').[451] In this study, Droz undertook a preliminary assessment of the problems raised by international child abduction by one parent,[452] i.e., of the potential needs of States that a convention on international child abduction should address.[453] Droz had come to the conclusion that a convention containing mere mechanisms for the recognition and enforcement of judgments would be insufficient to deal with all of the problems arising in connection with international child abduction.[454] For example, a classic recognition and enforcement convention would be unable to effectively address the situation in which a child had been brought to or retained in a country other than the country of its original habitual residence by one parent against the will of the other parent, when no custody decision had as yet been rendered.[455] Furthermore, the Note looked into the question of how difficult it would be to implement certain objectives.[456] By means of this study, a possible concept for a convention on child abduction had been established (during the 'concept phase' of the project).[457] The topic of child abduction was then discussed by the Fourth Commission of the Thirteenth Session on the basis of this short conceptual study, and eventually added to the agenda of the Hague Conference.[458] By adding the topic to the agenda of the next

450 Dyer, 'Report on international child abduction by one parent: Prel Doc No 1 of August 1978' (n 125) 12.
451 Droz, 'Note' (n 428) 121.
452 Ibid 122–23 [IV].
453 Ibid 121.
454 Ibid 123 [IV]; Beaumont/McEleavy, *Child Abduction* (n 68) 17.
455 Droz, 'Note' (n 428) 121, 123, [IV.2]; the treaty mechanism that could deal with this situation by creating an obligation for the court or the administrative authority of the State of the new residence of the child to return it to the State of its habitual residence (the 'summary return mechanism', 1980 Hague Convention on International Child Abduction (n 80), art 12) later became the centrepiece of the 1980 Hague Convention on International Child Abduction, and contributed significantly to its success, see Beaumont/McEleavy, *Child Abduction* (n 68) 17, 21–3.
456 Droz, 'Note' (n 428) 123, 124, [V]–[VII].
457 Association for Project Management (n 432) 3, 12–14.
458 'Final Act', in *Actes et Documents de la Treizième Session 1976, Tome I* (n 428), 23, 36; Dyer, 'Report on international child abduction by one parent: Prel Doc No 1 of August 1978' (n 125) 12.

Diplomatic Session, this preliminarily developed concept was approved by the Hague Conference Member States.

Adair Dyer, Secretary of the Hague Conference, then began the detailed planning for a new Hague Convention, and the project entered the definition phase (the phase of detailed planning).[459] Dyer began the work on the definition phase by preparing a questionnaire addressed to the Hague Conference Member States (hereafter 'Dyer Questionnaire'),[460] accompanied by an extensive report (Dyer Report).[461] Both the questionnaire and report addressed the two basic conceptual questions of the very first phase of planning a project, the question of the 'why' (the need for the project) and of the 'what' (the methods to be used to address the identified needs), in more detail. The purpose of the questionnaire and report was to confirm the need for a convention, and to establish viable solutions for an instrument to address the problems of international child abduction effectively that the Hague Conference Member States could choose from.[462] In this way, Dyer had set out to establish a plan of construction that the Special Commission could follow, highlighting the necessary components of a new convention text, and showing possible ways forward in terms of feasible solutions, called 'methods' in the Dyer Report (addressing the 'how').[463] Regarding the conceptual question of how exactly the problems could be addressed, the Dyer Questionnaire identified seven methods which could be used to tackle the problems that arose in cases of international child abduction.[464] For example, the Questionnaire suggested that an international convention on child abduction could include provisions to facilitate the enforcement of decisions,[465] provisions that could speed up the return of the child[466] or strengthen administrative

---

459 Association for Project Management (n 432) 14: '[d]uring the definition phase the preferred solution is further evaluated and optimised – often an iterative process. This phase requires a transition to strategic planning'.

460 Adair Dyer, 'Questionnaire on international child abduction by one parent: Prel Doc No 1 of August 1978' in *Actes et Documents de la Quatorzième Session, Tome III, Child Abduction* (n 125) 9–11.

461 Dyer, 'Report on international child abduction by one parent: Prel Doc No 1 of August 1978' (n 125) 12–51.

462 Dyer, 'Questionnaire' (n 460) 9, 9–11.

463 'Possible Methods for Reducing or Ameliorating Problems of Child Abduction through Action by the Conference', in Dyer, 'Report on international child abduction by one parent: Prel Doc No 1 of August 1978' (n 125) 12, 46.

464 Cf ibid 'Questions 25 and 26' in Dyer, 'Report on international child abduction by one parent: Prel Doc No 1 of August 1978' (n 125) 46–51.

465 Cf 'Question 25, option a)', in Dyer, 'Questionnaire' (n 460) 11.

466 Cf 'Question 25, option c)' ibid.

co-operation between the States.[467] In addition, the questionnaire had sought to establish whether the proposed methods would be acceptable to the Member States of the Hague Conference.[468]

By asking the Member States about their preferences regarding the possible methods a convention on international child abduction could introduce, and by communicating these answers to the States, the Special Commission meetings, which took place in March and November 1979,[469] were equipped with a clear idea of the viable methods.[470] Furthermore, both the report and questionnaire had helped the Member States to develop a clear understanding of the problems arising in cases of international child abduction by one parent and of the need for a convention. Due to this, the States had been able to develop a clear idea of the way forward during this pre-negotiation phase before the Diplomatic Session. The governments' answers to the Dyer Questionnaire showed that four methods were acceptable to the States: the recognition and enforcement of custody decisions, harmonisation of rules of international jurisdiction, enhanced cooperation between administrative authorities, and the acceleration of the return of a child.[471] In this way, effective discussions during the implementation phase of the project (during the Special Commission meetings) and eventually successful inter-state negotiations (at the Fourteenth Diplomatic Session in October 1980) were facilitated.[472] At the same time, the project managers themselves had refined their understanding of why a convention was needed, and which methods such a convention should employ to address those needs.[473] In particular, by researching the (regulatory) needs of States regarding international child abduction by one parent, the Permanent Bureau was able to assist the Member States in developing a solution to those cases where no custody

[467] Cf 'Question 25, option g)' ibid.

[468] Cf ibid 11.

[469] 'Conclusions drawn from the discussions of the Special Commission of March 1979 on legal kidnapping: Preliminary Document No 5 of June 1979', and 'List of participants in the Special Commission's meetings', in *Actes et Documents de la Quatorzième Session, Tome III, Child Abduction* (n 125), 162 and 160.

[470] '[The Special Commission] had before it Preliminary Document No 1, *Questionnaire and Report on international child abduction by one parent*, prepared by Mr C A Dyer of the Permanent Bureau', ibid 162; see also 'Question 25' in Dyer, 'Questionnaire' (n 460) 11; cf also Beaumont/McEleavy, *Child Abduction* (n 68) 18.

[471] Beaumont/McEleavy (n 68) 18.

[472] Cf Dyer, 'Report on international child abduction by one parent: Prel Doc No 1 of August 1978' (n 125) 51; Beaumont/McEleavy, *Child Abduction* (n 68) 16–23.

[473] Cf Dyer, ibid; see also Frame, *Managing Projects in Organizations* (n 60) 111–116.

decision had as yet been rendered: the 'summary return mechanism', which was meant to ensure the quick return of a wrongfully removed or retained child to the State of its habitual residence.[474] By including this mechanism, the convention provided an efficient method to solve an acute problem, and addressed a real need of the Hague Conference Member States.[475] This mechanism was decisive in making the 1980 Hague Child Abduction Convention a successful instrument.[476]

4.3. HAGUE CONFERENCE PROJECT MANAGEMENT FOR THE WORK ON THE 1993 HAGUE CONVENTION ON INTERCOUNTRY ADOPTION

As with the preparation of the 1980 Hague Convention on International Child Abduction, the preparatory work of the Permanent Bureau on what became the 1993 Hague Convention on Intercountry Adoption first focussed on developing a basic concept for drafting a new Hague Convention in this area. The Permanent Bureau began its research by concentrating on gaining a clear understanding of the problems raised in connection with intercountry adoption, and of the potential interests or needs of States in concluding a convention (management of the 'why').[477] This research was an essential element to ensure the Permanent Bureau was in a position to identify suitable methods, or solutions, to deal with these problems (management of the 'what'), and to develop a concept for creating a new Hague Convention on Intercountry Adoption.[478] Hans

474 1980 Hague Convention on International Child Abduction (n 80) art 12; the summary-return mechanism had its origin in a proposal of a Swiss expert made during the preparatory work on the Custody Convention of the Council of Europe, see Beaumont/McEleavy, *Child Abduction* (n 68) 17.

475 By consulting with the governments of the Member States and the International Social Service (an international NGO), the Permanent Bureau was able to establish that almost 50% of abductions or retentions by one parent into/in a State other than the State of the last habitual residence of the child took place where no judicial decision on the custody had as yet been made, see Adair Dyer, 'International Child Abduction by Parents' (1980) 168 Recueil des Cours de l'Académie de Droit International 252, 253; Beaumont/McEleavy, *Child Abduction* (n 68) 17.

476 See above (n 80) and Bruch, 'How to Draft a Successful Family Law Convention' (n 115) 49, 50; Beaumont/McEleavy, *Child Abduction* (n 68) 20, 21, 31.

477 Van Loon, 'Note' (n 428) [1]–[44], in particular [44], [45].

478 Ibid [49]–[58]; Van Loon, 'Report on Intercountry Adoption – Prel Doc No 1 of April 1990' (n 92) 14–101.

van Loon, then Secretary of the Hague Conference, had begun the work on the topic through a meticulous study of the social and legal problems surrounding the phenomenon of intercountry adoption. In particular, the study analysed new social and legal developments since the adoption of the 1965 Hague Convention on Intercountry Adoption, and the question of why this convention was not able to meet the present day's needs.[479] Already in the early stages of planning (the concept phase), the conceptual study (or short feasibility study) for a new Hague Convention on Intercountry Adoption – the 'Note' prepared by van Loon – had identified four potential needs that this new instrument should address:[480] the need to set up standards for intercountry adoptions, the need to establish a system of supervision to ensure adherence to these standards, the need for establishing channels of communication between authorities of countries of origin and receiving countries, and the need for cooperation between the aforementioned countries.[481]

The Note then made two concrete suggestions for the form of a new convention, i.e., two proposals regarding the methods a new Hague Adoption Convention could employ ('what'). As a first option, the Note suggested setting up a convention that would be 'limited to meeting only the needs for standards and for a system of supervision'.[482] As a second option, which the Note reported 'would be even more useful, but also more ambitious', it suggested creating a convention establishing 'a system of mutual information and co-operation between sending and receiving countries' which 'would by its very nature require the Conference to open its doors for non-Member, sending countries, to participate on an equal footing with the Member States'.[483]

The Note was considered by the Special Commission of General Affairs and Policy of the Conference, which recommended retaining the topic on the agenda of the Hague Conference.[484] In this way, the concept was

479 Van Loon, 'Note' (n 428) [1]–[43]; [48].

480 The 'old' Hague Convention on Intercountry Adoption, the Convention on Jurisdiction, Applicable Law and Recognition of Decrees Relating to Adoption (adopted 15 November 1964) had not – and still has not – entered into force, see Hague Conference on Private International Law, 'Convention of 15 November 1965 on Jurisdiction, Applicable Law and Recognition of Decrees Relating to Adoptions: Status table' <https://www.hcch.net/en/instruments/conventions/status-table/?cid=75> accessed 10 January 2024.

481 Van Loon, 'Note' (n 428) [44].

482 Ibid [57].

483 Ibid [59].

484 Ibid [3].

incidentally and provisionally approved by the Hague Conference Member States. Furthermore, the Special Commission 'invited the Secretary General to obtain assurances from those countries of origin which were not at that time Members of the Hague Conference that they would be willing to co-operate with the Conference, and to report back to the Sixteenth Session'.[485] After many non-Member States of the Hague Conference had signalled that they would be willing to work on a new Hague Adoption Convention, the First Commission of the Sixteenth Session of the Hague Conference decided on 19 October 1988 to include the topic of intercountry adoption with priority on the agenda of the Seventeenth Session of the Hague Conference.[486] The decision to add intercountry adoption to the agenda was directly linked to the agreement of the States of origin to participate in the negotiations of a new Hague instrument.[487] Van Loon's suggestion to invite countries of origin to the negotiations was an important step in the strategic planning which was necessary in order to successfully draft a new convention.

After the topic of intercountry adoption had been included in the agenda of the Hague Conference with priority, and the concept had been incidentally approved, the project entered the definition phase (the phase of detailed planning), the second phase of its life cycle. In this phase, the methods that had been preliminarily identified in the concept phase were confirmed and developed further (addressing the question of 'how').[488] This phase was prepared again by means of an extensive report by the Permanent Bureau ('Report on Intercountry Adoption', or Van Loon Report).[489] After a 'tour d'horizon'[490] of the issues raised by intercountry adoption, van Loon was able to confirm that a future convention should indeed achieve three objectives: ensuring that an intercountry adoption would only be allowed as a means of last resort; defining 'criteria and improv[ing] practices and procedures for intercountry adoption once it ha[d] been established that that [was] the only viable alternative to the child', and fighting abuses of intercountry adoption, in particular child trafficking.[491]

---

485 Ibid [3].

486 Ibid [3].

487 Van Loon, 'Report on Intercountry Adoption: Prel Doc No 1 of April 1990' (n 92) [2].

488 Association for Project Management (n 432) 14.

489 Van Loon, 'Report on Intercountry Adoption: Prel Doc No 1 of April 1990' (n 92) 14–101.

490 Ibid [169].

491 Ibid.

The Van Loon Report then made concrete suggestions for how exactly to address these needs, and engaged with the phase of detailed planning. The Report first suggested that the classical methods of harmonisation in private international law (i.e., harmonising rules of international jurisdiction and of the applicable law on intercountry adoptions) would not be able to ensure the best interest of the child in the process of intercountry adoption.[492] Other mechanisms would be needed to address these needs. The Report proposed that a convention should hold the authorities of the country of origin responsible for establishing whether an intercountry adoption was the last alternative for the child.[493] The Report also proposed that the convention should contain certain standards and principles for intercountry adoption that would improve practices and procedures for intercountry adoption worldwide.[494] Finally, the Report pointed out that the convention should help to tackle the problem of international child trafficking,[495] and noted that this would first and foremost require 'strict control over the activities of intermediaries, which should meet the criteria defined for them'.[496]

The Report then redefined (as compared to the Note) the suggestions for mechanisms that could put the identified objectives into practice: for example, it suggested installing a system of Central Authorities to coordinate the use of a future Hague Convention on Intercountry Adoption, and to ensure its proper application by the Contracting States.[497] The Report also advised that conflict-of-law problems could be reduced by defining certain criteria concerning the biological parents, the child and the adoptive parents in the convention, thereby reducing the need to apply possibly conflicting laws of the countries involved.[498] Also, the Report recommended that the recognition of adoption decrees and preliminary decisions should be ensured by means of the convention.[499] On the basis of this Report which had set out a roadmap for the experts for their future work on an adoption convention and which had concluded the phase

492 Cf ibid [169]–[187].

493 Ibid [170]; 1993 Intercountry Adoption Convention (n 80), art 4.

494 Van Loon, 'Report on Intercountry Adoption: Prel Doc No 1 of April 1990' (n 92) [171].

495 Ibid [172].

496 Ibid.

497 Ibid [173]–[179].

498 Ibid [180].

499 Ibid [181].

of detailed planning, the project entered into its implementation phase during the Special Commission meetings.[500]

It is interesting to note that the text finally adopted as the 1993 Hague Convention on Intercountry Adoption implemented the methods recommended by the van Loon Report to address regulatory problems raised in connection with intercountry adoption. For example, a system of Central Authorities was established.[501] Furthermore, Chapter II of the 1993 Hague Convention on Intercountry Adoption contained a list of requirements that had to be fulfilled before an intercountry adoption could take place according to the convention. The convention also prescribed in its Chapter V that an adoption certified by the competent authority of the State of the adoption as having been made in accordance with the convention should, in principle, be recognised by operation of law in the other Contracting States.[502]

By thoroughly researching the needs of States for a multilateral solution to the problems raised in connection with inter-country adoption, by suggesting the participation of non-Hague Conference Member States in the negotiations, and by recommending feasible methods to address these needs, Hans van Loon had enabled the Member States of the Hague Conference and the countries of origin to successfully engage in negotiations on a convention text on intercountry adoption.[503]

4.4. HAGUE CONFERENCE PROJECT MANAGEMENT FOR THE WORK ON THE HAGUE JUDGMENTS PROJECT

For the preliminary work on the Hague Judgments Project, the Permanent Bureau deviated from the project management techniques it had used for the 1980 Hague Convention on International Child Abduction and the 1993

500 Permanent Bureau, 'Conclusions of the Special Commission of June 1990 on intercountry adoption: Preliminary Document No 3 of August 1990', in Hague Conference on Private International Law, *Proceedings of the Seventeenth Session, 10 to 29 May 1993, Tome II, Adoption* (SDU Publishers 1994) 129, 129: '[t]he Special Commission on intercountry adoption met for the first time at the Peace Palace in The Hague from 11–21 June 1990'.

501 1993 Intercountry Adoption Convention (n 80), ch III.

502 Ibid art 23.

503 Gustavo Parra-Aranguren, 'Explanatory Report on the Convention on Protection of Children and Co-operation in Respect of Intercountry Adoption', in Hague

Hague Convention on Intercountry Adoption. Firstly, the Permanent Bureau did not prepare a general conceptual study for developing a global judgments convention. Secondly, it did not manage the general concept development phase during the Special Commission meetings in June 1994 and June 1996 with the same rigour it had employed for previous projects. Finally, it did not fully engage with the phase of detailed planning (the definition phase) before the Judgments Project entered its implementation phase (drafting a convention text) during the Special Commission meetings from 1997 to 1999.[504]

4.4.1. FAILURE TO DEVELOP A GENERAL CONCEPT FOR A CONVENTION ON JURISDICTION AND JUDGMENTS

The question of whether the topic of creating a new Hague Judgments Convention should be added to the agenda for future work of the Hague Conference was discussed during the Seventeenth Session of the Conference in 1993.[505] Normally, the Member States of the Hague Conference would have based this decision on a general conceptual study prepared by the Permanent Bureau (cf Note Droz[506] and Note van Loon[507]). This study would have provided a preliminary assessment of the needs, or interests, of the Member States in a global judgments convention, and recommended feasible methods to address the preliminarily identified needs. For the preparatory work on the Judgments Project, such a study should have focussed inter alia on the interests or needs of the US and the Member States of the EC concerning a judgments convention. These two groups of States represented the two largest economic areas at the time,[508] and a global judgments convention without the US or the EC Member States as Contracting States could not have been considered truly successful. Securing the acceptability of the convention text by these two stakeholders was therefore essential, as their non-acceptance of the draft

Conference on Private International Law, *Proceedings of the Seventeenth Session, 10 to 29 May 1993, Tome II, Adoption* (SDU Publishers 1994) 537 [2].

504 Addressed in Chapter 5.

505 'Final Act of the Seventeenth Session', in Hague Conference on Private International Law, *Proceedings of the Seventeenth Session, 10 to 29 May 1993, Tome I, Miscellaneous Matters* (SDU Publishers 1995) 29, 43.

506 Droz, 'Note' (n 428).

507 Van Loon, 'Note' (n 428).

508 See above, Section 2.2.

Convention would have led to a failure of the project. Therefore the US and the Member States of the EC were the main project stakeholders.[509] Moreover, a possible outcome of the negotiations could have been a judgments convention that would have entered into force *only* between States agreeing to establish treaty relations amongst each other (by means of what has been called the process of 'bilateralisation').[510] This made the needs analysis of the US and the EC Member States (and possibly the EFTA Member States) even more important when considering the creation of a treaty regime on jurisdiction and judgments between the European States and the US.

4.4.1.1. Preparations for the Seventeenth Diplomatic Session in May 1993

In reality, the Preliminary Document prepared by the Permanent Bureau in response to the US proposal to add work on a judgments convention to the agenda of the Hague Conference during its Seventeenth Session (Preliminary Document No 17 of May 1992; hereafter Prel Doc No 17),[511] was only able to 'sketch'[512] the problems raised by the planning of an international judgments convention, and of the interests of States involved.[513] Prel Doc No 17 conducted a preliminary needs analysis and initially recommended (based on a preliminary assessment of the possible methods) to work towards a single convention only (possibly enriched with a red list of indirect grounds of jurisdiction prohibiting the recognition and enforcement of judgments rendered on these bases).[514] This preliminary needs analysis was not based on a study of the actual needs or interests of the Hague Conference Members in general, however, or of the Member States of the EC and the US in particular. Prel Doc No 17 did not fully engage with the question of the 'why', i.e. why the Hague Conference Member States

---

509 See, e.g., Janet Walker, 'Canada's Position on a Multilateral Judgments Convention', in Carmody/Iwasawa/Rhodes (eds), *Trilateral Perspectives* (n 341) 127, 129.

510 See Fragistas, 'Rapport de la Commission spécial' (n 127) 24; Letter Edwin D Williamson to Georges Droz (n 25); Permanent Bureau, 'Some Reflections: Prel Doc No 17 of May 1992' (n 131) 237, 239.

511 Permanent Bureau, 'Some Reflections: Prel Doc No 17 of May 1992' (n 131) 231–239.

512 'Conclusions of the Special Commission of June 1992 on general affairs and policy of the Conference', in Hague Conference on Private International Law, *Proceedings of the Seventeenth Session, 10 to 29 May 1993, Tome I, Miscellaneous Matters* (SDU Publishers 1995) 245, 253.

513 Ibid 253.

514 Permanent Bureau, 'Some Reflections: Prel Doc No 17 of May 1992' (n 131) [13], [17]; Beaumont, 'The revived Judgments Project' (n 43) 532.

needed an international judgments convention.[515] Regarding the needs analysis, Prel Doc No 17 only undertook a mostly theoretical assessment of the possible needs for a global judgments convention: '[w]ith rapidly expanding commercial contacts worldwide [...], legal uncertainty, delays and costs caused by the absence of a general enforcement of judgments convention are likely to interfere increasingly with the needs of trade and business'.[516] The document then went on to state that not all the countries in the world would be as receptive to foreign judgments as the US, but that 'many countries impose restrictions such as jurisdiction tests, reciprocity, choice of law tests, revision au fond'.[517] Finally, countries like the Member States of the EC or the US would continue to render and enforce judgments based on exorbitant grounds of jurisdiction against defendants domiciled in a third State.[518] Prel Doc No 17 then presented a general overview of the available convention types for creating an international judgments convention (addressing the question of 'what'): the single convention, the double convention, and the mixed convention.[519]

Prel Doc No 17 also discussed the feasibility of the respective convention types, but not in great depth.[520] With regard to the mixed convention, Prel Doc No 17 confined itself to quote the letter from the US legal advisor Edwin D Williamson for an explanation of this convention type,[521] and concluded the discussion of the mixed-convention concept by listing its advantages and disadvantages:

> The main advantage of this proposal over a *traité simple* [a single convention], it would seem, is that it will achieve partial *uniformity* at the level of jurisdictional grounds among Contracting States. The uniformity will only be partial because countries would remain free to maintain existing non-exorbitant grounds of jurisdiction and, indeed, might create new ones which leaves room for new developments in response to new needs. This would mean, however, that the enforcing court, just as in the case of a *traité simple*, but unlike the Lugano Convention, could not dispense with controlling the grounds upon which the original court has based its jurisdiction. Moreover, if the grounds of jurisdiction offered by the new convention were to be direct, but not exclusive, this must mean that the parties were offered the choice between approaching different

515 Permanent Bureau, 'Some Reflections: Prel Doc No 17 of May 1992' (n 131) [2]–[4].
516 Ibid [2].
517 Ibid [4].
518 Ibid [4], [13].
519 Ibid [14]–[19].
520 Ibid.
521 Ibid [14].

> courts in different jurisdictions. This would mean opening the doors for forum shopping and it would lead to difficult problems of *lis pendens*.[522]

Prel Doc No 17 then pointed out some of the difficulties that could arise when creating unified grounds of international direct jurisdiction in general (i.e., both under a strict double convention and under a mixed convention) in a Hague Judgments Convention:

> One of the problems with a convention of the *traité double* type is that unless the new grounds of jurisdiction were to be framed very close to those of the Lugano Convention, one may expect some reluctance on the part of (some of) the Lugano countries to accept such grounds. [...] Additional pressure to stick as closely as possible to the existing Brussels and Lugano texts may come from the system of uniform interpretation.[523]

Nevertheless, Prel Doc No 17 noted that it could not be 'excluded that negotiations in the Hague Conference might lead to a new *traité double*', thereby preliminarily confirming the feasibility not only of a mixed convention, but also of a strict double convention (as both convention types are double conventions).[524] Prel Doc No 17 eventually concluded with an explicit recommendation of the Permanent Bureau for creating a single convention, which could be expanded to a double convention, provided sufficient progress was made on the single convention: '[t]he most cautious approach, however, it would seem would be to start with examining the possibility of a *traité simple* and see whether one could [make] a further step. This was also the course taken by the initial negotiators of the Brussels Convention.'[525]

A possible cause for neglecting these essential, preliminary steps of project planning (conducting an analysis of the concrete needs, and of a study of feasible solutions to address these needs through a judgments convention) by the Permanent Bureau was most likely the timing of the proposal by the US: the topic of the enforcement of judgments was first suggested to the Conference through a letter from the US Department of State Legal Adviser on 5 May 1992,[526] less than one month before the topic should have been discussed by a plenary meeting of the Hague Conference during the Special Commission on General Affairs and Policy, from 1–4 June 1992 in The Hague.[527]

522 Ibid [15].
523 Ibid [16].
524 Ibid [18]; see also above, Chapter 2.
525 Ibid [18].
526 'Conclusions of the Special Commission of June 1992 on GAP' (n 512) 253.
527 Ibid.

The purpose of the Special Commission meeting on General Affairs and Policy was to prepare for the decisions to be taken during the Seventeenth Diplomatic Session in May 1993 on which new projects should be placed on the agenda for future work of the Hague Conference.[528] As previously discussed, the work cycle of the Hague Conference normally lasted four years,[529] and the next four-year cycle was meant to begin after the Seventeenth Diplomatic Session in May 1993 (the Seventeenth Session also marked the centenary of the Hague Conference).[530] The US most likely regarded it as essential to start work on the convention as soon as possible since it originally intended to adopt the convention during the Eighteenth Diplomatic Session in 1996.[531] Due to the lack of time between receiving the letter from the US and the meeting of the Special Commission on General Affairs and Policy, the Permanent Bureau was only in a position to draft a 'preliminary report' on the topic (Prel Doc No 17) before the meeting in June 1992.[532] Since the US was a very important Member State of the Hague Conference, the Permanent Bureau most likely would not have been in a position to defer the proposal.[533]

Since Prel Doc No 17 did not (and could not) engage with the questions of 'why' and 'what' in great detail, 'the discussions [at the Special Commission meeting on General Affairs and Policy] were not able to go into great depth'.[534] Nevertheless, the States represented at the meeting 'recognized that the American proposal offered significant interest and deserved attention, though it would have been premature to take a decision immediately, even to recommend its rejection or its acceptance'.[535] Had the Permanent Bureau followed its established methods of project management, which had proven so successful in the past, then the next steps of the planning process would have been to establish the needs of

528 Ibid 245.

529 Original Statute Hague Conference (n 18) art 3(6) (now Statute Hague Conference (n 18) art 4(6)).

530 Cf Hague Conference on Private International Law, *Proceedings of the Seventeenth Session, 10 to 29 May 1993, Tome I, Miscellaneous Matters* (SDU Publishers 1995) 3.

531 Letter Edwin D Williamson to Georges Droz (n 25), 1. Eventually, however, the Judgments Project was indeed only put on the agenda of the Hague Conference during the Eighteenth Session in 1996, with a view to adopt a convention during the Nineteenth Session, see 'Final Act of the Eighteenth Session' (n 27) 47.

532 Permanent Bureau, 'Some Reflections: Prel Doc No 17 of May 1992' (n 131); cf also Paul Beaumont, 'The Hague Choice of Court Agreement Convention 2005: Background, Negotiations, Analysis and Current Status' (2009) 5 JPIL 125, 128.

533 See above, Section 2.2.

534 'Conclusions of the Special Commission of June 1992 on GAP' (n 512) 245, 253.

535 Ibid.

States for a judgments convention (researching the 'why') properly, and to conduct research into the possible methods for reaching the identified objectives, including their feasibility. The Permanent Bureau, however, considered the time too short for it to develop a strategy for creating a global judgments convention on its own before the Seventeenth Diplomatic Session of the Hague Conference in May 1993.[536] One reason may have been the enormous workload the Permanent Bureau was facing in the early stages of (and also throughout) the Judgments Project,[537] with the support of only four permanent lawyers at the Permanent Bureau.[538] In fact, a report prepared by a consulting agency in 2002 concluded that the Permanent Bureau lacked adequate resources to perform its tasks.[539]

---

536 'Intervention Mr van Loon', in 'Minutes No 3', in *Proceedings of the Seventeenth Session, Tome I* (n 530) 327: '[t]he proposal [for a judgments convention] had been submitted late and the Special Commission [on General Affairs and Policy of June 1992] had therefore set up a working party to consider whether the subject was an appropriate topic for the Hague Conference and, if so, what would be the advantage of a convention dealing only with the recognition and enforcement ("single" convention) rather than one which also includes the assumption of jurisdiction to adjudicate ("double" convention)'.

537 In 1992, the Permanent Bureau was busy preparing for the Seventeenth Session in 1993 during which the Hague Convention on Intercountry Adoption should be (and was) adopted; moreover, the Permanent Bureau was preparing topics that were to be discussed during the Seventeenth Session, including the revision of the Convention of 5 October 1961 concerning the powers of authorities and the law applicable in respect of the protection of minors (and a possible extension of the new convention's scope to the protection of incapacitated adults), and various other topics, see 'Final Act Seventeenth Session' (n 505) 43. In addition, the Permanent Bureau had been charged with other tasks, as for example, preparing for and convening the Special Commission meetings to review the Operation of the Hague Convention on the Civil Aspects of International Child Abduction in January 1993, see Permanent Bureau, 'Report of the Second Special Commission Meeting to Review the Operation of the Hague Convention on the Civil Aspects of International Child Abduction held 18–21 January 1993', <https://assets.hcch.net/upload/abdrpt93e.pdf> accessed 4 April 2023, [1].

538 'The Hague Conference on Private International Law on the Eve of the New Millennium: Some Concrete Suggestions for Strategic Action proposed by the Informal Group of Ambassadors of the Council of Diplomatic Representatives: Summary of the Discussions of the Group, prepared by the Chairman – Preliminary Document No 2 of March 2000', in Hague Conference on Private International Law, *Proceedings of the Nineteenth Session, 6 to 22 June 2001 – Part One, 2 to 13 December 2002 – Part Two, Tome I, Miscellaneous Matters* (Koninklijke Brill NV 2008) 67, 67 [7].

539 PriceWaterhouseCoopers, 'The Hague Conference on Private International Law: Resource Deficiencies and Strategic Positioning', in *Proceedings of the Nineteenth Session, Tome I* (n 538), 119, 121 [1]: '[o]ur research shows clearly that the Secretariat [...] of the Hague Conference has inadequate resources for the tasks it is currently required to perform. Our analysis shows an approximate 30% gap between the resources of the Secretariat and the workload [...]. We based our analysis on the assumption of four operative lawyers'.

Due to these constraints, the then Secretary General, Georges Droz, proposed to set up a Working Group that would meet before the Seventeenth Session, in order to make recommendations to this plenary meeting of the Hague Conference Member States.[540] The Special Commission on General Affairs and Policy approved this suggestion.[541] It was further decided that this Working Group would consist of

> experts in the field of judicial jurisdiction, and after consultation it was [also] decided that the group would be composed of an expert from Argentina or Venezuela, from China, from Egypt, from Finland, from France, from Hungary, from the United Kingdom and from the United States.[542]

Eventually, the Working Group was composed of 13 experts from nine Hague Conference Member States.[543] This Working Group was charged with the preparation of a report for the consideration of the Seventeenth Session, considering the general appropriateness of the topic for the Hague Conference, and also the respective advantages of a single, double and mixed convention.[544]

4.4.1.2. *The Consequences of Outsourcing the Planning of the Conceptual Phase to a Working Group: No Definite Decision on Including the Judgments Project in the Agenda of the Hague Conference*

The Working Group fulfilled its mandate and prepared a conceptual study which recommended the mixed convention[545] as the best method to create a global judgments convention. The conclusions of the Working Group were made available as Prel Doc No 19.[546] At the same time, the Working Group rejected a strict double convention as a viable strategy for drafting a global judgments convention: the Working Group reached the conclusion 'that a complete double convention of the Brussels/Lugano type, appropriate as it

---

540 'Conclusions of the Special Commission of June 1992 on GAP' (n 512) 253.

541 Ibid.

542 Ibid.

543 'Conclusions of the Working Group, Prel Doc No 19 of November 1992' (n 28) 257 [1]: Mr A Boggiano from Argentina, Mr Li Haopei and Mr Zhang Kening from China, Mr A Amer from Egypt, Mr G Möller from Finland, Mr J Lemontey from France, Mr T Bán from Hungary, Mr J A C Watherston and Mr P M Beaton from the United Kingdom, Mr P H Pfund, Mr A T von Mehren and Mr P D Trooboff from the United States, and Mr G Parra-Aranguren from Venezuela.

544 Ibid [2].

545 For a definition of the term 'mixed convention', see above, Section 2.1.

546 'Conclusions of the Working Group – Prel Doc No 19 of November 1992' (n 28) 257.

may be in a regional framework, would be overly ambitious in the context of the broad Hague Conference membership'.[547] As a result, the Working Group 'expressed a preference for a convention which would offer some of the advantages of a double convention, while at the same time having a greater degree of flexibility than that available with the convention of the Brussels/Lugano type'.[548] This means that the Working Group had expressed a preference for a mixed convention, based on the proposal of the distinguished private international law expert, Professor Arthur T von Mehren, who was also a member of the US delegation to the Special Commission meetings on the Judgments Project and of the Working Group.[549] What the Working Group had done, therefore, was to research the feasibility of the different convention types that were available for concluding a global judgments convention. The Working Group had made a recommendation for what was the only method that had a reasonable chance to lead to the adoption of an international convention, regulating at the same time the recognition and enforcement of judgments as well as international direct jurisdiction: the mixed convention.[550]

However, the fact that it had not been the Permanent Bureau itself which had prepared the conceptual study proved problematic. Without a neutral, well-reasoned recommendation by the project managers (the Permanent Bureau) in favour of the mixed convention, the Member States of the Hague Conference represented at the Seventeenth Session in May 1993 could not be convinced of first, the general desirability (i.e., the need) for concluding a judgments convention, and second, of the attractiveness and the feasibility of the mixed-convention model (the only method for concluding a judgments convention with a reasonable chance of success).[551] Although the Working Group had identified the best and in fact the *only* viable approach for concluding a judgments convention on a global level,[552] the validity of these recommendations was not accepted by the plenary meeting of the Hague Conference Member States during the Seventeenth Session. Two reasons can be identified: first, the validity of these recommendations was questioned because the neutrality of the

---

547 Ibid [5].

548 Ibid [5].

549 See above (n 543); 'Conclusions of the Special Commission of June 1994' (n 446) 4.

550 See above, Sections 2.3.2. and 2.4.

551 Peter D Trooboff, 'Proposed Hague Conference General Convention on Jurisdiction and the Recognition and Enforcement of Judgments – Some Thoughts on Finding Solutions to Tough Issues', in Alegría Borrás et al (eds), *E Pluribus Unum: Liber Amicorum Georges A L Droz* (Martinus Nijhoff Publishers 1996) 461, 470.

552 See Chapters 2 and 3.

Working Group was doubted; and second, the preparation of the conceptual strategy failed to convince in its substance due to a lack of depth of the conclusions by the Working Group.[553]

The limited size of the Working Group raised concerns regarding the fairness of this process,[554] as it comprised only nine Member States of the Hague Conference (Argentina, China, Egypt, Finland, France, Hungary, the United Kingdom, the US and Venezuela),[555] representing only roughly 25% of the total number of the then 35 Member States.[556] The recommendation for a mixed convention by the Working Group was therefore not perceived as the result of a neutral study of the needs or interests of all Member States (study of the 'why'), and of a study of appropriate methods to conclude a global judgments convention (study of the 'what'). The perceived lack of neutrality and procedural fairness made it difficult for the other Member States to accept the Working Group's conclusions,[557] even though the Working Group had indeed recommended the one convention type with the best chances of securing the adoption of a convention text on jurisdiction and judgments.[558] Rather, as the Swiss delegate noted, the recommendation of the Working Group to conclude a mixed convention was perceived to be an expression of merely American interests[559] or concerns.[560] Equally, the delegate of

553 For example, the Danish delegate to the Seventeenth Session of the Hague Conference, Mr Allan Philip, noted that the Working Group proposal lacked depth regarding the study of the general need for a convention, see 'Minutes No 3' in *Proceedings of the Seventeenth Session, Tome I* (n 530) 327. In fact, the Conclusions of the Working Group had apparently not even convinced all the members of the group itself, see 'Intervention Mr Parra-Aranguren', ibid at 330, noting that he 'would not insist on the need for a convention concerning recognition and enforcement of foreign judgments', thereby questioning the why; see also 'Intervention Mr Boggiano', ibid, noting that he 'favoured the approach suggested by the Danish delegation [starting with the consideration of exorbitant jurisdiction and using Article 59 of the Brussels Convention as a starting point]'; Mr Boggiano then suggested that the Permanent Bureau should prepare a report focussing on the question of the convention type, see ibid.

554 Rebecca Hollander-Blumoff, Tom R Tyler, 'Procedural Justice in Negotiation: Procedural Fairness, Outcome Acceptance, and Integrative Potential' (2003) 33(2) Law & Social Inquiry 473, 492.

555 'Conclusions of the Working Group: Prel Doc No 19 of November 1992' (n 28) 257 [1].

556 Cf 'Statute of the Hague Conference on Private International Law: Status table' (n 72).

557 Hollander-Blumoff, Tyler (n 554) 491, 492, 494.

558 See above, Chapter 2.

559 See the intervention of Mme Jametti Greiner in 'Minutes No 3', in *Proceedings of the Seventeenth Session, Tome I* (n 530) 328.

560 Bucher, 'Vers une convention mondiale' (n 173) 77, fn 2: 'Les débats préliminaires [until the Special Commission meeting of June 1996] étaient en revanche inspirés

Portugal, Ms Magalhães Collaço, questioned whether the Working Group was the right vehicle to advance the project, due to the limited number of States represented in it.[561]

The recommendations of the Working Group failed to attract agreement from the other Member States of the Hague Conference not only due to neutrality concerns. Additionally, the depth of analysis by the Working Group regarding the general need for a judgments convention (the 'why'), as well as the analysis of the available methods (the 'what') was questioned; when the question of whether and with what priority the topic of recognition and enforcement of foreign judgments should be placed on the agenda was discussed during the Seventeenth Session, out of 35 States represented, 16 States expressed reservations about the project. Out of these 16 States, 4 States expressly requested further studies on the general need for a convention,[562] and 8 States requested further studies on the method (including the feasibility of the possible methods for concluding a global judgments convention).[563]

Indeed, these concerns had some merit. Due to the limited size of the Working Group, it naturally could comment mainly on the needs for, or at the least, the interests of the States represented in the Group in a global judgments convention. Moreover, Prel Doc No 19 (the Conclusions of the Working Group) had not studied the feasibility of concluding a mixed convention, or a double convention, in detail. In fact, the Working Group had not researched in great depth the reasons why a convention of the

des préoccupations américaines.' (The preliminary discussion [until the Special Commission meeting of June 1996] however had been inspired by American concerns.') (Translation provided by the author.).

561 See the intervention of Mme de Magalhães Collaço in 'Minutes No 3' in *Proceedings of the Seventeenth Session, Tome I* (n 530) 329.

562 See the interventions from the delegates of the following countries during the Meeting of Thursday, 20 May 1993, 'Minutes No 3' and 'Minutes No 4', in *Proceedings of the Seventeenth Session, Tome I* (n 530) 327–336, all not insisting on the need for a convention: Denmark (Mr Philip), 327; Japan (Mr Shimizu), 328; Switzerland (Ms Jametti Greiner), 328; Venezuela (Mr Parra-Aranguren), 330.

563 Ibid 327–336: Denmark (Mr Philip) and Germany (Mr Wagner), both suggesting Article 59 Brussels Convention 1968 as a starting point; Japan (Mr Shimizu), 328; Canada (Ms Verdon), 328; Mexico (Mr Siqueiros, questioning the feasibility of even a global single convention), 330; Israel (Mr Goldwater), 330; Egypt (Mr Mubarak), 330; Argentina (Mr Boggiano), 330; Sweden (Mrs Hagelberg), 330: 'although the Working Party had drawn up an interesting and valuable document, more work was required. An in-depth analysis and suggestions on the direction which should be taken by such a convention was necessary. She welcomed the Danish approach as being a valuable contribution'.

strict double-convention type would be technically unfeasible on a global level. Prel Doc No 19 merely stated that 'it felt that a complete double convention of the Brussels/Lugano type, appropriate as it may be in a regional framework, would be overly ambitious in the context of the broad Hague Conference membership.'[564] Moreover, the Working Group noted

> that it would be attempting too much in a worldwide context [...] to require the court of origin to assume jurisdiction only on the grounds specified in the convention; and to require the court requested to enforce the judgment to do so without examination of the grounds of jurisdiction on which the original court had based its judgment – even if it were an 'exorbitant' ground of jurisdiction.[565]

It did not stress, however, the enormous challenge that unifying direct grounds of jurisdiction posed.[566] It also did not point out the difficulties the unification of direct jurisdiction would raise from the point of view of the US: due to constitutional constraints, the possibilities for unifying grounds of international direct jurisdiction were limited.[567] A comprehensive study of the feasibility of a global double convention was not covered by the remit of the Working Group's mandate, however, which only asked for a report from the Group to answer the following questions:

> [I]s the topic an appropriate one for the Conference to take up? If so, what are the advantages of an approach in the form of a convention dealing only with recognition and enforcement (a so-called *convention simple*, 'single' convention) as compared with one in the form of a convention that addresses not only recognition and enforcement, but also the assumption of jurisdiction to adjudicate (a so-called *convention double*, 'double convention')? Or, as the United States had proposed to the Special Commission, and explained in more detail in a paper submitted to the Working Group, would a mixed form, incorporating elements of both single and double conventions, be preferable?[568]

Had the Permanent Bureau itself taken charge of developing a convention concept, and had it employed the same rigour as for the work on other conventions, it would have preliminarily assessed the feasibility of creating

564 'Conclusions Working Group: Prel Doc No 19 November 1992' (n 28) [5].
565 Ibid.
566 See Section 2.2.
567 Ibid.
568 'Conclusions Working Group: Prel Doc No 19 November 1992' (n 28) [2].

both a strict double convention and a mixed convention. Moreover, such preparations should have entailed the production of a comparative report on the domestic rules on international direct jurisdiction existing in the Hague Conference Member States, potentially based on questionnaires, in order to assess the feasibility of unifying grounds of direct jurisdiction in general, and between the US and the EC Member States in particular.[569] The study of the feasibility of the possible methods for concluding a judgments convention would have revealed that the mixed-convention concept was in fact the only viable option with a real chance to positively regulate not only the recognition and enforcement of foreign judgments, but also the exercise of international jurisdiction,[570] and that the strict double convention approach was in fact unfeasible.[571]

In reality, since a significant number of delegates had expressed doubts about the need for or the correct approach to the project during the Seventeenth Session, a compromise solution regarding the question of whether the topic should be included in the agenda of the Hague Conference was sought on the basis of a proposal by the delegation of Denmark.[572] The topic of the enforcement of judgments was tentatively added to the agenda of the Conference, with the understanding that further work on conceptual planning was needed before the Member States could decide whether they wanted to work towards a Diplomatic Conference or not. The Seventeenth Session decided to

> include in the Agenda for the work of the Conference the question of the recognition and enforcement of foreign judgments in civil and commercial matters [...] and [r]equest[ed] the Secretary General to convene as soon as is feasible a Special Commission charged with [...] studying further the problems involved in drafting a new convention, on the basis of a document prepared by the Permanent Bureau, taking into account the discussions of the Seventeenth Session, [...] making proposals with respect to the work which might be undertaken, [and] suggesting the timing of such work.[573]

As a result, the following two meetings of the Special Commission on the recognition and enforcement of foreign judgments in civil and commercial matters in June 1994 and June 1996 were regarded as 'exploratory'

569 Cf Beaumont/McEleavy, *Anton's Private International Law* (n 68) [3.17].
570 See Chapter 3.
571 See Chapter 2.
572 'Work Doc No 7', in *Proceedings of the Seventeenth Session, Tome I* (n 530) 310.
573 'Final Act Seventeenth Session' (n 505) 17.

meetings, without the intent to begin the process of drafting a convention text.[574] Effectively, the Seventeenth Session had deferred the task of preparing the strategy for creating a global judgments convention to a Special Commission, a forum to which all interested Member States of the Hague Conference could send experts in the subject matter.[575] That means that while traditionally only the Permanent Bureau as the project managers would have been involved in preparing the conceptual strategy for creating a Judgments Convention, now the project customers, the Hague Conference Member States, also became involved in the strategic planning. The strategic planning had been partially outsourced, therefore, to the project customers themselves (with detrimental effects, as discussed below).[576]

4.4.1.3. *Further Consequences of Outsourcing the Planning of the Conceptual Phase to a Working Group: Lack of Understanding of the Mixed-Convention Concept on the Part of the Project Managers*

A further consequence of the fact that the Permanent Bureau had not developed the mixed-convention concept itself was that this concept had also not been fully appreciated by the project managers themselves. As a result, the project managers were not in a position to advise the Hague Conference Member States about what strategic decisions would be necessary in order to develop a mixed convention. This meant that the project managers could not support the first meeting of the Special Commission on the recognition and enforcement of foreign judgments in civil and commercial matters in June 1994 with advice on how to construct a mixed convention. Since the topic of a mixed convention had not been prepared by the Permanent Bureau in a way that would have made the

---

574 David McClean, 'The Hague Conference's Judgments Project', in James Fawcett (ed), *Reform and Development in Private International Law – Essays in Honour of Sir Peter North* (OUP 2002) 255, 259 ('[The Special Commission meeting in June 1994] began with statements from a spokesman of the parties to the Lugano Convention and from a delegation from a Brussels Convention party; each emphasized the exploratory nature of the meeting and expressed coded hesitations about the whole project. Other delegations expressed concerns about the level of damages in United States judgments, and gave voice to doubts as to the wisdom of tackling both contractual and other issues in the same text, and about the feasibility of a full double Convention. The mood of the room was interpreted, perhaps surprisingly, as showing strong support for a double Convention').

575 See further below, Section 4.4.2.4.

576 Ibid.

mixed-convention concept accessible to the participants of the meetings on the Judgments Project, the majority of the Member States of the Hague Conference equally had never developed a full appreciation of the mixed-convention concept.[577] This lack of appreciation of and information about the mixed-convention approach seems to have influenced the (pre-) negotiation process on the Judgments Project negatively in two ways.[578] First, it is likely to have contributed directly to the fact that the mixed convention was rejected three times in the course of the Judgments Project: the first time incidentally during the Seventeenth Diplomatic Session by the delegations of the Hague Conference Member States,[579] the second time by the majority of the experts present during the Special Commission on the question of the recognition and enforcement of foreign judgments in civil and commercial matters in June 1994,[580] and then again by the experts represented during the meeting of the Special Commission on international jurisdiction and the effects of foreign judgments in civil and commercial matters in June 1997.[581] Second, as neither the project managers nor the majority of the Member States had developed a comprehensive appreciation of the mixed-convention concept, no viable strategy to save the Judgments Project could be developed after the double-convention concept had eventually been cast aside in the Special Commission meeting of June 1999.[582]

4.4.2. FAILURE OF THE PERMANENT BUREAU TO MANAGE THE GENERAL CONCEPT-DEVELOPMENT PHASE DURING THE SPECIAL COMMISSION MEETINGS OF JUNE 1994 AND JUNE 1996

As discussed above, the Hague Conference Member States eventually had transferred developing a strategy for creating a Hague Judgments

577 Cf von Mehren, 'Theory and Practice of Adjudicatory Authority' (n 141) 409.

578 Cf Dupont/Faure, 'The Negotiation Process', in Kremenyuk (n 65) 53.

579 'Minutes No 3', 'Minutes No 4', in *Proceedings of the Seventeenth Session, Tome I* (n 530) 327–333.

580 'Conclusions of the Special Commission of June 1994' (n 446) [6].

581 Kessedjian, 'Synthesis of the Work of the Special Commission of June 1997 on International Jurisdiction and the Effects of Foreign Judgments in Civil and Commercial Matters: Prel Doc No 8 of November 1997' (n 288) 81 [4d].

582 Von Mehren, 'Theory and Practice of Adjudicatory Authority' (n 141) 410; see further below, Chapter 5.

Convention to a Special Commission.[583] The topic had been included in the agenda of the Conference under the condition that the Permanent Bureau would develop a document in preparation of this Special Commission meeting, 'taking into account the discussions of the Seventeenth Session, [and] making proposals with respect to the work which might be undertaken'.[584] As analysed above, during the Seventeenth Session the delegates had inter alia questioned both the need for a global judgments convention, and the appropriate method. The Seventeenth Session therefore charged the Permanent Bureau with subsequently developing a concept for creating a global judgments convention because the concept created by the Working Group had been rejected by a significant number of Member States.

Although the Seventeenth Session had expressly tasked the Permanent Bureau with drafting a working document that would take into account the concerns of the Session regarding the need and method for creating a judgments convention, the conceptual planning for the project was not re-developed. The document that was drafted for the attention of the first Special Commission meeting on the Judgments Project in June 1994 was the 'Annotated checklist for Issues to be discussed at the meeting of the Special Commission on Jurisdiction and Enforcement of Judgments (20–24 June 1994)'[585] (hereafter Prel Doc No 1). Prel Doc No 1 neither re-assessed the practical needs or interests of the Hague Conference Member States in a judgments convention, nor did it analyse the feasibility of the available methods for creating a global convention on jurisdiction and judgments (i.e., creating a strict double convention, or a mixed convention). Rather, Prel Doc No 1 only repeated the description of the mixed-convention concept which had been provided already by Prel Doc No 19 (the conclusions of the Working Group), in almost the same wording.[586] The fact that no feasibility study regarding both the mixed convention and strict double convention was developed is all the more surprising since some of the delegations present at the Seventeenth Diplomatic Session had explicitly questioned the actual feasibility of the

---

583 See Section 4.4.1.2.

584 'Final Act Seventeenth Session' (n 505) 43.

585 Permanent Bureau, 'Annotated Checklist of Issues to be Discussed at the Meeting of the Special Commission on Jurisdiction and Enforcement of Judgments: Prel Doc No 1 of May 1994' <https://assets.hcch.net/docs/5a2b5a48-65bb-4272-8a01-cd43117068f3.pdf> accessed 4 April 2023.

586 Ibid 6, 7; 'Conclusions Working Group: Prel Doc No 19 November 1992' (n 28) [6].

mixed-convention concept itself (the delegates from Denmark,[587] Japan,[588] Germany[589] and Egypt[590]), or, like the delegation from Mexico, the feasibility of drawing up a global judgments convention under any method (i.e., under a single, strict double or mixed-convention concept).[591]

4.4.2.1. *No Re-Assessment of the Concrete Needs*

As discussed previously, the first step in developing a project consists of analysing the practical needs of the project customers in the project. Prel Doc No 1, the document prepared for the Special Commission meeting in June 1994 remained however on the level of a theoretical analysis of the needs of the Hague Conference Member States without researching whether these theoretical needs for a judgments convention reflected actual practical needs or interests. Prel Doc No 1 stated that the lack of a global multilateral instrument for regulating the recognition and enforcement of judicial decisions 'leaves international commerce and trade with a situation which is basically unsatisfactory: legal uncertainty, delays and costs are interfering increasingly with the needs of trade and business'.[592] Prel Doc No 1 then concluded that

> an orderly international framework for recognition and enforcement of judgments is in the general interest. A convention will increase predictability for litigants in determining the jurisdictional bases on which they may bring a suit, and whether or not there is likely to be recognition and enforcement in other Contracting States. It will also enable plaintiffs to know where to bring suit and where enforcement is possible, and allow defendants to know where they cannot be sued. As a result, cost is reduced for parties and courts, business planning is facilitated and overburdened court systems are relieved.[593]

Since again no concrete assessment of the practical needs of the Hague Conference Member States in a judgments convention had taken place, the Permanent Bureau was not in a position to translate these needs into a viable method for concluding a global judgments convention, and it could

587 'Minutes No 3' in *Proceedings of the Seventeenth Session, Tome I* (n 530) 327.
588 Ibid 328.
589 Ibid 328.
590 Ibid 330.
591 Ibid 329.
592 Permanent Bureau, 'Annotated Checklist' (n 585) 4.
593 Ibid.

not make a neutral recommendation for an appropriate convention type addressing those needs. By merely copying the recommendations of the Working Group, the Permanent Bureau missed the opportunity to make an independent recommendation for adopting the mixed-convention concept for the Hague Judgments Project.[594]

4.4.2.2. *Best Convention Type According to the Needs Analysis: Mixed Convention*

The mixed convention would have been a viable convention type to address the needs of in particular the US and the EC Member States at the same time. In theory, the main interest of the US in the Judgments Project, to secure the recognition and enforcement of US judgments in Europe, could have been addressed by concluding a single convention on the recognition and enforcement of foreign judgments. A single convention[595] could have overcome some of the main obstacles that hindered the recognition and enforcement of US judgments in Europe, such as the requirement of reciprocity[596] (which existed, for example, in German law).[597] Furthermore, concluding a single convention could also have ensured the recognition and enforcement of US judgments in those States that did not recognise and/or enforce foreign judgments without a treaty (Austria, Denmark, Norway, Sweden, the Netherlands),[598] and it could have prohibited a review of the merits.[599] By unifying rules of indirect jurisdiction, a single convention also could have helped to overcome the requirement of a check of the international jurisdiction of the court of origin, one of the main obstacles to the recognition and enforcement of

594 Ibid 6, 8.

595 For a definition of the term 'single convention', see above, Section 2.1.

596 Droz, 'Mémoire sur la question de la reconnaissance et de l'exécution des jugements étrangers en matière patrimoniale' (n 170) 11; Fragistas, 'Rapport de la Commission spécial' (n 127) 25.

597 German Code of Civil Procedure, art 328(1); Behr (n 332) 221–223; see also Wurmnest (n 292) 182, 188; some have argued, however, that Germany seldom denied recognition of US judgments due to lack of reciprocity (as German judgments were generally recognised and enforced in the US), see Behr (n 332) 223.

598 For the Netherlands, see references above (n 344); for Denmark and Norway, see Behr (n 332) 217; for Sweden, and generally, see Lutz (n 345) 432; see also Samuel P Baumgartner, 'Understanding the Obstacles to the Recognition and Enforcement of US Judgments Abroad' (2013) 45 NYUJ Int'l L & Pol 965, 970.

599 Belgian Judicial Code (Code Judiciaire), art 570 (now revised); Fevery (n 348) 95; see also Behr (n 332) 219; Dogauchi, 'The Hague Draft Convention from the Perspective of Japan' (n 322) [III a].

foreign judgments in general.[600] Moreover, a single convention could have helped to provide clearer rules for the treatment of multiple or punitive damage awards,[601] thereby speeding up the recognition and enforcement process.[602] Finally, a single convention could have restricted the effects of exorbitant grounds of jurisdiction to a certain extent. By means of a list of prohibited grounds of indirect jurisdiction (a red list of indirect grounds of jurisdiction),[603] a single convention could have prevented judgments rendered on an exorbitant basis in the court of origin from circulating under the convention.[604]

However, only a mixed convention concept could have accommodated both the interest of the US in securing the recognition and enforcement of foreign judgments in Europe, and the interests of the US and the EC Member States in regulating international direct jurisdiction at the same time. A mixed convention had all the advantages of a single convention in terms of fostering the recognition and enforcement of foreign judgments. At the same time, the mixed-convention concept could have addressed the interests of the EC Member States in advancing legal certainty and predictability in international civil proceedings by means of the green list of accepted grounds of jurisdiction.[605] Through these unified grounds of jurisdiction, litigants in proceedings within the convention's scope would know where they could sue and be sued respectively.[606] Admittedly, creating

600 Fragistas, 'Rapport de la Commission spécial' (n 127) 29.

601 Cf von Mehren, 'Recognition of United States Judgments Abroad' (n 70) 458.

602 The 1976 UK-US draft convention, for example, excluded judgments from its scope to the extent that they concerned punitive or multiple damages, see 1976 UK-US draft Convention (n 387) art 2 (2) (b); eventually, a provision on multiple and punitive damage awards was included in the 2001 Interim Text, providing that a judgment awarding non-compensatory damages should only be recognised and enforced to the extent that a court in the State addressed for the recognition and enforcement of a judgment could have awarded similar or comparable damages, see 2001 Interim Text (n 36) art 33; see also 2005 Hague Choice of Court Convention (n 3), art 11; 2019 Hague Judgments Convention (n 53) art 10.

603 'Conclusions Working Group: Prel Doc No 19 November 1992' (n 28) [6]; von Mehren, 'Recognition of United States Judgments Abroad' (n 70) 458; von Mehren, 'New Approach' (n 1) 283, 285, speaking of 'list of excluded bases'.

604 Cf 1971 Hague Judgments Convention (n 22); Supplementary Protocol to the Hague Convention on the Recognition and Enforcement of Foreign Judgments in Civil and Commercial Matters (adopted 1 February 1971; entered into force 20 August 1979) 1144 UNTS 271.

605 Von Mehren, 'Enforcing Judgments Abroad' (n 6) 19 ('permitted bases'); see also above, Section 2.1.

606 'Conclusions Working Group: Prel Doc No 19 November 1992' (n 28) [4]–[6]; von Mehren, 'New Approach' (n 1) 287.

a non-exhaustive green list would not have advanced legal certainty and predictability to the same extent as a strict double convention.[607] Under a strict double convention, litigants knew that they could sue and be sued only according to the provisions of the green list.[608] Compared to the status quo of international civil cooperation between the US and the EC Member States, however, where no common rules on the exercise of international direct jurisdiction existed at all, a mixed convention would have increased legal certainty for litigants and courts involved in civil proceedings to a significant extent.[609]

In addition, through a red list of direct grounds of jurisdiction, the mixed-convention concept could have prohibited domestic courts from exercising jurisdiction on exorbitant bases, thereby ensuring that defendants would not be subjected to the excessive jurisdictional reach of a foreign court. Both the US and the European States had an interest in restricting the use of exorbitant direct grounds of jurisdiction.[610] According to von Mehren's concept of a mixed convention, the Contracting States to a mixed convention would include the grounds of direct jurisdiction in the red list on which consensus existed that jurisdiction should not be exercised on these bases because of their clearly exorbitant nature.[611] As stated above, as with a single convention, the Contracting States to a mixed convention could have mitigated the effects of exorbitant jurisdiction also indirectly by prohibiting Contracting States from recognising and enforcing judgments rendered on such a basis (through a red list of indirect jurisdiction).[612]

Finally, and most importantly, only the mixed-convention concept could have satisfied the interest of the US of maintaining its flexibility in being able to regulate international direct jurisdiction by means of domestic rules. For the US, it was in fact essential that a judgments convention would not infringe excessively upon its sovereign power to regulate the exercise of jurisdiction in international civil proceedings by means of domestic law.[613] The US regarded it as vital that their flexibility

---

607 Cf Tell, 'Can a Mixed Convention Work?' (n 148) 37–39.

608 Von Mehren, 'Enforcing Judgments Abroad' (n 6) 23.

609 Von Mehren, 'New Approach' (n 1) 287; von Mehren, 'The Case for a Convention-mixte Approach' (n 266) 92; Nygh, 'Arthur's Baby' (n 266) 162.

610 See above, Chapter 2.

611 Von Mehren, 'New Approach' (n 1) 278, 279 ('black list').

612 'Conclusions Working Group: Prel Doc No 19 November 1992' (n 28) [6]; von Mehren, 'Recognition of United States Judgments Abroad' (n 70) 458; von Mehren, 'New Approach' (n 1) 285, speaking of 'list of excluded bases'.

613 Special Commission on general affairs and policy of the Conference (1–4 June 1992), 'Work Doc No 1 – distributed 1 June 1992 – Document submitted by the United States

and autonomy regarding the possibility to create new rules of jurisdiction would be maintained, in order to be able to adapt to changes in law and society.[614] In this context, in a Working Document submitted to the meeting of the Special Commission on General Affairs and Policy of the Hague Conference in 1992, the US had stated explicitly that it regarded the exhaustive regulation of international direct jurisdiction by means of a strict (or closed) double convention as 'stultifying'.[615] Moreover, the US had noted in the Working Document that it wanted to remain able to 'revise its jurisdictional practices to take into account changes in legal and economic circumstances', which would not have been possible if the convention had regulated the exercise of international direct jurisdiction exhaustively by means of a strict double convention.[616] The mixed-convention concept would have restricted this power only to a limited extent.[617] While a closed double convention removed the sovereign power of Contracting States to create new rules on jurisdiction since it regulated the exercise of international direct jurisdiction exhaustively,[618] the mixed convention was far less invasive in this regard.[619] A mixed convention only obliged its Contracting Parties to make the grounds

---

Delegation (Lc ON No 15(92)' (on file with author) 3; von Mehren, 'Recognition of United States Judgments Abroad' (n 70) 457; von Mehren, 'New Approach' (n 1) 287.

614 Special Commission on general affairs and policy of the Conference (1–4 June 1992), 'Work Doc No 1 – distributed 1 June 1992 – Document submitted by the United States Delegation (Lc ON No 15(92)' (on file with author) [II]: '[u]nder the proposed approach [the true mixed convention approach], each Contracting State retains, where jurisdictional bases that the convention neither prohibits as exorbitant nor specifies as acceptable are in question, flexibility in its jurisdictional and recognition and enforcement practices. This flexibility permits a degree of experimentation and adaptation that seems desirable. A measure of ambiguity and uncertainty results, of course. However, under the proposed approach overall practices with respect to both jurisdiction and recognition would be far clearer and much more easily ascertained than is today the case when litigation or recognition abroad is in question'; see also 'Conclusions of the Working Group: Prel Doc No 19 of November 1992' (n 28) 257, 258 [5]; cf also Bucher, 'Vers une convention mondiale' (n 173) 80; cf also von Mehren, 'New Approach' (n 1) 272, 287.

615 Special Commission on general affairs and policy of the Conference, 'Work Doc No 1 June 1992' (n 613) 3.

616 Ibid 3; see also Matthew H Adler, Michele Crimaldi Zarychta, 'The Hague Convention on Choice of Court Agreements: The United States Joins the Judgment Enforcement Band' (2006) 27 Nw J Int'l L & Bus 1, 11: '[t]he United States, however, proposed a so-called "mixed convention" from the outset because it would provide the United States with more flexibility'.

617 See, e.g., von Mehren, 'Recognition of United States Judgments Abroad' (n 70) 458.

618 See, e.g., 1968 Brussels Convention (n 140) art 2(1), art 3(1).

619 von Mehren, 'Recognition of United States Judgments Abroad' (n 70) 458.

of direct jurisdiction on the green list available to claimants.[620] As opposed to the green list of an exhaustive double convention, the mixed-convention concept would not have prevented the Contracting States from creating new jurisdictional provision.[621] In addition, the green list of a mixed convention would not have restricted the courts of the Contracting States in their use of the existing domestic grounds of direct jurisdiction.[622] Under the true mixed-convention concept, the domestic rules of international direct jurisdiction (the 'grey area', or 'permitted area') would have co-existed with the unified jurisdictional provisions of the Hague Judgments Convention.[623] The mixed-convention concept only limited domestic jurisdiction by means of the red list, banning the use of certain domestic jurisdictional provisions regarded as exorbitant by the Contracting States.[624]

4.4.2.3. *No Detailed Study of Feasible Methods for or of Challenges in Regulating Direct Jurisdiction*

The second aspect of developing a concept for a project was to research the (technical, political and/or legal) feasibility of the possible methods that could address the identified needs of the project customers, or the identified problems.[625] Regarding the discussions of the possible convention types, Prel Doc No 1 of 1994 only listed the advantages and disadvantages of

620 'Conclusions Working Group: Prel Doc No 19 November 1992' (n 28) [6].
621 Von Mehren, 'New Approach' (n 1) 287.
622 'Conclusions Working Group: Prel Doc No 19 November 1992' (n 28) [6]; von Mehren, 'Recognition of United States Judgments Abroad' (n 70) 458; von Mehren, 'New Approach' (n 1) 283; Tell, 'Can a Mixed Convention Work?' (n 148) 37–39.
623 Von Mehren, 'Recognition of United States Judgments Abroad' (n 70) 458; von Mehren, 'New Approach' (n 1) 283; the mixed convention concept therefore could have resulted in a situation in which the jurisdiction provisions in the green list of the convention were drafted in a similar or even identical way to the national jurisdictional provisions in the grey area. The difference between the jurisdictional provisions in the green list and in the grey area was that the existence of the provisions in the green list was guaranteed by the convention, that the Contracting Parties were obliged to exercise international direct jurisdiction on these bases if the relevant conditions for their application were fulfilled, and that the provisions in the green list should be interpreted in the same way in all the Contracting Parties, thereby fostering legal certainty and predictability for litigants.
624 von Mehren, 'Recognition of United States Judgments Abroad' (n 70) 458; von Mehren, 'New Approach' (n 1) 283 ('black list'); 'Conclusions Working Group: Prel Doc No 19 November 1992' (n 28) [6].
625 See above, Section 4.1.

the mixed-convention concept, without assessing the actual feasibility of creating a global convention of this type, and without discussing the feasibility of the only alternative for creating a convention on jurisdiction and judgments – the strict double convention – at all.[626] Rather, the double-convention concept was used as a point of reference in describing the mixed-convention concept: for example, it was noted that the mixed convention would

> like the double convention, contain a list of grounds upon which the court of origin, at least in principle, would be required to assume jurisdiction, [and] unlike the complete double convention, but like the single convention, allow the court of origin to assume jurisdiction on grounds neither approved by the convention in the 'white list' nor disapproved in the 'black list' (the 'grey area').[627]

In this way, the Permanent Bureau had also indirectly confirmed the technical feasibility of creating a strict double convention on a global level. Furthermore, by merely listing the similarities and differences of a mixed and double convention, the effect produced was that the mixed-convention model seemed to be less prestigious and at the same time far more complicated than a strict double convention.[628] Regarding the question of the feasibility of creating a binding instrument unifying rules of international direct jurisdiction, Prel Doc No 1 noted that

> [f]rom a technical point of view, the problems [regarding international direct jurisdiction] are familiar and the exercise could draw inspiration from a wealth of multilateral and bilateral conventions. For this reason, the present document can be relatively short and focus on concrete questions and issues with references to various possible answers and solutions contained in existing international instruments.[629]

As shown in Chapter 2, the unification of grounds of international direct jurisdiction raised technical challenges as well as challenges regarding its political feasibility, which made a closed double convention unfeasible for creating a global judgments convention.

---

626 Cf Permanent Bureau, 'Annotated Checklist' (n 585) 4–8.
627 Ibid 6.
628 Trooboff, 'Some Thoughts on Finding Solutions to Tough Issues' (n 551) 470.
629 Permanent Bureau, 'Annotated Checklist' (n 585) 4.

4.4.2.4. *The False Start of the Special Commission Meeting in June 1994*

A study of the feasibility of the available convention types would have shown that only the mixed convention was a viable method with a chance for successfully creating a convention with rules on both the recognition and enforcement of judgments *and* jurisdiction. If the Permanent Bureau had furthermore conducted a needs analysis, it would have shown that the mixed convention was not only the only convention type that was technically and politically feasible, but also the only type with a reasonable chance to address the needs of the two main stakeholders in the project (the US and the EC Member States) at the same time.

Since the concept phase of the Judgments Project had not been prepared with the same rigour as applied in other convention projects, the majority of experts meeting at the Special Commission in June 1994 and the governments they represented had no clear idea of the challenges involved in creating a strict double convention on a global level, nor of the feasibility or desirability of the mixed-convention concept. Moreover, since no needs analysis had taken place, the experts were not aware that creating a strict double convention was not only technically and politically unfeasible, but that this convention type was also unable to address the needs of, in particular, the US in a Hague Judgments Convention.[630] Due to this lack of information, the Member State governments were unable to make an informed policy decision on whether they should support creating a strict double convention or a mixed convention, which negatively influenced the pre-negotiation phase.[631] Moreover, without the Permanent Bureau as a neutral body having explained in an objective conceptual study that the only theoretical alternative to the mixed-convention concept, i.e., the strict double convention, was unfeasible, it is not surprising that the mixed-convention concept – this structurally complicated and less prestigious method for creating a global judgments convention compared to a strict double-convention – was rejected as the convention type that should be pursued in June 1994:[632]

> The experts agreed that if a convention were to be drawn up it would be desirable to go further than a 'simple convention' such as the Hague Convention of 1 February 1971 [...]. It was agreed that it would be preferable

630 See above, Section 4.4.2.2.

631 Dupont/Faure, 'The Negotiation Process', in Kremenyuk (n 65) 52.

632 Trooboff, 'Some Thoughts on Finding Solutions to Tough Issues' (n 551) 470.

> to establish not only rules on the enforcement of decisions, but also rules on judicial jurisdiction at the stage of the initial litigation. It seemed that in such a convention there might be established a list of bases for assuming jurisdiction which might be accepted and a list of bases, the utilization of which might be prohibited. The issue was discussed as to whether it should be provided in addition that each State might utilize bases for assuming jurisdiction which would be neither accepted nor prohibited by the convention [i.e., whether a mixed convention should be created]. *Finally, the tendency was to reject such a possibility and to favour the preparation of a double convention limiting itself, as do the Conventions of Brussels and Lugano, to bases for assuming jurisdiction which are accepted and those which are rejected.*[633]

The mixed-convention concept had not been abandoned completely, however, but was not meant to be pursued as a priority.[634] Catherine Kessedjian, who participated in the Special Commission meeting of June 1994 as an expert for France,[635] and in 1996 joined the Hague Conference to replace Secretary General Georges Droz as the French-speaking member of the Permanent Bureau,[636] reported that creating a strict double convention was regarded as the 'maximum goal' in 1994 by a 'relatively large number of experts'.[637] It was perceived as

> the most ambitious objective, i.e., abolishing the largest possible number of exorbitant grounds of jurisdiction, and specifying in as many cases as possible which kinds of jurisdiction are authorised under the Convention, so as to clarify in as many instances as possible the international jurisdiction of the courts.[638]

Moreover, 16 out of the 32 expert groups which were present during the Special Commission meeting of June 1994 were familiar with the convention

---

633 'Conclusions of the Special Commission of June 1994' (n 446) [6]. Emphasis added.

634 Kessedjian, 'Prel Doc No 7 of April 1997' (n 141) [152]–[156]; '[w]hen this point [the question of the convention type] was discussed during the Special Commission of June 1994, a relatively large number of experts expressed their preference for negotiation *a priori* a double Convention […]. These same experts were afraid that were negotiations […] to start with the idea that it would be a "mixed" Convention, there might be too little desire to compromise on the part of some delegations when it came to the overall objective of the negotiations'. Ibid at [152], [153].

635 Ibid 4.

636 'Minutes of the Opening Session', Permanent Bureau of the Hague Conference on Private International Law (eds), *Proceedings of the Eighteenth Session 30 September to 19 October 1996), Tome I, Miscellaneous Matters* (SDU Publishers 1999) 19.

637 Kessedjian, 'Prel Doc No 7 of April 1997' (n 141) 12, 57, [156], [153].

638 Ibid [153].

type of a strict double convention: at this date, the Hague Conference had 41 Member States, out of which 32 participated in the Special Commission meeting,[639] 16 States of which were a Contracting State to either the 1968 Brussels Convention and/or the 1988 Lugano Convention: Belgium, Denmark, Finland, France, Germany, Greece, Ireland, Italy, Luxembourg, the Netherlands, Norway, Portugal, Spain, Sweden, Switzerland and the United Kingdom.[640] Moreover, Austria had signed the Lugano Convention in June 1994.[641] In total, in June 1994 there were 17 States connected by a common regional regime on international jurisdiction and the recognition and enforcement of foreign judgments, and 15 others.[642]

Not only were the Brussels/Lugano States in the majority during the Special Commission meeting in June 1994, but the discussions of the meeting also started with statements from representatives from Brussels/Lugano States (i.e., from representatives of Member States adhering to a closed double-convention),[643] thereby setting the tone of the meeting. These representatives questioned the general feasibility of the project.[644] Apparently, the same experts who had recommended to pursue the strict double convention as a first priority 'were afraid that were negotiations for the future Convention to start with the idea that it would be a "mixed" Convention, there might be too little desire to compromise on the part of some delegations when it came to the overall objective of the negotiations'.[645] This statement also shows that the decision of the Special Commission in June 1994 to primarily pursue the development

639 Argentina, Australia, Austria, Belgium, Canada, Chile, China (People's Republic of), Czech Republic, Denmark, Finland, France, Germany, Greece, Ireland, Israel, Italy, Japan, Latvia, Luxembourg, Mexico, the Netherlands, Norway, Poland, Portugal, Romania, Slovenia, Spain, Sweden, Switzerland, the United Kingdom, the United States of America and Uruguay see <https://www.hcch.net/en/instruments/conventions/status-table/print/?cid=29> accessed 4 April 2023; 'Conclusions of the Special Commission of June 1994' (n 446) 3–6.

640 1968 Brussels Convention (n 140) preamble; 1988 Lugano Convention: Parties (n 194); Convention on the accession of the Kingdom of Spain and the Portuguese Republic to the Convention on jurisdiction and the enforcement of judgments in civil and commercial matters and to the Protocol on its interpretation by the Court of Justice with the adjustments made to them by the Convention on the accession of the Kingdom of Denmark, of Ireland and of the United Kingdom and the adjustments made to them by the Convention on the accession of the Hellenic Republic (89/535/EEC)(1) (1989 San Sebastián Convention).

641 1988 Lugano Convention: Parties (n 194).

642 Von Mehren, 'Theory and Practice of Adjudicatory Authority' (n 141) 410, 411.

643 McClean (n 574) 255, 259.

644 Ibid.

645 Kessedjian, 'Prel Doc No 7 of April 1997' (n 141) [153].

of a strict double convention was maybe not mainly a decision *for* the double convention, but in fact a decision *against* the mixed-convention concept. This demonstrates the negative effects of the fateful decision of the Seventeenth Session to defer the conceptual planning to the Special Commission meetings in 1994 and 1996. During the Special Commission meetings, two factors came into play: first, the mixed convention concept had not been prepared in a way that would have highlighted its importance to the success of the project. And second, the fact that also the Hague Conference Member States, the project customers, had been involved in the conceptual planning during the Special Commission meetings unduly influenced this phase due to the particular constitution of the Hague Conference membership.[646] The Brussels-Lugano Member States were in the majority and with their bias for a strict double convention were able to influence the phase of conceptual planning with a detrimental effect for the project by leading the Special Commission down the path of creating a strict double convention as first priority, a convention type without a reasonable chance of success. Based on the discussions of the Special Commission meetings, the Hague Judgments Project was officially put on the agenda of the Hague Conference: 'The Eighteenth Session […] [d]ecides to include in the Agenda of the Nineteenth Session the question of jurisdiction, and recognition and enforcement of foreign judgments in civil and commercial matters.'[647] The general concept developed by the Special Commission meetings was thereby incidentally approved.

4.5. CONCLUSION

The Permanent Bureau deviated from established patterns of Hague Conference project management during the conceptual phase of the Judgments Project between 1992 and 1996. The Permanent Bureau had not developed the general concept for creating a Judgments Convention itself during the concept phase, but the development of a conceptual study had been outsourced, first to a Working Group, then to the two Special Commission meetings that met in 1994 and 1996. The general concept developed by these Special Commission meetings had been inherently flawed, since the strict double convention – an unfeasible convention type

646 Cf Zartmann,' Negotiation as a search for justice' (n 93) 71, 73, 84; Albin, Druckman (n 93) 1017.

647 'Final Act of the Eighteenth Session' (n 27), 47.

for a global judgments convention – had been chosen as the convention type that should be pursued as a first priority. The fact that no needs analysis and no feasibility study of the available methods had taken place led to the ill-fated recommendation of the Special Commission meeting in June 1994 to reject an attempt to create a mixed convention as a first priority, and to work towards a strict double convention. However, the creation of a strict double convention was not only unwanted by at least one of the main stakeholders in the project, but it was also practically unachievable on a global level. The recommendation to pursue a strict double convention as a priority might be seen as procedurally unfair as well since the decision seemed to have been influenced by those Hague Conference Member States that were members of the Brussels-Lugano regime. As will be shown in Chapters 5 and 6 in more detail, the failure to properly develop a viable general concept for creating a global judgments convention lay at the heart of the failure of the Judgments Project.

CHAPTER 5

DID THE JUDGMENTS PROJECT FAIL DUE TO A LACK OF PREPARATION OF THE SPECIAL COMMISSION MEETINGS BETWEEN 1997 AND 1999?

After the Special Commission meeting in 1996, the Hague Judgments Project was officially added to the agenda of the Hague Conference during its Eighteenth Session. In project management terms, and according to previous Hague Conference practice,[648] the Hague Judgments Project now entered the 'implementation phase', i.e., the phase in which the drafting of a convention text began during further Special Commission meetings set up for this purpose.[649] For this phase, which lasted from June 1997 – October 1999, in total five further Special Commission meetings took place: in June 1997, March 1998, November 1998, June 1999 and October 1999 (originally, only four Special Commission meetings were scheduled).[650] The draft convention text created by those Special Commission meetings was meant to serve as the basis for official negotiations between the Hague Conference Member States during the Nineteenth Diplomatic Session, which originally was scheduled to take place in the year 2000.[651]

In theory, during this 'implementation phase', the plan to develop a judgments convention should have been executed.[652] To recall, the general concept that had been developed during the Special Commission

---

648 See above, Sections 4.2 and 4.3.

649 Association for Project Management (n 432) 15; Kessedjian, 'Synthesis of the Work of the Special Commission of June 1997 on International Jurisdiction and the Effects of Foreign Judgments in Civil and Commercial Matters: Prel Doc No 8 of November 1997' (n 288) [3].

650 Nygh/Pocar Report (n 29) 211; Kessedjian, ibid.

651 Kessedjian, ibid; see also McClean (n 574) 259.

652 Association for Project Management (n 432) 15.

meetings in 1994 and 1996 consisted of pursuing the creation of a strict double convention as a first priority (but without having abandoned the mixed convention concept completely).[653] However, an important project management step in the creation of a plan for developing a global judgments convention had been missed. According to good project management practice and previous usages of the Permanent Bureau, the general concept for creating a Hague Judgments Convention that had been developed and incidentally approved by the Hague Conference Member States during the Eighteenth Session should have been developed further in a 'definition phase' of the project.[654] During this definition phase, detailed planning should have taken place in order to enable the general plan to be implemented, i.e., the question of 'how' to create a judgments convention based on a strict double convention concept should have been addressed.[655] Moreover, the possibility that a mixed convention would be concluded had not been ruled out during the general concept development phase.[656] For this reason, detailed planning for how to construct a mixed convention should have taken place as well. The documents prepared by the Permanent Bureau in preparation of the implementation phase did however not engage fully with this phase of detailed planning for creating a strict double convention and a mixed convention, as will be discussed in the following.

5.1. PREPARATIONS FOR THE SPECIAL COMMISSION MEETING OF JUNE 1997

In order to be able to implement the general concept developed during the Special Commission meetings from 1994–1996, the Permanent Bureau would have needed to generate a more detailed plan of how exactly a strict double convention could be created on a global level. However, in reality, no comprehensive strategy advising on the construction of a strict double convention was developed in preparation for the Special Commission meeting in June 1997. The document prepared by the Permanent Bureau for the Special Commission of June 1997 was Prel Doc No 7, also known

653 'Conclusions of the Special Commission of June 1994' (n 446) [6]; Kessedjian, 'Prel Doc No 7 of April 1997' (n 141) [152]–[156]; Section 4.4.2.4.
654 Association for Project Management (n 432) 14.
655 Association for Project Management (n 432) 14.
656 Kessedjian, 'Prel Doc No 7 of April 1997' (n 141) [152]–[156].

as the Kessedjian Report. This report can be compared to the Dyer Report and the van Loon Report in terms of project management, the purpose of which should have been to reconfirm the needs of the Member States and to refine the methods that the convention would employ to address these identified needs in the detailed planning phase of creating a global judgments convention.

5.1.1. NEEDS ASSESSMENT BY PRELIMINARY DOCUMENT NO 7

Prel Doc No 7 did perform a needs assessment, and made an independent recommendation for a convention concept on the basis of the needs the report had identified. The report concluded that only a convention regulating international jurisdiction directly and exhaustively would be able to meet the needs of today's litigants.[657] According to Prel Doc No 7, the need to regulate international jurisdiction was even greater than the need to secure the recognition and enforcement of foreign judgments.[658] The report based this conclusion on the assumption that the 1971 Hague Judgments Convention was not successful because it did not regulate direct jurisdiction.[659] Furthermore, the report also based the success of the Brussels and Lugano Conventions on the fact that both were strict double conventions, regulating international jurisdiction directly (and exhaustively).[660] The report did not confirm, however, whether this perceived need of private litigants for almost absolute legal certainty (a need that could have only been addressed by a strict double convention) was also a real need for the Hague Conference Member States. Instead, the Permanent Bureau assumed that it knew best what its Member States

657 Ibid [8].

658 Ibid: '[i]f we consider the needs of litigants in international litigation, we see that although it is vital to secure for a judgment obtained in any one country effects in one or more other countries, the first priority is to ascertain which court has international jurisdiction to adjudicate initially on the merits of the case'.

659 Ibid.

660 Ibid [9]: '[i]t seems beyond doubt that the Brussels Convention and its sister instrument, the Lugano Convention, have enjoyed the success they have because […] they have one common characteristic by comparison with the endeavours of the Hague Conference: they are double conventions, in the sense that they primarily define direct jurisdiction of courts in the subjects with which they deal, treating this as a vital preliminary to the effects which arise from the resulting judgments'.

needed, without having conducted a full analysis of the actual needs.[661] Based on the success of the 1968 Brussels Convention and the 1988 Lugano Convention, the Permanent Bureau assumed that concluding a strict double convention was the best way to address their customers' (the Hague Conference Member States) needs. At the same time, the Permanent Bureau had ignored in particular the resistance of one of its customers (the US) to an exhaustive regulation of international direct jurisdiction by means of a new Hague Judgments Convention.[662]

Regarding the selection of the convention type (the method for addressing the identified needs of the Hague Conference Member States in regulating the exercise of international direct jurisdiction and securing the recognition and enforcement of judgments), Prel Doc No 7 concluded that only a strict double convention would be able to address those needs it had identified (the needs of litigants in international civil litigation for almost absolute legal certainty). Prel Doc No 7 concluded with the recommendation that

> [i]t is important to spell out that the maximum goal (a strict double Convention) could continue to underlie the programme of work, in order not to sap the will for compromise on the part of delegations, and to secure at the outcome of the negotiations the adoption of a text which will give litigants the greatest possible degree of predictability.[663]

5.1.2. NO UNEQUIVOCAL DECISION FOR ONE CONVENTION TYPE (NO DETERMINATION OF THE METHOD)

Another issue in the preparation of the implementation phase (in the phase of detailed planning) was that no definite decision on the convention type was taken at the outset of this phase. As with all documents previously prepared by the Permanent Bureau on the Judgments Project, Prel Doc No 7 did not highlight the vital importance of making a definite decision on the question of the convention type (the method for creating a global

---

661 In this way, the Permanent Bureau seems to have employed what has been called a 'father-knows-best approach' in project-management literature regarding the needs analysis and the needs articulation, Frame, *Managing Projects in Organizations* (n 60) 131.

662 Cf ibid 131, 132.

663 Kessedjian, 'Prel Doc No 7 of April 1997' (n 141) [156].

judgments convention) at the very beginning of the implementation phase (the drafting phase), so that a workable draft convention text as a basis for the actual negotiation phase could be developed.

The provisions of a convention, as well as the decision-making process required in order to determine which provisions should be included in a draft convention text, all depended on the convention type.[664] This had already been pointed out by Georges Droz during the preparation of the Judgments Convention of 1971.[665] During the Ninth Session of the Hague Conference, no State had expressed a wish to regulate international jurisdiction directly.[666] Even though it seemed as if the Member States of the Hague Conference were only interested in concluding a single convention merely regulating the recognition and enforcement of foreign judgments, Droz nevertheless regarded the question of the convention type as so vital that he asked the Member States to re-confirm their favoured convention type, in order to elicit an explicit answer.[667] As a result, the Special Commission that was set up for the work on the 1971 Convention discussed this fundamental question of the convention type right at the beginning of the deliberations as the second question (after discussing the question of bilateralisation).[668] It concluded that although a double convention would be preferable from a theoretical point of view, the experts represented at the Special Commission nevertheless thought that time was not ripe yet for a double convention: the degree of judicial and practical integration of the Hague Conference Member States did not seem to allow the creation of a system to distribute the exercise of direct international jurisdiction among the Member States through rules of direct jurisdiction yet.[669]

As shown in Chapter 4, no unequivocal decision regarding the convention type had been made during the first two Special Commission

664 See also below, Section 6.3.

665 Droz, 'Mémoire sur la question de la reconnaissance et de l'exécution des jugements étrangers en matière patrimoniale' (n 170) 10.

666 Ibid 10, 11.

667 Droz, 'Mémoire sur la question de la reconnaissance et de l'exécution des jugements étrangers en matière patrimoniale' (n 170) 11; during the Ninth Session, it was discussed whether a single convention could also provide for one ground of direct jurisdiction for choice of court, see ibid 14; if such a provision providing for direct jurisdiction on choice of court could have been agreed upon, then the 1971 Hague Judgments Convention (n 22) would have become the first mixed convention. This option was ultimately rejected, however, see above (n 170) and Fragistas, 'Rapport de la Commission spécial' (n 127) 32.

668 Fragistas, ibid, 25.

669 Ibid.

meetings in 1994 and 1996. In theory, Prel Doc No 7 therefore should have encouraged the Hague Conference Member States to decide which convention type should be pursued. In practice, Prel Doc No 7 treated the mixed-convention concept as a fallback option that could be pursued in case the strict double convention should fail. Prel Doc No 7 also recommended that the creation of a strict double convention should be pursued as the primary objective.[670] As a result, no definite decision on the question of which convention type to pursue was taken by the experts represented at the Special Commission meeting in June 1997:

> As to the structure of the future Convention, although some delegations stressed that the proceedings would probably result in a mixed convention, most of the delegations which expressed a position preferred to negotiate a [strict] double convention, which should be the premise underlying the reasoning and the negotiations conducted by the Special Commission.[671]

5.1.3. INSUFFICIENT DETAILED PLANNING BY PRELIMINARY DOCUMENT NO 7 FOR A STRICT DOUBLE CONVENTION

Prel Doc No 7 did not sufficiently emphasise the detailed planning needed for developing a strict double convention. Even though the majority of experts participating in the Special Commission meetings wanted to primarily pursue a strict double convention from June 1994 onwards, Prel Doc No 7 did not entail detailed planning for constructing this type of convention. Instead of identifying its necessary components, Prel Doc No 7 and other preparatory material prepared by the Permanent Bureau used the 1968 Brussels Convention as a plan for creating a strict double convention on a global level. Both Prel Doc No 7[672] and the 'Information Document – Enforcement of Judgments – June 1997 – Examples of Treaty Provisions'[673] relied heavily on the Brussels Convention (and the 1988

---

670 Kessedjian, 'Prel Doc No 7 of April 1997' (n 141) [156].

671 Kessedjian, 'Synthesis of the Work of the Special Commission of June 1997 on International Jurisdiction and the Effects of Foreign Judgments in Civil and Commercial Matters: Prel Doc No 8 of November 1997' (n 288) [4d].

672 Ibid 13–69.

673 Permanent Bureau, 'Examples of Treaty Provisions on International Jurisdiction – Info Doc June 1997' (n 298).

Lugano Convention) for guidance on how to construct a strict double convention text. These documents suggested that the Special Commission should discuss all the provisions on international direct jurisdiction which were also contained in these instruments.[674]

Due to this, it was overlooked that a strict double convention on a global level has different requirements than the 1968 Brussels Convention, which was a purely regional instrument. Applying good project management practice, the Permanent Bureau should have focussed the attention of the experts on the necessary components for creating a strict double convention on a global level, and on the structural issues of this convention type, in order to give the experts a clear a picture as possible of the technical requirements of a global double convention right at the beginning of the drafting phase. Two structural issues in particular should have been discussed by the Permanent Bureau, had it drawn up a plan of the necessary elements of a global double convention: the need to include special grounds of direct jurisdiction (in particular, contract jurisdiction), and the need to address situations where no court was available in case a negative conflict of jurisdiction should arise.[675] Without this plan of construction, the experts of the Special Commission meetings entered into the drafting phase of a convention text without the necessary guidance on the components of a double convention, hindering the efficiency of the phase.[676]

---

674 Kessedjian, 'Prel Doc No 7 of April 1997' (n 141) 29, 35–55, and Permanent Bureau, 'Examples of Treaty Provisions on International Jurisdiction: Info Doc June 1997' (n 298), which suggested that the following provisions on international direct jurisdiction should be discussed as candidates for the inclusion into the green list of the Hague Judgments Convention: jurisdiction with respect to immovable property; jurisdiction with respect to rent contracts for immovables; jurisdiction with respect to companies/corporations; jurisdiction with respect to public registers; jurisdiction with respect to intellectual property; jurisdiction with respect to the enforcement of judgments; jurisdiction with respect to work contracts; jurisdiction in matters of insurance; jurisdiction in matters of consumer protection; choice of court (express choice); choice of court (tacit choice); jurisdiction in contract (except work, insurance and consumer contracts); jurisdiction in tort; jurisdiction in matters concerning branches; jurisdiction in matters relating to a trust; jurisdiction for related actions; jurisdiction for provisional and protective measures; jurisdiction in matters regarding to maintenance obligations; jurisdiction of the defendant's habitual residence; jurisdiction in the case of plurality of defendants; jurisdiction for counter-claims; and jurisdiction for actions relating to a warranty or guarantee or any other third-party proceeding.

675 See also above, Section 2.3.1.

676 Cf Dupont/Faure, 'The Negotiation Process', in Kremenyuk (n 65) 52.

5.1.3.1. *Necessary Components of a Strict Double Convention: Special Grounds of Jurisdiction*

Under a strict double convention, courts in a Contracting State could have exercised jurisdiction over matters within the convention's scope only on the basis of the connecting factors contained in the convention text.[677] Already existing domestic grounds of direct jurisdiction cannot be used anymore.[678] Due to the vast geographic distances covered by the jurisdictional provisions of a global judgments convention, access to justice under a strict double convention could not be ensured if the claimant could bring proceedings in only one forum, for example in the defendant's home forum.[679] If the defendant's home forum was geographically distant from the claimant's domicile, the costs and the inconvenience associated with having to travel to the defendant's home forum could have deterred potential litigants from pursuing a legitimate claim altogether, thereby inhibiting access to justice.[680] Access to additional forums provided by special grounds of jurisdiction were able to alleviate the burden associated with litigation for the claimant.[681] For these reasons, special grounds of jurisdiction were necessary components of a strict double convention in order to ensure access to justice.[682] As discussed above, contract jurisdiction was one of the most important jurisdictional provisions in a strict double convention,[683] and a convention without such a provision would have had little attraction for potential Contracting States.[684]

The question of whether such a provision on contract jurisdiction was needed was discussed by the experts during the Special Commission meetings.[685] It was argued that most parties to an international commercial

677 Von Mehren, 'Enforcing Judgments Abroad' (n 6) 19; see also 1968 Brussels Convention (n 140) art 2(1), (2); art 3(1).
678 Von Mehren, 'Enforcing Judgments Abroad' (n 6) 19.
679 Cf Johnson (n 244) and Jacobs (n 244).
680 Jacobs (n 244); Johnson (n 244).
681 Johnson (n 244).
682 Cf Weser, 'Bases of Judicial Jurisdiction' (n 244).
683 Section 2.3.1.1.; see also Droz, 'Preliminary Draft of the Convention on Jurisdiction and Foreign Judgments' (n 243), 18: 'A Preliminary Draft of an international convention on jurisdiction in civil and commercial matters could not "politically" abstain from formulating rules applicable to contracts'; Weser, ibid 331, 332; Gaudemet-Tallon (n 246) 67.
684 Cf Droz, ibid.
685 Nygh/Pocar Report (n 29) 235 [97].

contract would include a choice-of-court clause in their agreement and that contract jurisdiction was therefore not essential.[686] This argument was invalid under a strict double-convention concept, however, since such a convention regulated the exercise of international direct jurisdiction exhaustively. A provision on jurisdiction in contractual matters could not have been substituted by other jurisdictional provisions, for example through a provision guaranteeing the effectiveness of choice-of-court agreements as suggested during the Special Commission. Including a jurisdictional provision guaranteeing the effectiveness of choice-of-court agreements could not always replace the need for a contractual forum, as parties could simply forget to include an agreement into their contract, the agreement could be invalid, the parties might not have been able to reach an agreement, or they might simply not have wanted to agree on the jurisdiction of a particular forum.[687] In all of these cases, default rules for contractual jurisdiction needed to be included in the double-convention text.

The importance of including a provision on contract jurisdiction within a strict double convention on a global level had not been highlighted in the preparatory material of the Permanent Bureau. Instead, Prel Doc No 7 listed the 'various admissible grounds of jurisdiction' which should be discussed by the Special Commission meetings 'in descending order of their weight of the imperative character'.[688] This 'weight of the imperative character' had been determined on the basis of the hierarchy of the jurisdictional provisions in the 1968 Brussels Convention. As a result, contract jurisdiction was discussed by Prel Doc No 7 only towards the end of the document,[689] after discussing 'exclusive jurisdiction',[690] 'protective jurisdiction'[691] and 'choice of court'.[692] This order shows that the significance of a provision on contract jurisdiction for concluding a strict double convention had not been highlighted by the preparatory material of the Permanent Bureau, and this issue had not been brought to the attention of the private international law experts participating in the Special Commission meeting.

---

686 ibid.

687 Regarding the latter point see Andreas F Lowenfeld, 'Transatlantic Business Transactions: Some Questions for the Lawyers' (2004) 26 Hous J Int'l L 251, 258.

688 Kessedjian, 'Prel Doc No 7 of April 1997' (n 141) [82].

689 Ibid [118]–[120].

690 Ibid [83]–[90].

691 Ibid [103]–[114].

692 Ibid [103]–[114].

The second preparatory document that was drafted by the Permanent Bureau in order to support the discussion during the Special Commission meeting of June 1997, 'Information Document of June 1997', which contained examples of treaty provisions on international jurisdiction, followed the same order.[693] Also in this document, 'jurisdiction in contract' only featured on page 33 out of 61 pages in total. When contract jurisdiction was discussed two days before the end of the Special Commission meeting in June 1997, the First Secretary 'highlighted the need to determine *whether* such a ground of jurisdiction should be included in the Convention and provided the Commission with an extensive list detailing various forms of contracts. [...] The discussion then focussed on the *appropriateness* of including contract jurisdiction within the text of the Convention [...]'.[694] Although it was not clear at the time that Prel Doc No 7 was prepared whether the further work of the Special Commission meetings would really result in a strict double convention,[695] Prel Doc No 7 should have pointed out the importance of a jurisdictional provision on contract jurisdiction in case the experts decided to work towards a strict double convention.

5.1.3.2. *The Need to Include a Mechanism that Ensures Access to Justice in a Strict Double Convention*

Regarding the detailed planning for creating a strict double convention on a global level, the Permanent Bureau should furthermore have linked the viability of a strict double convention to the availability of a system that was able to interpret the convention text to avoid negative conflicts of jurisdiction.[696] A plan of construction for a global double convention should have made the Special Commission aware that a double convention without a common court would stand little chance of becoming a workable convention, and as a result would unlikely be accepted by the Hague Conference Member States. None of the preparatory material of the Permanent Bureau discussed the need to avoid

693 Permanent Bureau, 'Examples of Treaty Provisions on International Jurisdiction: Info Doc June 1997' (n 298).

694 See Special Commission June 1997, 'Minutes No 14' (on file with author) (emphasis added).

695 Kessedjian, 'Prel Doc No 7 of April 1997' (n 141) [156].

696 See above, Section 2.3.1.3.

negative conflicts of jurisdiction, however. This is surprising, since the risk of negative conflicts of jurisdiction was one of the reasons for the Contracting States of the 1968 Brussels Convention to vest the European Court of Justice with the power to interpret the jurisdictional provisions of this strict double convention in 1972.[697]

Several options could have been considered to ensure access to justice in cases of negative conflicts of jurisdiction: besides establishing a common court (or a functional equivalent), another option would have been to include a 'forum of necessity' provision (*forum necessitatis*) in the convention text. In order to avoid a denial of justice, such a provision would exceptionally allow Contracting States to assume jurisdiction in those cases where no forum was available under the convention. Prel Doc No 7 had discussed the forum of necessity in a questionnaire addressed to the Hague Conference Member States in preparation of the Special Commission of June 1997, asking inter alia whether a forum of necessity would exist in the national law of the Member States.[698] The importance of such a provision for the viability of a strict double convention text was not discussed, however. As a result, the Permanent Bureau received only six responses to the questionnaire, and in general the question of 'denial of justice' did not invoke 'much enthusiasm from the experts'.[699] Moreover, according to the discussions during the Special Commission meeting of March 1998, it seemed as if 'the experts generally favour[ed] not including such a provision in the future Convention.'[700] Detailed planning would have required the project managers to highlight the connection between a viable strict double convention and a common

697 Cf 'Gemeinsame Erklärung' (n 260); von Bülow, 'Vereinheitlichtes Internationales Zivilprozessrecht in der Europäischen Wirtschaftsgemeinschaft' (n 260) 508; cf also Arthur T von Mehren, 'The Hague Jurisdiction and Enforcement Convention Project Faces an Impasse – A Diagnosis and Guidelines for a Cure' (2000) IPRax 465, 467; eventually, negative conflicts of jurisdiction did materialise under the Brussels regime, see Case C-327/10 *Hypoteční banka as v. Udo Mike Lindner* EU:C:2011:745; Case C-292/10 *G v. Cornelius de Visser* EU:C:2012:142, [42].

698 Kessedjian, 'Prel Doc No 7 of April 1997' (n 141) Annex III.

699 Catherine Kessedjian, 'Synthesis of the Work of the Special Commission of March 1998 on International Jurisdiction and the Effects of Foreign Judgments in Civil and Commercial Matters: Prel Doc No 9 of July 1998 for the attention of the Special Commission of November 1998 on the question of jurisdiction, recognition and enforcement of foreign judgments in civil an commercial matters', in *Proceedings of the Twentieth Session, Tome II* (n 29) 109, 133 [83].

700 Ibid 133 [84].

court at the beginning of the work on the project. The project managers should have made clear that a commitment to creating a strict double convention also demanded a commitment to establishing a functional equivalent to the ECJ. The question of establishing a common court should therefore have been discussed at the beginning of the phase of detailed planning.

5.1.4. INSUFFICIENT DETAILED PLANNING FOR THE MIXED-CONVENTION CONCEPT

Besides engaging in detailed planning for a strict double convention, the Permanent Bureau should have also engaged in the detailed planning for creating a mixed convention, since the mixed-convention concept had not been abandoned completely.[701] A proper plan of construction for a mixed convention would have highlighted that work on this convention type entailed in particular identifying common grounds of jurisdiction which all States regarded as acceptable for exercising international direct jurisdiction (the green list).[702] Identifying the direct grounds of jurisdiction for the green list was one of the key aspects of the mixed-convention concept as envisaged by von Mehren.[703] These grounds of jurisdiction would have reflected the 'legal traditions' of all Hague Conference Member States participating in the work on the Judgments Project.[704] As a result, the green list would have most likely been rather limited.[705] Furthermore, a mixed convention could have also entailed a red list of those grounds of jurisdiction which were regarded as exorbitant, i.e., inappropriate for exercising international jurisdiction.[706] This red list of prohibited grounds

---

701 Kessedjian, 'Prel Doc No 7 of April 1997' (n 141) [152]–[156].

702 Von Mehren, 'New Approach' (n 1) 287 ('[bases] so clearly appropriate as to be recommended for this white list [i.e., the green list]'); von Mehren, 'Enforcing Judgments Abroad' (n 6) 27; von Mehren, 'The Case for a Convention-mixte Approach' (n 266) 92; 'Work Doc No 33: Proposal by the delegation of United States of America', in *Proceedings of the Twentieth Session, Tome II* (n 29) 405; cf also Nygh, 'Arthur's Baby' (n 266) 154, 155; see also above, Chapter 2.

703 Ibid.

704 Jeffrey D Kovar, Letter to Hans van Loon (n 34) 5.

705 Ibid; Nygh, 'Arthur's Baby' (n 266) 155; see also Brand, 'Restructuring the Preliminary Draft Convention Text' (n 267) 77; 'Work Doc No 33: Proposal by the delegation of United States of America', in *Proceedings of the Twentieth Session, Tome II* (n 29) 405.

706 Von Mehren, 'New Approach' (n 1) 283, 287 ('black list'); von Mehren, 'Enforcing Judgments Abroad' (n 6) 19 ('prohibited bases'); see also above, Section 2.1.

of jurisdiction presumably would have been also rather limited.[707] Apart from the green list and the red list, the domestic grounds of jurisdiction would have remained unregulated by the mixed convention, and would have constituted the grey area.[708] Moreover, the recognition and enforcement of judgments would have been guaranteed only for those judgments that had been rendered based on a jurisdictional provision on the green list.[709] This means that the true mixed-convention concept also had a different purpose from a strict double convention regarding the question of regulating direct jurisdiction: while the strict double convention aimed at achieving as much legal certainty as possible, the mixed convention merely aimed at improving legal certainty regarding the exercise of direct jurisdiction, while maintaining the flexibility of its Contracting States.[710] It would have been vital for the Permanent Bureau to make this distinction in terms of purpose between these two convention concepts clear as part of the conceptual planning for creating a mixed convention.

Since the inclusion in the green or in the red list respectively depended on the 'universal acceptance' of the negotiating States, creating a mixed convention would have also required a decision-making process during the preparatory stages that could have given effect to such universal acceptance. For this reason, the Permanent Bureau should have recommended a decision-making process on the basis of consensus. Taking decisions on this basis would have entailed seeking general agreement in negotiations 'without resorting to vote'.[711] In order to achieve consensus, participants in international negotiations would normally make 'every effort possible to achieve a generally acceptable decision'[712] by making concessions and seeking compromises.[713] There was no consensus when a State (or a

---

707 'Work Doc No 33: Proposal by the delegation of United States of America', in *Proceedings of the Twentieth Session, Tome II* (n 29) 405.

708 Ibid; cf also von Mehren, 'New Approach' (n 1) 287; see also above, Section 2.1.

709 Von Mehren ibid.

710 See above, Chapter 2; von Mehren, 'New Approach' (n 1) 287; von Mehren, 'The Case for a Convention-mixte Approach' (n 266) 92; Nygh, 'Arthur's Baby' (n 266) 162.

711 Roy S Lee, 'Multilateral Treaty Making and Negotiating Techniques: An Appraisal', in Bin Cheng, E D Brown (eds), *Contemporary Problems of International Law: Essays in Honour of Georg Schwarzenberger on his Eightieth Birthday* (Stevens & Sons Limited 1988) 157, 165; Walker, *Manual for UN Delegates* (n 120) 74.

712 Lee, ibid 165, 166.

713 Walker, *Manual for UN Delegates* (n 120) 80; see also Rolf Wagner, 'Die Haager Konferenz für Internationales Privatrecht zehn Jahre nach der Vergemeinschaftung der Gesetzgebungskompetenz in der justiziellen Zusammenarbeit in Zivilsachen' (2009) 73 RabelsZ 215, 224.

qualified minority of States)[714] openly opposed a decision. For this reason, the consensus principle would have ensured that minorities could not be outvoted (which was possible under a system of majority voting), as they had the power to block a decision by vetoing it.[715] Although the decision-making process of the Hague Conference traditionally took place on the basis of majority voting, the working methods were flexible and would have allowed for a decision-making process on the basis of consensus.

Moreover, the preparatory work of the Permanent Bureau also should have clarified the relationship between the green list of direct grounds of jurisdiction and the grey area in a true mixed convention. According to the true mixed-convention approach as envisaged by Arthur von Mehren, the grey area (the domestic grounds of jurisdiction) would not have been limited by the green list in any way. Rather, these jurisdictional provisions in the green list of the convention would have existed in addition to the national grounds of direct jurisdiction. The only component of the mixed convention that would have been able to restrict the grey area was the red list of prohibited grounds of direct jurisdiction, directly prohibiting Contracting States to use certain grounds of jurisdiction regarded as exorbitant.[716]

5.2. THE EFFECTS OF THE FAILURE TO MANAGE THE IMPLEMENTATION PHASE, JUNE 1997–OCTOBER 1999

In reality, Prel Doc No 7 did not provide a detailed plan of construction for a strict double convention, or a true mixed convention. Instead, Prel Doc No 7 (the Kessedjian Report) reconfirmed the general concept that had been established during the first two Special Commission meetings of 1994 and 1996.[717] This entailed attempting to create a strict double convention as a first priority, with the mixed-convention approach as the fallback option.[718] This plan was implemented from the beginning of the

714 Walker, *Manual for UN Delegates* (n 120) 74.

715 Anthony Aust, *Modern Treaty Law and Practice* (3rd edn, CUP 2013) 81; Lee (n 711) 157, 165; Wagner, 'Vergemeinschaftung Gesetzgebungskompetenz' (n 713) 224.

716 Von Mehren, 'New Approach' (n 1) 283, 285, 287.

717 Kessedjian, 'Prel Doc No 7 of April 1997' (n 141) [156].

718 Ibid [152]–[156]; Permanent Bureau of the Hague Conference on Private International Law, 'Preliminary Results of the Work of the Special Commission Concerning the Proposed Convention on International Jurisdiction and Foreign Judgments in Civil

Special Commission meeting of June 1997.[719] By beginning its work with the attempt to create a strict double convention on the basis of Prel Doc No 7 of April 1997, the Special Commission essentially pursued a 'trial and error' approach: trying to achieve as much unification of jurisdictional provisions as possible by primarily working towards the creation of a strict double convention. The mixed convention concept was regarded as the safety net, i.e., the default option that could always be pursued in case the attempt to draft a strict double convention should prove unattainable after all.[720] The Preliminary Document reporting on the preliminary conclusions of the Special Commission meeting in June 1997 records that

> [t]he negotiations began with an attempt to obtain a *convention double*, i.e., a convention which proposes a closed list of direct jurisdictional grounds which the litigants must have at their disposal to file a substantive claim. However, it is not certain that such a closed convention is attainable. In such a case, the future Convention could be 'mixed', i.e. it would provide a list of authorised jurisdictional grounds and a list of prohibited grounds. Use of other jurisdictional grounds existing in national laws could continue but without any guarantee that the judgment so rendered would have effect abroad.[721]

Accordingly, the Chair of the Special Commission meetings (the expert from Canada, Mr T Bradbrooke Smith)[722] noted in his report on the Special Commission meeting in March 1998 that

> our study of the subject matter has been predicated on the *convention double* concept – a list of required jurisdictional bases, perhaps together with an illustrative list of prohibited grounds, that would exhaust the reach of the

---

and Commercial Matters: Information Document, Enforcement of Judgments, September 1997' (Preliminary Results Special Commission 1997) [2.1]–[2.3] (on file with author).

719 Kessedjian, 'Prel Doc No 8 of November 1997' (n 288) 81 [4d]; see also Special Commission on the question of jurisdiction, recognition and enforcement of foreign judgments in civil and commercial matters (3–13 March 1998), 'Chairman's Report with respect to the meeting of 3–13 March 1998' (on file with author) 3, 4; see also Special Commission of June 1997, 'Report of Meeting No 1' (on file with author) at 2: '[s]everal experts suggested that the primary goal of the Convention should be a double convention *stricto sensu*. However, they stated that if this proved unattainable it would remain possible to negotiate a mixed or even a single convention'.

720 Permanent Bureau, 'Preliminary Results Special Commission 1997' (n 718) [2.1]–[2.3].

721 Ibid.

722 Special Commission on the question of jurisdiction, recognition and enforcement of foreign judgments in civil and commercial matters (3–13 March), 'Final list of participants' (on file with author) 2.

> proposed Convention. It remains to be determined by the Special Commission, in light of its examination of the range of potential grounds of jurisdiction for inclusion or exclusion, whether this approach is practical or desirable or whether, as suggested by some delegations, a more appropriate format is a *convention mixte*, an approach which additionally would allow for jurisdiction in relation to certain subject-matters the recognition and enforcement of judgments in respect to which would be discretionary in the State addressed. Much hinges on this issue in terms of the type of the convention to be prepared but it is premature to suggest at what precise stage it might, or should, be resolved. The draft which it is hoped will emerge from the November 1998 meeting may assist markedly in this regard.[723]

Underlying this plan was an erroneous understanding of the mixed convention and its regulation of jurisdiction. The mixed convention was seen mainly as a restricted or reduced version of a strict double convention;[724] it was mistaken for being like a strict double convention (a convention with a broad green list of unified jurisdictional provisions), but with the additional option for States to exercise jurisdiction on the basis of national jurisdictional provisions (the grey list), provided that the use of jurisdiction was not prohibited.[725] As Prel Doc No 7 had recommended, by primarily pursuing the creation of a strict double convention, the Special Commission attempted to achieve agreement on as many jurisdictional provisions as possible first (as a broad list of jurisdictional provisions was required in order to ensure access to justice).[726] Moreover, the preparatory work of the Permanent Bureau erroneously assumed that if the discussions during the meetings would show that agreement on a broad list of direct grounds of jurisdiction was in fact unattainable, then the draft convention text could still be turned into a mixed convention by simply allowing Contracting States to exercise international direct jurisdiction on the basis of national grounds of direct jurisdiction.[727]

Indeed, when it became clear during the process of drafting a convention text during the penultimate session of the Special Commission in June 1999 that a strict double convention on a global level was indeed

723 'Chairman's Report March 1998' (n 719) 3, 4.

724 Ibid; Permanent Bureau, 'Preliminary Results Special Commission 1997' (n 718) [2.1]–[2.3].

725 'Chairman's Report March 1998' (n 719) 3, 4.

726 Cf Kessedjian, 'Prel Doc No 7 of April 1997' (n 141) [156].

727 Permanent Bureau, 'Preliminary Results Special Commission 1997' (n 718) [2.1]–[2.3]; cf also 'Chairman's Report March 1998' (n 719) 3, 4.

unfeasible, the experts abandoned this convention type and attempted to shift towards creating a mixed convention by adding Article 19 into the draft convention text.[728] Article 19 of the June 1999 Draft ('Jurisdiction based on national law') (later: Article 17 of the October 1999 Preliminary Draft Convention; Article 17 of the 2001 Interim Text) allowed States to have recourse to their domestic grounds of jurisdiction for proceedings within the convention scope (the grey area).[729]

Simply allowing Contracting States the use of domestic grounds of jurisdiction, however, did not turn the draft convention text into a true mixed convention. As has been shown above, the convention type (strict double convention or mixed convention) was not only the end result of the negotiation process, but also at the same time the roadmap guiding the negotiations. Creating a mixed convention would have required a different decision-making process with regard to creating the green list of grounds of international direct jurisdiction. To create a true mixed convention, only the jurisdictional provisions on which consensus existed (among the negotiating States or experts) that exercising international direct jurisdiction on these bases was clearly appropriate would have been included in the green list.[730] Since reaching consensus on provisions on international direct jurisdiction is very difficult to achieve, this green list developed on the basis of consensus would have been rather small, presumably.[731] That means, a true mixed convention also had a different structure, i.e., a different architecture, from a strict double convention, namely an architecture which would have secured for the future Contracting States a sufficient amount of flexibility regarding the exercise of international direct jurisdiction (a side effect resulting from

728 Von Mehren, 'Theory and Practice of Adjudicatory Authority' (n 141) 410; June 1999 Draft (n 313) Article 19.

729 June 1999 Draft (n 313), Article 19: '[s]ubject to Articles 4 [Choice of court], 5 [Appearance by the defendant], 7 [Contracts concluded by consumers], 8 [Employment contracts], 13 [Exclusive jurisdiction] and [14] [Provisional and protective measures], the Convention does not prevent the application by Contracting States of rules of jurisdiction under national law, provided that this is not prohibited under Article 20'; Nygh/Pocar Report (n 29) 263 [203]–[206].

730 Von Mehren, 'New Approach' (n 1) 287; von Mehren, 'Enforcing Judgments Abroad' (n 6) 27; von Mehren, 'The Case for a Convention-mixte Approach' (n 266) 92; Nygh, 'Arthur's Baby' (n 266) 154, 155.

731 Cf von Mehren, 'New Approach' (n 1) 287; cf Nygh, 'Arthur's Baby' (n 266) 155, 157; see also Brand, 'Restructuring the Preliminary Draft Convention Text' (n 267) 77; 'Work Doc No 33: Proposal by the delegation of United States of America', in *Proceedings of the Twentieth Session, Tome II* (n 29) 405; Jeffrey D Kovar, Letter to Hans van Loon (n 34) 5.

the decision-making process on the basis of consensus).[732] The Special Commission meetings did not proceed on the basis of consensus, however, but on the basis of majority voting during the last two Special Commission meetings in June and October 1999.[733] The effects of the decision-making process on the basis of voting, coupled with a lack understanding of the purpose of a true mixed convention, are discussed in the following.

5.3. THE EFFECT OF A LACK OF PREPARATION COUPLED WITH A DECISION-MAKING PROCESS ON THE BASIS OF MAJORITY VOTING

The Special Commission took decisions on the basis of voting during the last two Special Commission meetings of the drafting phase in June and October 1999.[734] Under this decision-making process, a provision was included into the draft convention text if it 'received support of a majority of the delegations present and voting'[735] (indicative votes were taken during the November 1998 session of the Special Commission).[736] Due to the decision-making process on the basis of majority voting, some jurisdictional provisions were included in the green list of the October 1999 Preliminary Draft Convention that were deemed appropriate by only a simple majority of participating experts, while a strong minority in fact did not deem them to be appropriate for exercising jurisdiction. For example, the Special Commission decided to include a provision regulating

[732] Cf Jeffrey D Kovar, Letter to Hans van Loon (n 34) 5; von Mehren, 'Theory and Practice of Adjudicatory Authority' (n 141) 409, 410.

[733] See, e.g., Special Commission on international jurisdiction and the effects of foreign judgments in civil and commercial matters (25–30 October 1999), 'Report of Meeting No 74' (on file with author); Trooboff, 'Ten (and Probably More) Difficulties' (n 298) 276.

[734] Original Rules of Procedure (n 90), art 3; cf also Permanent Bureau, 'Conclusions of the Special Commission on GAP of May 2000' (n 35) 12; 'Chairman's Report March 1998' (n 719) 3: '[d]uring the November meeting [...], we shall be taking indicative votes on many issues, while in 1999 a more formal procedure will obtain so as to resolve all outstanding matters'; see also Jeffrey D Kovar, Letter to Hans van Loon (n 34) 2: 'an incipient tendency at the November 1998 session toward bloc voting in support of established positions became fully developed and overwhelmed the two 1999 sessions'.

[735] Original Rules of Procedure (n 90), art 3; see also Ronald A Brand, 'Community Competence for Matters of Judicial Cooperation at the Hague Conference on Private International Law: A View from the United States' (2002) 21 JL & Com 191, 193.

[736] 'Chairman's Report March 1998' (n 719) 3.

jurisdiction in matters relating to individual contracts of employment in the October 1999 Preliminary Draft Convention.[737] Only half of the votes cast were in favour of including employment contracts within the scope of the convention in the first place, however, while almost a third of the votes were cast against: out of 28 votes cast, 14 votes were in favour of including employment contracts, 8 votes were against and 6 delegations abstained from casting a vote.[738] Another example was the discussion of the question of whether tenancies of immovable property should be included within the grounds of exclusive jurisdiction:[739] 15 votes were cast in favour of such a provision, 7 were cast against and 2 delegations abstained.[740] Had the Special Commission undertaken to negotiate a true mixed convention, a provision regulating international direct jurisdiction for tenancies regarding immovable property would not have been included in the draft convention text, as there was no consensus among the experts that exercising international direct jurisdiction on this basis would be clearly appropriate. Another example was whether the draft convention text should include a ground of exclusive jurisdiction for proceedings which have as their object the decisions of the organs of a legal person: 12 votes were cast in favour of such a provision and 9 against (with 3 abstentions).[741] A strong minority also rejected the proposal to attribute exclusive direct jurisdiction to the courts of a Contracting State in which a legal person had its seat if the proceedings had as their object the validity or nullity of the decisions of its organs: 12 votes were cast in favour, 9 against and there were 3 abstentions.[742]

Once the Special Commission began to take decisions on the basis of voting, it had therefore unwittingly abandoned the possibility of creating a true mixed convention; taking decisions on the basis of voting also had the effect that jurisdictional provisions were included in the green list on which no consensus existed that exercising jurisdiction on these bases would be clearly appropriate. As a result, the implementation phase (the phase of drafting of a convention text) began to disadvantage the proponents of a true mixed convention (in particular the US) once the Special Commission

737 October 1999 Preliminary Draft Convention (n 32), art 8.

738 'Report of Meeting No 74' (n 733).

739 Special Commission on the question of jurisdiction, recognition and enforcement of foreign judgments (7–18 June 1999), 'Report of Meeting No 61' (on file with author).

740 Ibid.

741 Ibid 1.

742 Ibid.

started to take decisions on the basis of voting in June and October 1999.[743] It can be said, therefore, that the decision-making process was unfair for the proponents of the true mixed convention, and that the phase of creating a draft convention text lacked justice in this regard: the proponents of the true mixed-convention model did not have the same chance to contribute to the outcome of the negotiations as the proponents of the other convention type.[744] Eventually, taking decisions on the basis of voting had the effect that the October 1999 Preliminary Draft Convention[745] became structured almost exactly like the 1968 Brussels Convention and the 1988 Lugano Convention, as it contained most of the jurisdictional provisions that were also used in the texts of Brussels and Lugano:[746] defendant's forum (Article 3), Choice of court (Article 4), Appearance by the defendant (Article 5), Contracts (Article 6), Contracts concluded by consumers (Article 7), Individual contracts of employment (Article 8), Branches [and regular commercial activity] (Article 9), Torts or delicts (Article 10), Trusts (Article 11), Exclusive jurisdiction (Article 12(1)–(5)), Provisional and protective measures (Article 13), Multiple defendants (Article 14), Counter claims (Article 15), and Third-party claims (Article 16). This means that the green list of the October 1999 Preliminary Draft Convention almost exactly matched the green list of the Brussels Convention (and the Lugano Convention) in its structure.[747] Although the minutes prepared during the

---

743 See above (n 734).

744 Zartmann, 'Negotiation as a search for justice' (n 93) 71, 73, 84; Albin, Druckman (n 93) 1017.

745 October 1999 Preliminary Draft Convention (n 32) 190.

746 Cf von Mehren, 'Theory and Practice of Adjudicatory Authority' (n 141) 410.

747 The only jurisdictional topics found in the Brussels and Lugano texts which were not included in the October 1999 Preliminary Draft Convention were 1968 Brussels Convention (as amended [1990] OJ C189/2)/1988 Lugano Convention (n 144), art 5(4) (jurisdiction with regard to a civil claim for damages or restitution based on an act giving rise to criminal proceedings); art 5(7) (jurisdiction with regard to a dispute concerning the payment of remuneration claimed in respect of the salvage of a cargo or freight); art 6(4) (jurisdiction in matters relating to a contract if the action may be combined with an action against the same defendant in matters relating to rights in rem in immovable property); and art 16(5) (jurisdiction in matters concerned with the enforcement of judgments). Jurisdiction in matters relating to maintenance (1968 Brussels Convention/1988 Lugano Convention, art 5(2)), and jurisdiction in matters relating to liability from the use or operation of a ship, ibid art 6a, were excluded from the scope of the October 1999 Preliminary Draft Convention under its art 1(2)(b) and (h); jurisdiction in matters relating to insurance, finally (1968 Brussels Convention/1988 Lugano Convention, Title II, s 3), was regarded as being covered by the provision on jurisdiction in consumer matters of the October 1999 Preliminary Draft Convention, cf Kessedjian, 'Synthesis of the Work of the Special Commission of June 1997 on International Jurisdiction and the Effects of Foreign Judgments in Civil and Commercial Matters: Prel Doc No 8 of November 1997' (n 288) 81 [48].

Special Commission meetings do not specify which experts supported the relevant proposals, it is interesting to note that the Contracting Parties to the Brussels Convention and the Lugano Convention constituted an absolute majority of the participants during the Special Commission meeting in June 1999, with 15 of 28 participants being a Contracting Party to either the 1968 Brussels Convention and/or the 1988 Lugano Convention.[748] During the Special Commission meeting in October 1999, 33 Hague Conference Member States participated, with 16 of them belonging to the Brussels-Lugano group, thereby constituting almost an absolute majority.[749] The US, on the other hand, rejected the strict double-convention structure of the October 1999 Preliminary Draft Convention: since its green list would have regulated the exercise of international direct jurisdiction in so many instances, the 1999 Draft Convention had been regarded as being too restrictive of the possibility of the Contracting States to regulate the exercise of international direct jurisdiction by means of domestic rules.[750]

Moreover, the properties and requirements of a true mixed convention had not been fully appreciated by at least some of the participating experts until the beginning of the Diplomatic Session in 2001, which most likely hindered the efficiency of the drafting process.[751] Until then, some experts believed, for example, that the 'grey area', the national grounds of

---

748 28 Hague Conference Member States were present during the Special Commission meeting in June 1999, and 14 of these were also Contracting Parties to the 1968 Brussels Convention: Austria, Finland, Sweden, Denmark, Ireland, United Kingdom, Spain, Portugal, Germany, France, Italy, Belgium, Luxembourg and the Netherlands, see above (n 640); Switzerland was a Contracting Party to the 1988 Lugano Convention, see 1988 Lugano Convention – Parties (n 194). The 13 non-Brussels-Lugano States were Argentina, Australia, Canada, China (People's Republic of), Cyprus, Republic of Korea, Croatia, United States of America, Israel, Japan, Morocco, Slovakia and the Czech Republic, see Hague Conference on Private International Law, 'Final list of participants – Special Commission on international jurisdiction and the effects of foreign judgments in civil and commercial matters 7–18 June 1999' (on file with author); see also Brand, 'Community Competence' (n 735) 197.

749 In addition to the participants of the June 1999 meeting, the following Hague Conference Member States participated in the Special Commission meeting in October 1999: Hungary, Mexico, Monaco, Norway, Romania, Turkey and Uruguay, see Special Commission on international jurisdiction and the effects of foreign judgments in civil and commercial matters (25–30 October 1999), 'Final list of participants' (on file with author); 14 of the participants were Contracting Parties to the 1968 Brussels Convention, see above (n 748); besides Switzerland, Norway was also a Contracting Party to the 1988 Lugano Convention, see above (n 748).

750 Special Commission meeting of November 1998, 'Report No 53' (on file with author).

751 Cf Dupont/Faure, 'The Negotiation Process', in Kremenyuk (n 65) 52.

jurisdiction which were not included in the green list, would nevertheless be limited by the green list in the convention.[752]

5.4. CONCLUSION

The preparatory work undertaken by the Permanent Bureau on the Judgments Project also deviated from the project management techniques that it had used for preparing the work on the 1980 Hague Convention on Child Abduction and the 1993 Hague Convention on Intercountry Adoption in preparation of and during the implementation phase (the phase during the Special Commission meetings from 1997–1999 with the purpose of creating a draft convention text). The conceptual strategy of pursing the creation of a strict double convention, which had been developed during the first two Special Commission meetings in 1994 and 1996, had not been tested for its viability before the Judgments Project entered into its drafting phase (from 1997 onwards). Moreover, no sufficient detailed planning had taken place for creating a strict double convention on a global level and no detailed planning on how to create a mixed convention had taken place.

Despite the insufficient preparation of its definition phase, the Judgments Project was allowed to enter into the implementation phase, i.e., drafting a convention text during the Special Commission meetings from 1997 onwards in order to prepare the adoption of a convention text during a Diplomatic Conference. The use of Preliminary Documents as a basis of the discussions during the implementation phase (the Special Commission meetings from 1997–1999) which followed the structure of the 1968 Brussels Convention (a strict double convention), and the use of a decision-making process on the basis of majority voting, coupled with a lack of understanding of the mixed-convention concept, led the Special Commission meetings to develop a draft convention text (the 'project deliverable') that satisfied, in particular, the needs of those Hague Conference Members which were also Contracting Parties to the 1968 Brussels Convention and the 1988 Lugano Convention:[753] the October 1999 Preliminary Draft Convention.

---

[752] Tell, 'Can a Mixed Convention Work?' (n 148) 37; 'Intervention Peter Nygh (co-Reporter)', in 'Minutes No 1', in *Proceedings of the Twentieth Session, Tome II* (n 29) 479; see also below, Chapter 6.

[753] Paul Beaumont, 'UK Position on the Hague Preliminary Draft Convention on Jurisdiction and Foreign Judgments in Civil and Commercial Matters adopted by the Special Commission on 30 October 1999' (on file with author), 1; Wagner,

The October 1999 Preliminary Draft Convention did not, however, address the needs of the US. As von Mehren noted, '[i]n spirit and inspiration, the [Special] Commission's product was not a mixed convention but a close-knit double convention with none of the flexibility and room for development that a mixed convention could have provided.'[754] The October 1999 Preliminary Draft Convention would have restricted the flexibility of the Contracting States to regulate the exercise of international direct jurisdiction autonomously to a significant extent (as a strict double convention would have done). Since this need for flexibility was overlooked by the project managers, the Special Commission meetings failed to produce a draft convention text that could have served as an acceptable starting point for the multilateral negotiations during a Diplomatic Session.[755] Without an underlying strategy giving guidance on how to create a global judgments convention, at the end of the phase of the Special Commission meetings in October 1999, the Judgments Project had therefore failed to produce the project deliverable, a draft convention text suitable to be sent to a Diplomatic Conference.

'Gerichtsstandsvereinbarungen' (n 19) 104, 105; Brand, 'Community Competence' (n 735) 197.

754 Von Mehren, 'Theory and Practice of Adjudicatory Authority' (n 141) 410.

755 Brand, 'Community Competence' (n 735) 198.

CHAPTER 6

DID THE JUDGMENTS PROJECT FAIL BECAUSE THE BASIS FOR CONSENSUS-BUILDING WAS MISSING DURING THE DIPLOMATIC SESSION?

After the final Special Commission meeting had taken place in October 1999, the US declared that it could not support the October 1999 Preliminary Draft Convention as a basis for multilateral negotiations in a Diplomatic Session, and the Judgments Project had reached an impasse.[756] The Legal Advisor to the US Department of State, Jeffrey D Kovar, informed the then Secretary General of the Hague Conference, Hans van Loon, in February 2000 that the October 1999 Preliminary Draft Convention[757] which had been produced by the Special Commission meetings on the Judgments Project stood 'no chance of being accepted in the United States'.[758] According to this letter, the October 1999 Preliminary Draft Convention raised various issues regarding its scope of application,[759] the rules on recognition and enforcement,[760] Article 37 October 1999 Preliminary Draft Convention (Relationship with other conventions),[761] and Article 41 October 1999 Preliminary Draft Convention (Federal clause).[762] The letter also raised concerns regarding the specific content of some of the jurisdictional provisions of the green list.[763] The most

756 Jeffrey D Kovar, Letter to Hans van Loon (n 34); cf also Permanent Bureau, 'Conclusions of the Special Commission on GAP of May 2000' (n 35) 10–12.

757 October 1999 Preliminary Draft Convention (n 32) 190.

758 Jeffrey D Kovar, Letter to Hans van Loon (n 34) 3; the quoted part of the letter is also reproduced in von Mehren, 'Can the Hague Conference Project Succeed?' (n 31) 192.

759 Jeffrey D Kovar, Letter to Hans van Loon (n 34) 5.

760 Ibid 10.

761 Ibid 10.

762 Ibid.

763 Ibid 6–8; in particular, the letter raised issues with the connecting factors employed by the following provisions of the October 1999 Preliminary Draft Convention (n 32): Article 3 (Defendant's Forum), Article 6 (Contracts), Article 7 (Consumer Contracts),

significant concerns of the US, however, related to the structure of the draft convention text, i.e., the convention type pursued, which was a mixed convention in name only as discussed above in Chapter 5:

> [D]espite nearly eight years of discussion of the fundamental importance and need for a mixed convention, and agreement by vote that the Special Commission would work to that end, what we see in the present text [the October 1999 Preliminary Draft Convention] is for all intents and purposes a narrow double convention.[764]

From the point of view of the US, the green list of the October 1999 Preliminary Draft Convention was too broad,[765] and as a result did not allow sufficient room for 'growth and development in the future' regarding domestic rules on international direct jurisdiction.[766] Such a broad green list would have resulted in a very narrow unregulated area, and would not have provided for enough flexibility for Contracting States to adapt their jurisdictional rules in order to react to changes in law and society.[767] Moreover, this grey area would have been restricted even further by Article 18 of the October 1999 Preliminary Draft Convention (the provision containing the red list): Article 18 would have prohibited not only the use of certain connecting factors included in the red list),[768] but it also contained a general and very broad definition of exorbitant jurisdiction.[769] This definition prohibited the use of any other domestic rule on international direct jurisdiction beyond the red list of Article 18(1) which met this definition of exorbitant jurisdiction.[770]

Since the October 1999 Preliminary Draft Convention did not meet its needs, the US requested to postpone the Diplomatic Conference in

---

Article 8 (Employment Contracts), Article 9 (Branches [and Regular Commercial Activity]), Article 10 (Torts), and Article 12 (Exclusive Jurisdiction).

764 Ibid 4; see also Sections 5.2–5.4 above.

765 Ibid 5: '[i]n our view there should be carefully defined bases of required jurisdiction reflecting all delegations' legal traditions'.

766 Ibid 5.

767 Ibid 5: '[i]n our view there should be [...] a substantial permitted area that will provide the flexibility for the convention to adapt to changing circumstances'.

768 October 1999 Preliminary Draft Convention, art 18(2).

769 October 1999 Preliminary Draft Convention, art 18(1): '[w]here the defendant is habitually resident in a Contracting State, the application of a rule of jurisdiction provided for under the national law of a Contracting state is prohibited if there is no substantial connection between that State and the dispute'.

770 Nygh/Pocar Report (n 29) 263 [208]–[209]; Jeffrey D Kovar, Letter to Hans van Loon (n 34) 5: '[i]n our view there should be [...] a limited list of well-known exorbitant grounds of jurisdiction'.

February 2000.[771] This request was supported by the Ambassadors of Australia, Japan, and the Republic of Korea,[772] as well as the Ambassador of the People's Republic of China, who 'all indicated that the negotiations had reached a critical phase and that more time was needed'.[773] The Member States of the EC, however, 'insisted that everything should be done to complete the Convention at the Diplomatic Session which should be held before the end of 2001'.[774] In response to the letter sent by the US, the Special Commission meeting on General Affairs and Policy of the Hague Conference in May 2000 decided to split the Diplomatic Session (the plenary meeting of the Hague Conference Member States during which new conventions are adopted) into two parts, and to use a decision-making process on the basis of consensus instead of majority voting (for the first time in the history of the Hague Conference).[775] Furthermore, it was agreed that no binding decisions would be taken unless consensus or near consensus existed on the relevant question.[776] The second part of

771 Permanent Bureau, 'Conclusions of the Special Commission on GAP of May 2000' (n 35) 10, 11: '[t]he United States delegation explained why it had requested that the Hague Conference postpone the Diplomatic Session. Following consultation with various interest groups in the United States, a consistent view had emerged that there would be difficulty in accepting the text of the preliminary draft Convention in the United States. To achieve enough Congressional support for acceptance it would be necessary to present a more balanced text and a flexible mixed Convention would be the best solution. However, the US delegation was aware that, on the one hand, some delegations had argued that it would be difficult to accept even a limited grey area, and on the other hand, some American lawyers were not yet ready to accept the proposed list of prohibited bases of jurisdiction'.

772 By means of a letter written together with the Ambassador of the United States, see Permanent Bureau, 'Conclusions of the Special Commission on GAP of May 2000' (n 35) 10.

773 Ibid 10, 11.

774 Ibid 11.

775 This proposal was made by the delegations of Denmark and the United Kingdom after 'extensive informal discussions had taken place', and was 'unanimously accepted' by the participants of the Special Commission on General Affairs and Policy in May 2000, see Permanent Bureau, 'Conclusions of the Special Commission on GAP of May 2000' (n 35) at 11. Not only had the United States asked to postpone the Diplomatic Session but also 'a letter from the Ambassadors of Australia, Japan, the Republic of Korea and the United States and a letter from the Ambassador of the People's Republic of China all indicated that the negotiations had reached a critical phase and that more time was needed. A letter from the 15 European Union Member States meanwhile, while admitting that the work might be delayed by some months, insisted that everything should be done to complete the Convention at the Diplomatic Session which should be held before the end of 2001' ibid 10, 11.

776 Permanent Bureau, 'Conclusions of the Special Commission on GAP of May 2000' (n 35) 11.

the Diplomatic Session, originally intended to be held at the end of the year in 2000, was postponed until either late 2001 or 2002.[777] Moreover, it was agreed that the second part of the Diplomatic Session would then be conducted according to the standard rules of procedure of the Hague Conference, i.e., on the basis of majority voting.[778] In order to prepare for the consensus process, the Hague Conference Member States furthermore agreed to convene several informal meetings between themselves in order to foster 'the consideration and drafting of proposals for resolving important substantive and technical issues'.[779] In total, six such informal meetings took place:[780] in Washington (30 October – 1 November 2000), The Hague (11–12 December 2000), Basle (13–15 December 2000), Geneva (1 February 2000), Ottawa (26 February – 2 March 2001), and Edinburgh (23–26 April 2001).

During the final informal meeting in Edinburgh, some discussions on the formal convention structure took place. During this meeting, three proposals on the question of the formal structure were distributed: one proposal stemmed from the US scholar Ronald Brand, one from a scholar from New Zealand (David Goddard), and one from the Swiss scholar Andreas Bucher.[781] When these proposals were discussed under the topic 'Agenda [for the Diplomatic Session]/Structure of the Convention' in the afternoon of 25 April 2001, the penultimate day of the informal meeting, some experts in fact requested to reconsider the convention purpose: '[t]here were some requests that there be an opening statement or lecture on the work that had been carried out to date and what it was hoped the future Convention would achieve.'[782] However, this request was rejected according to the report: '[o]thers disagreed and favoured a short discussion on the structure of the instrument to help to introduce the debate.'[783] Even

---

777 Ibid.

778 Ibid.

779 Ibid.

780 Permanent Bureau, 'Informational note on the work of the informal meetings held since October 1999 to consider and develop drafts on outstanding items: Prel Doc No 15 of May 2001', in *Proceedings of the Twentieth Session, Tome II* (n 29) 363, 363.

781 Permanent Bureau, ' Prel Doc No 15 of May 2001, Annex VII' (n 780) 374–379; Peter E McEleavy, 'Towards a Worldwide Convention on Jurisdiction and Foreign Judgments in Civil and Commercial Matters: Edinburgh Informal Meeting 23–26 April 2001 – Scottish Executive Justice Department & Lord Chancellor's Department – Report on the Proceedings' (McEleavy Report) (on file with author) 18.

782 McEleavy Report, ibid 18.

783 Ibid.

though the experts 'concluded that it would be unavoidable to have a short controlled debate on the opening day on the nature of the Convention, and during this statements could be made as to how the instrument might be structured',[784] the question of the convention type was not seriously reconsidered before or during the Diplomatic Session in 2001.[785]

A reconsideration of the convention type at the outset of the Diplomatic Session would have been required, however, for the official negotiations to have a chance of leading to a successful outcome by working towards a true mixed convention. Merely changing the decision-making process from majority voting to one based on consensus was not sufficient to produce a true mixed convention. Even though a decision-making process based on consensus was required for creating a true mixed convention as suggested by Arthur T von Mehren,[786] it would have been necessary for the Hague Conference Member States to agree on the purpose of the convention, i.e., the convention type, in order for the consensus process to be successful, as the convention purpose has a direct influence on the convention structure and its content, as analysed above in Chapter 5.[787]

However, different understandings of the mixed-convention concept existed, in particular between the US and the European bloc. While the US pursued the concept of a true mixed convention, the European bloc clung to the structure of the October 1999 Preliminary Draft Convention, which was a mixed convention in only a technical sense. In spirit and purpose, the October 1999 Preliminary Draft Convention was more akin to a strict double convention. From the point of view of the European bloc, the mere fact that the October 1999 Preliminary Draft Convention allowed the use of non-unified, domestic grounds of international direct jurisdiction in addition to the green list had turned the draft convention text into a mixed convention.[788] As shown in Chapter 5, the true mixed convention concept required more than the mere option for States of being allowed to use their domestic grounds of jurisdiction in addition to the provisions on the green list, and the October 1999 Preliminary Draft Convention developed by the Special Commission meetings was a

784 Ibid; a list of participants for the informal meetings in Ottawa and Geneva is available in *Proceedings of the Twentieth Session, Tome II* (n 29) 324–325 and 342–343.

785 'Minutes No 1: Meeting of Wednesday 6 June 2001 (afternoon)', in *Proceedings of the Twentieth Session, Tome II* (n 29) 478–483.

786 See above, Section 5.1.4.

787 See above, Sections 5.1.4. and 5.2.

788 Wagner, 'Gerichtsstandsvereinbarungen' (n 19) 105; see also Bucher, 'Vers une convention mondiale' (n 173) 80.

mixed convention only in a technical sense, but not in spirit.[789] Based on the conceptual and detailed planning of the Permanent Bureau that had recommended creating a strict double convention as a first priority, and which used the 1968 Brussels Convention as the plan of construction, the Special Commission meetings had created their own version of a mixed convention which was more akin to a strict double convention.[790] One of the participants of the Special Commission meetings even had described the October 1999 Preliminary Draft Convention fittingly as a 'restricted double convention' ('*convention double restreinte*').[791]

These two different views on the meaning of the term 'mixed convention' (the true mixed convention and the restricted double convention) between in particular the US and the European bloc became obvious on the very first day of the Diplomatic Session. When the question of the nature of the future convention was discussed on 6 June 2001, the US repeated that the October 1999 Preliminary Draft Convention would stand 'no chance of acceptance in the United States', and called for a replacement of this draft 'in a consensus building way' in order to create a true mixed convention.[792] Ms Renfors, the Swedish delegate speaking on behalf of the European Community, on the other hand, noted during the discussions that 'it was essential [for the European Community] that the Convention be a mixed instrument, containing grounds of required, white list [green list], jurisdiction, grounds of prohibited, black list [red list], jurisdictions as well as certain existing national grounds of jurisdiction'.

This lack of agreement on the meaning and purpose of the mixed convention concept inevitably resulted in a lack of consensus on the question on whether the green list should be able to restrict the unregulated grey area. This lack of common understanding of the purpose of the grey area had been highlighted by the Co-Reporter Mr Nygh when he discussed the nature of the convention at the beginning of the Diplomatic Session as it had been requested during the Edinburgh meeting.

789 Von Mehren, 'Theory and Practice of Adjudicatory Authority' (n 141) 410; see above, Sections 5.2–5.4.

790 Bucher, 'Vers une convention mondiale' (n 173) 79 ('Convention double restreinte'); Brand, 'Community Competence' (n 735) 197.

791 See Bucher, ibid.

792 'Intervention Mr Kovar', in 'Minutes No 1', in *Proceedings of the Twentieth Session, Tome II* (n 29) 479; 'Working Document No 11: Statement by the delegation of the United States of America', in *Proceedings of the Twentieth Session, Tome II* (n 29) 395, 396.

The Co-Reporter 'stated that the nature of this final "grey", or "status quo", list was not always properly understood. It was regarded by some as being a residual group, but on the other hand, could be viewed as the starting point, allowing courts in Contracting States to exercise their existing bases of jurisdiction'.[793] Under the true mixed-convention concept, the domestic rules of international direct jurisdiction (the 'grey area', or 'permitted area') would have co-existed with the unified jurisdictional provisions of the Hague Judgments Convention and therefore would have been the 'starting point'.[794] That means the green list of the mixed convention would not have restricted the courts of the Contracting States in their use of the existing domestic grounds of direct jurisdiction,[795] as was assumed sometimes erroneously by those participants in the Judgments Project who pursued the mixed convention in form of a restricted double convention. Under the true mixed convention, the jurisdictional provisions in the grey area would have existed in addition to the green list.

Due to this lack of agreement on the purpose and nature of the convention, the negotiations could have only moved forward if a decision on the true mixed convention had been made on the first day of the Diplomatic Session. However, the issue was left unresolved, and after the initial discussions about the nature of the convention, the negotiations shifted towards a discussion of the scope of the convention.[796] The fact that the mixed-convention concept had not been prepared comprehensively during the concept phase and the phase of detailed planning now unfolded its full effects. Since there was no agreement on the convention type and its purpose, it was in fact impossible for the US and the EC and its Member States to achieve sufficient agreement on provisions during the first part of the Diplomatic Session in 2001 that would have justified scheduling the second part of the Diplomatic Session. In particular, this lack of agreement on structure and purpose hindered reaching consensus in three particular ways: First, no consensus was reached on the content of the green list of the 2001 Interim Text.[797] Second, no consensus was reached regarding

793 'Intervention Mr Nygh (co-Reporter)', in 'Minutes No 1', in *Proceedings of the Twentieth Session, Tome II* (n 29) 478, 479.

794 Von Mehren, 'Recognition of United States Judgments Abroad' (n 70) 458; von Mehren, 'New Approach' (n 1) 283.

795 'Conclusions Working Group: Prel Doc No 19 November 1992' (n 28) [6]; von Mehren, 'Recognition of United States Judgments Abroad' (n 70) 458; von Mehren, 'New Approach' (n 1) 283; Tell, 'Can a Mixed Convention Work?' (n 148) 37–39.

796 'Minutes No 1', in *Proceedings of the Twentieth Session, Tome II* (n 29) 480.

797 See below, Section 6.1.

the extent to which a Hague Judgments convention should prohibit States from exercising international direct jurisdiction.[798] And third, the lack of agreement on the purpose of the convention (i.e., the lack of agreement on the convention type) also called into question the validity of the results of the consensus process in general.[799]

6.1. NO AGREEMENT ON THE CONTENT OF THE GREEN LIST OF THE 2001 INTERIM TEXT

To some extent, employing a consensus-based decision-making process during the Diplomatic Session had seemingly identified several grounds of jurisdiction that should be included in the green list.[800] At the same time, however, no consensus was reached for several other jurisdictional provisions with regard to whether these provisions should be included in the green list at all, or which connecting factor would be appropriate. For example, no consensus could be reached on whether jurisdictional provisions for matters relating to consumer contracts should be included in the convention text.[801] Equally, no consensus could be reached on whether the provision on tort jurisdiction should include the activity of the defendant as a connecting factor (i.e., allow jurisdiction in tort matters on the basis of the activities of the defendant in the forum state).[802] Neither could consensus be reached on whether the convention should provide

798 See 2001 Interim Text (n 36), art 18, fn 104: '[t]here was no consensus on this provision'; further discussed in Section 6.2.

799 See below, Section 6.3.

800 Jurisdiction based on an exclusive choice-of-court agreement of the parties for disputes arising out of a particular legal relationship, 2001 Interim Text (n 36), art 4(1); jurisdiction based on the express acceptance of jurisdiction, 2001 Interim Text, art 4(3); jurisdiction in matters relating to torts regarding the place where the act or omission that caused the injury occurred, 2001 Interim Text, art 10(1)(a); exclusive jurisdiction based on a trust agreement in proceedings concerning the validity, construction, effects, administration or variation of a trust created voluntarily and evidenced in writing, 2001 Interim Text, art 11; and exclusive jurisdiction concerning the validity of entries in public registers (other than those dealing with intellectual property rights) of the courts of the Contracting State in which the register was kept, 2001 Interim Text, art 12(3); moreover, consensus existed that it would be appropriate for a court which had jurisdiction according to the convention to determine a claim to also determine a counter-claim arising out of the transaction or occurrence on which the original claim was based, see 2001 Interim Text, art 15; fn 98.

801 2001 Interim Text (n 36), art 7; fn 43.

802 Ibid art 10(2), fn 67.

for jurisdiction in tort matters in the State where an act, omission or an injury might occur.[803] Nor could consensus be reached on whether the convention should provide for exclusive jurisdiction in matters which had as their objects rights in rem in immovable property, tenancies of immovable property,[804] the validity, nullity, or dissolution of a legal person, or the validity or nullity of the decisions of its organs.[805] Also, there was no consensus on the appropriate connecting factors for the home forum of the defendant (the defendant's forum), or for jurisdiction in contractual matters.[806] All of these provisions were included in the 2001 Interim Text within square brackets (sometimes also containing several alternative provisions) in order to indicate lack of consensus.[807]

If the Diplomatic Session had worked towards creating a true mixed convention, then the jurisdictional provisions on which no consensus existed regarding whether they should be included in the green list should have been removed from the convention text from a conceptual point of view.[808] By removing the controversial jurisdictional provisions from the green list, the Hague Conference Member States would have chosen not to regulate international direct jurisdiction for these matters (i.e., the jurisdictional topics would have remained in the unregulated grey area).[809] The EC and its Member States, however, rejected such a reduction of the scope of the green list. This can be demonstrated by the discussions of Working Document No 97 (Work Doc No 97), a joint proposal submitted during the Diplomatic Session on 18 June 2001 (i.e., four days before its end).[810] With Work Doc No 97, the delegations from Argentina, Australia,

---

803 Ibid art 10(4), fn 69.

804 Ibid art 12(1), fn 78.

805 Ibid art 6, Alternative A and Alternative B; Alternative A of Article 6 focused on the connection between the defendant and the forum and reflected the US-American approach to international direct jurisdiction, see above, Section 2.2.1.; Alternative B of Article 6 reflected the European approach to international direct jurisdiction, see Section 2.2.2.; see also 2001 Interim Text (n 36), fn 33; 2001 Interim Text, art 12(2), fn 79.

806 2001 Interim Text (n 36) art 3(1); 2001 Interim Text (n 36) art 6, Alternative A and Alternative B; see also 2001 Interim Text (n 36), fn 33.

807 See, e.g., Wagner, 'Sachstandsbericht' (n 346) 536.

808 See, e.g., 'Work Doc No 33: Proposal by the delegation of United States of America', in *Proceedings of the Twentieth Session, Tome II* (n 29) 405; Von Mehren, 'New Approach' (n 1) 287.

809 See, e.g., Von Mehren, 'New Approach' (n 1) 287; Nygh, 'Arthur's Baby' (n 266) 155.

810 'Work Docs Nos 90–97: Distributed on Monday 18 June 2001', in *Proceedings of the Twentieth Session, Tome II* (n 29) 437.

New Zealand[811] and Norway[812] suggested employing a new approach in working towards a Judgments Convention. This new approach had been deemed necessary by its proponents since it had become apparent during the meeting that major areas of disagreement, in particular regarding the green list and the red list, remained and that the possibility of achieving a sufficient degree of consensus on a convention text was out of reach.[813] In particular, Work Doc No 97 proposed that negotiations proceed by employing a three-step approach: as a first step, those grounds of direct jurisdiction should be identified on which consensus or near-consensus existed (as 'core provisions of the Convention');[814] second, those jurisdictional provisions should have been further refined, and other jurisdictional provisions on which consensus could be achieved should have been added;[815] and as a third, it suggested 'to conduct periodic reviews of the Convention, with a view to building on the initial Convention over time'.[816] As a starting point regarding the unification of grounds of international direct jurisdiction, Work Doc No 97 named four provisions as the core of the future work on a judgments convention: jurisdiction based on the defendant's forum, jurisdiction based on a choice of court, jurisdiction in branch matters, and jurisdiction based on a counter claim.[817] Effectively, Work Doc No 97 recommended building a true mixed convention as envisaged by Arthur T von Mehren. In line with von Mehren's vision, Work Doc No 97 proposed to focus on identifying those jurisdictional provisions for inclusion into the green list on which consensus existed between the Hague Conference Member States that exercising jurisdiction over defendants on these bases

---

811 New Zealand only became a Member State of the Hague Conference on 5 February 2002, see <https://www.hcch.net/en/instruments/conventions/status-table/?cid=29> accessed 5 April 2023. It only had the status of an observer during the Diplomatic Session, therefore, see 'Members of the Second Commission', in *Proceedings of the Twentieth Session, Tome II* (n 29) 386, 389. Observers had a weaker position in the negotiations than Hague Conference Members since they were not allowed to take part in the decision-making process of the Hague Conference, see, e.g., van Loon, Schulz, 'The European Community and the Hague Conference on Private International Law' (n 100) 258.

812 'Work Doc No 97: Proposal of the delegations of Argentina, Australia, New Zealand and Norway', in *Proceedings of the Twentieth Session, Tome II* (n 29) 440–3.

813 'Work Doc No 97' ibid 442; according to one of the participants of the Diplomatic Session, David McClean, this Working Document 'was an expression of the frustration felt by many delegations, to which the Norwegian delegation had earlier given expression', see McClean (n 574) 266.

814 'Work Doc No 97' (n 812) 442.

815 Ibid.

816 Ibid.

817 Ibid 443.

would be appropriate.[818] For this reason, Work Doc No 97 was welcomed by the US delegate Jeffrey D Kovar as a 'basic mixed convention' when this proposal was briefly discussed at the Diplomatic Session on 18 June 2001.[819] When this proposal was discussed again, however, during the meeting of Commission I on General Affairs and Policy of the Conference (the meeting following the conclusion of the Commission II on the Judgments Project, during which the negotiations on the judgments convention had taken place), the EC and its Member States refused to restrict the green list of the Judgments Project in this way. On 21 June 2001, the delegate speaking on behalf of the EC, Ms Cecilia Renfors,[820] declared that the EC was not willing to settle for a more modest judgments convention in form of a true mixed convention as proposed by Work Doc No 97. Ms Renfors noted that

> the European Community wanted the Convention project to remain on the Agenda [...] and that the amount of time and resources expended on it already, as well as the joint effort of enormous talent in the past two weeks, were reason enough to continue. [...] [T]he suggestion that ambitions be limited in order to reach a safer, more achievable aim held no interest for her. She was not willing to abandon the original objectives of the preliminary draft Convention.[821]

Even though the negotiations during the first part of the Diplomatic Session had revealed major areas of disagreement regarding the green list

---

818 Von Mehren, 'New Approach' (n 1) 287 ('[bases] so clearly appropriate as to be recommended for this white list' [green list]); von Mehren, 'Enforcing Judgments Abroad' (n 6) 27; von Mehren, 'The Case for a Convention-mixte Approach' (n 266) 92; Nygh, 'Arthur's Baby' (n 266) 154, 155.

819 'Minutes No 19', in *Proceedings of the Twentieth Session, Tome II* (n 29) 589, 592.

820 Sweden held the presidency in the Council of the European Union during the time of the Diplomatic Session, see 'Minutes No 1', in *Proceedings of the Twentieth Session, Tome II* (n 29) 478, 479.

821 'Minutes of the First Commission – Minutes No 1 – Meeting of Thursday 21 June 2001 (Morning)', in Hague Conference on Private International Law, *Proceedings of the Nineteenth Session, 6 to 22 June 2001 – Part One, 2 to 13 December 2002 – Part Two, Tome I, Miscellaneous Matters* (Koninklijke Brill NV 2008) 586, 586. Besides the EC, also the Canadian delegation rejected restricting the ambitions of the Judgments Project in this way. Ms Sanderson, the delegate from Canada, 'expressed her continued commitment to the development of a broad Convention' and noted that 'the suggestion of limiting the scope of the Convention initially with a view to potential expansion at a later date was of limited interest to most States. However, Ms Sanderson acknowledged that it was important to leave this option open at the moment. She did maintain that it would be premature to jettison the broader objectives entirely', see 'Intervention Ms Sanderson' ibid 587.

(and the red list), as further discussed in the following, the EC and its Member States refused to reconsider the type and purpose of the future convention and the attempt to create a true mixed convention.

6.2. NO CONSENSUS ON THE 2001 INTERIM TEXT, ARTICLE 18(1) AND ARTICLE 18(2)

Due to the lack of agreement on the type and purpose of the future convention, no agreement on Article 18 of the 2001 Interim Text, the provision dealing with prohibited grounds of jurisdiction, could be reached during the Diplomatic Session of 2001. The US rejected a general definition of exorbitant jurisdiction as contravening the purpose of a true mixed convention and proposed to delete Article 18(1) in its entirety during the first part of the Diplomatic Session.[822] The relevant US Working Document (Work Doc No 33) noted that

> [t]he problem with this Article is not simply a matter of drafting but goes to the core of what this Convention is all about. The basic concept of a mixed convention is that there be a limited number of jurisdictional provisions so universally accepted that they exist on the white list, a limited number of jurisdictional bases so universally disapproved of that they exist on the black list and everything else remains in the grey area. We suggest a return to this basic structure with the deletion of paragraph 1.[823]

In addition, during the first part of the Diplomatic Session, Jeffrey D Kovar stressed that 'it was fundamental not to have a general standard of exclusion as in [Article 18] paragraph 1'.[824] This proposal, which would have reflected a true mixed convention structure, was rejected by the EC and its Member States. Since the EC Member States had entered the Diplomatic Session with their own understanding of the mixed convention concept (the 'restricted double convention' concept), including a broad red list and a general definition of exorbitant jurisdiction in the convention text was regarded as the precondition by the European bloc for allowing the exercise of jurisdiction on the basis of national grounds of jurisdiction in the grey

---

822 'Work Doc No 33: Proposal by the delegation of United States of America', in *Proceedings of the Twentieth Session, Tome II* (n 29) 405.

823 Ibid.

824 'Intervention Mr Kovar', in 'Minutes No 7' in *Proceedings of the Twentieth Session, Tome II* (n 29) 512.

area. This means that the European bloc was only ready to accept the mixed convention model, even in a purely technical sense, if the possibility for courts to exercise jurisdiction based on domestic provisions was severely restricted.[825] From the point of view of one of the delegates representing the European Commission during the Diplomatic Session, Olivier Tell,[826] a mixed convention would have been a worthwhile undertaking only if a (broad) 'black list [i.e., a red list]' restricted the scope of the grey area.[827] In Tell's opinion, without such a red list, the application of the convention could easily be circumvented and the convention would as a result lose its appeal in terms of legal certainty and security.[828] Equally, in the view of one of the delegates of Switzerland (a Contracting Party to the 1988 Lugano Convention),[829] Andreas Bucher,[830] a mixed convention whose grey area was not restricted by a red list would not have constituted any real progress regarding the regulation of international direct jurisdiction.[831] Accordingly, Ms Cecilia Renfors, the delegate from Sweden speaking on behalf of the EC, remarked that 'the European Community kept to the view that there must be a general rule so that unknown exorbitant jurisdictional rules might be outlawed' when this issue was discussed during the Diplomatic Session.[832] This view was also supported by the delegation from Switzerland, which highlighted the necessity of limiting the grey area (the area of domestic grounds of jurisdiction unregulated by the convention) by excluding those grounds of domestic jurisdiction which were as exorbitant as those already included in the closed list of Article 18(2) of the 2001 Interim Text.[833] As a

---

825 Olivier Tell, 'La construction de l'espace unique européen en matière de justice face à l'harmonisation universelle de la procédure civile: propos réalistes d'un acteur européen' (2003) 8 Unif L Rev 453, 460 fn 14; Bucher, 'Vers une convention mondiale' (n 173) 81.

826 'Members of the Second Commission', in *Proceedings of the Twentieth Session, Tome II* (n 29) 389; Tell, ibid 453.

827 Tell, ibid. Ibid 460 fn 14.

828 Ibid.

829 1988 Lugano Convention: Parties (n 194).

830 'Members of the Second Commission', in *Proceedings of the Twentieth Session, Tome II* (n 29) 388.

831 Bucher, 'Vers une convention mondiale' (n 173) 81.

832 'Intervention Ms Renfors', 'Minutes No 7', in *Proceedings of the Twentieth Session, Tome II* (n 29) 512.

833 'Intervention M Bucher', 'Minutes No 7', in *Proceedings of the Twentieth Session, Tome II* (n 29) 513: 'M. Bucher souligne par ailleurs les mérites d'une clause général du type de celle propose dans l'actuel paragraphe 1 de l'article 18. La zone grise étant fondée sur le droit national des État parties, il est nécessaire d'empêcher ces derniers de faire déborder cette zone de manière excessive [...]. La liste prévue à l'article 18 est fermée; il convient donc d'empêcher les États d'introduire d'autres chefs de compétence

result, there was no consensus on the 2001 Interim Text, Article 18(1), by the end of the Diplomatic Session.[834]

Due to the lack of agreement on the convention type, equally no consensus on the red list of Article 18(2) could be reached during the Diplomatic Session, even though some provisions of this list were generally regarded as exorbitant. An analysis of the minutes and the Working Documents of the first part of the Diplomatic Session shows that there had been no specific proposals (either written or oral) to delete the following provisions from the red list of the October 1999 Preliminary Draft Convention: jurisdiction exercised on the basis of the nationality of the claimant (2001 Interim Text, Article 18(2)(b)); jurisdiction exercised on the basis of the nationality of the defendant (2001 Interim Text, Article 18(2)(c)); jurisdiction exercised on the basis of the domicile, habitual or temporary residence, or presence of the claimant in that State (2001 Interim Text, Article 18(2)(d)); and jurisdiction exercised on the basis of the service of a writ upon the defendant in that State (2001 Interim Text, Article 18(2)(f)).[835] The lack of specific proposals to delete these provisions suggests that consensus in fact

également choquants' ('Among other things, Monsieur Bucher underlined the merits of a general clause of the type proposed by Article 18(1). Since the grey zone was based on the national law of the Contracting States, it would be necessary to hinder them to make use of this zone in an excessive manner. […] The list provided by Article 18 was closed; for this reason, States must not be allowed to introduce other grounds of jurisdiction that are equally shocking.' (Translation provided by the author.).

834 2001 Interim Text (n 36) fn 106. The delegation of the Republic of Korea had proposed to narrow the definition of exorbitant jurisdiction by prohibiting jurisdiction as exorbitant only if there was no substantial connection either between the forum state and the dispute or between the forum state and the defendant (see 'Work Doc No 29' in *Proceedings of the Twentieth Session, Tome II* (n 29) 404), in order for the convention to 'take account of the fact that there might be a substantial relationship between the State and the defendant [which] would be of importance to those States where personal jurisdiction referred only to the connection between the court and the defendant', see 'Minutes No 7' (n 824) 512. Although Ms Renfors, the delegate representing the EC, had initially signaled openness towards this proposal, see ibid, there was no immediate support for the proposal when it was discussed again during the morning session on Friday, 15 June 2001, and the proposal was included into the draft convention text with square brackets, see 'Minutes No 16', in *Proceedings of the Twentieth Session, Tome II* (n 29) 573; 2001 Interim Text (n 36) fn 105. Even if the definition of exorbitant jurisdiction would have been narrower according to the Korean proposal, nevertheless a general definition of exorbitant jurisdiction would still have contravened the spirit of a true mixed convention, see 'Work Doc No 33: Proposal by the delegation of United States of America', in *Proceedings of the Twentieth Session, Tome II* (n 29) 405.

835 See also 'Work Doc No 98: Provisional Summary of the Outcome of the Discussion in Commission II', in *Proceedings of the Twentieth Session, Tome II* (n 29) 444, 453, fn 69–71, fn 74.

existed among the Hague Conference Member States that exercising jurisdiction over defendants on these bases would be inappropriate, i.e., exorbitant. Had the true mixed-convention concept been followed, these provisions would have been included in the red list.[836]

At the same time, the US proposed to delete the following jurisdictional provisions from the red list as exercising jurisdiction on these bases was regarded as *not* being clearly inappropriate: jurisdiction exercised on the basis of carrying on of commercial or other activities by the defendant in that State, except where the dispute was directly related to those activities (2001 Interim Text, Article 18(2)(e)); jurisdiction exercised on the basis of the unilateral designation of the forum by the defendant in that State (2001 Interim Text, Article 18(2)(g)); jurisdiction exercised on the basis of the temporary residence or presence of the defendant in that State (2001 Interim Text, Article 18(2)(i)); and jurisdiction exercised on the basis of the signing in that State of the contract from which the dispute arose (2001 Interim Text, Article 18(2)(j)).[837] If a true mixed convention structure had been pursued, then those provisions would have been removed from the convention text as no consensus existed that they were in fact exorbitant. This means that the provisions would have remained in the grey area, and States would have been allowed to continue exercising jurisdiction on these bases.[838]

Eventually, no consensus was reached on either of the proposed deletions from the red list in Article 18(2) (i.e., on the deletion of Article 18(2)(e), (g), (i), and (j)), nor on Article 18 as a whole.[839] Since the Member States of the EC (and the EC itself) did not pursue a true mixed convention, the US proposal to delete Article 18(2)(e) from the red list[840] – a proposal entirely reflecting a true mixed-convention approach[841] – was misinterpreted by some of the other delegates as an attempt to destroy a previously reached agreement on the red list as a

---

836 Von Mehren, 'New Approach' (n 1) 283 ('black list').

837 'Work Doc No 33: Proposal by the delegation of United States of America', in *Proceedings of the Twentieth Session, Tome II* (n 29) 405, 406.

838 Ibid.

839 2001 Interim Text (n 36) fn 112, fn 113, fn 116, fn 117 and fn 104.

840 Article 18(2)(e) was meant to ban the exercise of general jurisdiction on the basis of business contacts; the US regarded general jurisdiction on the basis of doing business as a vital component of its jurisdictional system, see 'Work Doc No 33: Proposal by the delegation of United States of America', in *Proceedings of the Twentieth Session, Tome II* (n 29) 405.

841 'Intervention Mr Kovar', in 'Minutes No 7', *Proceedings of the Twentieth Session, Tome II* (n 29) 512, 514; see also above, Section 2.1.

package deal.[842] At the same time, those States which were not pursuing a true mixed convention regarded this red list as an essential precondition to being able to accept a mixed convention in the first place.[843] For these reasons, the German delegation retaliated by proposing to delete Article 18(2)(a) from the red list during the morning session of the penultimate day of the meeting of the Second Commission on the Judgments Project.[844] This proposal was in turn dismissed by the US delegation as a rejection of the mixed convention concept as such, as the German proposal 'would signal the ability of every delegation to target and bracket separate elements of jurisdiction'.[845] These interventions demonstrate once more

---

842 See, e.g., 'Intervention Mr Musger (Austria)', in *Proceedings of the Twentieth Session, Tome II* (n 29) 514: 'Mr Musger (Austria) recognised the importance of the doing business ground for the United States of America, but he pointed out that the other bases in paragraph 2 were fundamental in other States. […] He stated that European States could only give up these grounds if there was consensus on the list as a whole'; 'Intervention Mr Wagner (Germany)', in ibid: '[Mr Wagner] recognized that the general doing business ground was of great importance in the United States of America. However, he suggested that it was not quite so important in practice. He invited the meeting not to destroy what had been elaborated at the previous meeting. He pointed out that he could argue about sub-paragraph a) [of Article 18(2)] in the same way as the United States of America had done over e) [of Article 18(2)]. He agreed with the Delegate of Austria that Article 18 had to be balanced'; see also 'Intervention Mr Beaumont (United Kingdom)', in 'Minutes No 20' in *Proceedings of the Twentieth Session, Tome II* (n 29) 601: '[h]e noted that the United States of America had submitted Working Document No 33 earlier in an attempt to eliminate certain aspects of the black list. Such an approach was abandoned because of the realization that the list of prohibited grounds of jurisdiction was a package and had to be dealt with as such. Any attempt to break it into parts would be moving backwards'.

843 See 'Intervention M Bucher', in 'Minutes No 7', in *Proceedings of the Twentieth Session, Tome II* (n 29) 514: 'M Bucher (Suisse) rappelle que la nécessité d'une zone de fors prohibés a toujours été admise par le professeur von Mehren (États-Unis d'Amérique), à l'origine de l'idée fructueuse de convention mixte. Si l'on accepte de laisser la liberté aux États, c'est à la condition qu'il existe des fors prohibés. Le principe d'une liste noire est indiscutable' (Monsieur Bucher recalled that the necessity of a zone of prohibited grounds of jurisdiction had always been admitted by Professor von Mehren (USA) to be at the origin of the successful idea of a mixed convention. If one accepts some freedom of the [Contracting] States, then only under the condition that prohibited grounds of jurisdiction exist. The existence of a [red] list was indisputable as a matter of principle). (Translation provided by the author).

844 'Work Doc No 96 (Germany)' in *Proceedings of the Twentieth Session, Tome II* (n 29) 440; 'Intervention Mr Wagner (Germany)', in 'Minutes No 20', ibid, 600; Article 18(2)(a) reflected a domestic rule as existing, for example, in Germany, allowing the exercise of international direct jurisdiction over a defendant on the basis of the location of assets in the forum State, see German Code of Civil Procedure, art 23.

845 'Minutes No 20', in *Proceedings of the Twentieth Session, Tome II* (n 29) 600, 601; the proposal to delete Article 18(2)(a) was also rejected by the Mexican delegation: 'Mr Siqueiros (Mexico) expressed surprise at Working Document No 96 and its

the detrimental effect which the lack of agreement on the convention type had on the negotiations: the US had proposed to delete Article 18(2)(e) because it regarded exercising jurisdiction on this basis as clearly appropriate; the proposal to delete Article 18(2)(e) therefore reflected the true mixed convention concept. The delegate from Germany on the other hand had proposed to delete Article 18(2)(a) from the red list (and thereby to allow the application of corresponding domestic jurisdictional rules) not because exercising international direct jurisdiction on this basis was regarded as clearly appropriate, but because the German delegation had understood the US proposal to delete Article 18(2)(e) (and Article 18(1) and 18(2)(g), (i), (j)) as an attempt to destroy what had been perceived as a previously reached compromise.[846] The US delegation in turn threatened to propose to delete also the provision on jurisdiction exercised on the basis of the service of the claim on the defendant (2001 Interim Text, Article 18(2)(f)) from the red list, but eventually suggested to put the whole of Article 18 into square brackets.[847] Putting Article 18 into square brackets indicated that no consensus had been reached on this provision during the Diplomatic Session.[848] This proposal was accepted to mark the status quo of the negotiations.[849]

6.3. DOUBTFUL VALIDITY OF THE RESULTS OF THE CONSENSUS PROCESS DUE TO THE LACK OF AGREEMENT ON THE CONVENTION TYPE

What is more, the fact that there was no agreement on the convention type and its purpose during the diplomatic negotiations also casts doubt on the validity of the results of the decision-making process on the basis of consensus in general. Until the end of the first part of the Diplomatic Session in 2001, the Hague Conference Members had not agreed on which convention type should be pursued (i.e., whether a true mixed convention

---

proposal to delete Article 18(2)(a). […] He could not conceive of the purpose of excluding it from the black list', see ibid 601; as a result, there was no consensus on the proposal to delete Article 18(2)(a), see 2001 Interim Text (n 36) fn 110.

846 'Intervention Mr Wagner (Germany)', in 'Minutes No 7', in *Proceedings of the Twentieth Session, Tome II* (n 29) 514.

847 'Minutes No 20', in *Proceedings of the Twentieth Session, Tome II* (n 29) 600, 601.

848 Wagner, 'Sachstandsbericht' (n 346) 536.

849 'Minutes No 20', in *Proceedings of the Twentieth Session, Tome II* (n 29) 601.

should be created, or rather a mixed convention in the form of a restricted double convention).[850] Since there was no agreement on this vital issue, some of the results of the consensus process were doubtful in general: the purpose of the convention (the convention type) was a negotiating position which directly affected the question of whether States were willing to accept a jurisdictional provision for inclusion into either the green list (and thereby being obligated to ensure the availability of this provision) or the red list (and thereby being obligated to prohibit its use). Evidence suggests that the fact that the purpose of the convention had not been agreed upon from the beginning of the Diplomatic Session hindered reaching consensus in at least two further instances. First, the US did not consent to a jurisdictional provision it most likely would have consented to if the Hague Conference had worked towards a true mixed convention in at least one instance: the 2001 Interim Text shows that there was no consensus on the proper connecting factor for the defendant's forum.[851] The US rejected employing the connecting factor of habitual residence for the defendant's forum (the forum which has general jurisdiction over a defendant for all claims), and argued for a connecting factor of mere residence of the defendant.[852] At the end of the first part of the Diplomatic Session, no agreement was reached on this basic and essential jurisdictional provision, which was the only jurisdictional provision allowing general jurisdiction over the defendant (i.e., jurisdiction for all types of claims).[853] If the Hague Conference Members had agreed to negotiate a true mixed convention, however, it is likely that the US would have accepted 'habitual residence' as a connecting factor for the defendant's forum, in order to ensure that its domestic judgments could be recognised and enforced abroad in general in the other Contracting Parties to the Hague Judgments Convention.

Furthermore, it is equally questionable whether the red list as contained in Article 18(2) of the 2001 Interim Text accurately reflected all of the provisions which States would have been willing to include into the red list if the Hague Conference Member States had pursued a true mixed convention. Under a true mixed convention, jurisdictional provisions

---

850 See Introduction to Chapter 6 above.

851 2001 Interim Text (n 36) art 3(1).

852 'Work Doc No 13: Proposal of the delegations of Japan, New Zealand and the United States of America', in *Proceedings of the Twentieth Session, Tome II* (n 29) 396, 397, and 'Intervention Mr Kovar', in 'Minutes No 3', ibid 489, 493; see also 2001 Interim Text (n 36) fn 17.

853 2001 Interim Text (n 36) art 3(1).

would have been included into the red list only if States generally had regarded them as inappropriate as a basis for exercising international direct jurisdiction. As analysed above, the delegate from Germany proposed to delete Article 18(2)(a) from the red list (and thereby to allow the application of domestic jurisdictional rules using the connecting factor of the location of assets in the forum State) not because the delegation was convinced that exercising international direct jurisdiction on this basis would be clearly appropriate. Instead, they had understood the US proposal to delete Article 18(2)(e) (and Article 18(1) and 18(2)(g), (i), (j)) from the convention text as an attempt to destroy a previously reached compromise.[854]

6.4. CONCLUSION

As shown by these examples, the fact that the mixed-convention concept had not been prepared comprehensively by the project managers during the phases of conceptual and detailed planning unfolded its effects fully during the Diplomatic Session: no common understanding of the true mixed convention concept and its purpose existed, and the US and the EC pursued two different variants of the mixed convention concept: while the US pursued the creation of a true mixed convention as envisaged by von Mehren, the EC and its Members States pursued a mixed convention in form of a strict double convention as embodied in the October 1999 Preliminary Draft Convention (a '*convention double restreinte*'). Since these two types of a mixed convention pursued different purposes (flexibility and protection of sovereignty under the true-mixed-convention concept; as much legal certainty as possible under the strict-double-convention concept), it was impossible for the negotiating States to achieve a sufficient amount of consensus on a convention text during the first part of the Diplomatic Session.

---

854 'Intervention Mr Wagner (Germany)', in 'Minutes No 7', *Proceedings of the Twentieth Session, Tome II* (n 29) 514.

CHAPTER 7

DID THE JUDGMENTS PROJECT FAIL BECAUSE THE UNITED STATES VOICED THEIR CONCERNS ABOUT THE PROJECT TOO LATE IN TIME?

7.1. INTRODUCTION

As discussed in Chapter 6, the term 'mixed convention' had a different meaning for the US delegation than for the EC and its Member States. The next question that has to be explored in order to understand why the Judgments Project failed, therefore, is whether the US delegation potentially contributed to this misunderstanding by not making their understanding of a mixed convention (the true mixed convention as originally proposed by the US delegation and the Working Group in 1992) clear enough during the pre-negotiation phase of the Special Commission meetings. In fact, the concerns raised by the US delegation in the letter to Hans van Loon, the then Secretary General of the Hague Conference, that was sent after the Special Commission meeting in October 1999 seemed to have taken some of the other delegations, especially from Member States of the EC, by surprise. One of the experts of the United Kingdom delegation to the Special Commission meetings from 1996 onwards, Paul R Beaumont,[855] remarked that Jeffrey D Kovar's letter had interrupted 'the relatively smooth path to a Diplomatic Conference'.[856]

[855] Permanent Bureau, 'Conclusions of the second Special Commission meeting on the recognition and enforcement of foreign judgments in civil and commercial matters: Prel Doc No 6 of August 1996, List of Participants in the Special Commission Meeting', <https://assets.hcch.net/docs/a0062ce0-96bb-4132-9cc3-65f0671c370f.pdf> accessed 5 April 2023 2, 4; Special Commission on the question of jurisdiction, recognition and enforcement of foreign judgments in civil and commercial matters (3–13 March), 'Final list of participants' (on file with author) 10.

[856] Beaumont, 'UK Position on the Hague Preliminary Draft Convention' (n 753) 1.

Equally, the Portuguese ambassador and permanent representative to the EU, Vasco Valente, declared in a fax to the Secretary General of the Hague Conference that Portugal had taken note of the Kovar letter 'with apprehension'.[857] If the US had voiced their concerns about the structure of the convention only after the elaboration of the final version of the preliminary draft convention text in October 1999, then they would also have contributed to the failure of the Judgments Project to a certain extent. It would have been unreasonable to expect the other participants to accommodate concerns they had no knowledge of.

An analysis of the discussions of the preparatory stages of the Judgments Project shows, however, that the US delegation had made their opposition to a closed double-convention structure (which later developed into the restricted double convention concept)[858] clear throughout the whole course of the project. The preparation of the October 1999 Preliminary Draft Convention took place in two stages, as discussed previously: the first stage began with the consideration of the US proposal by the Special Commission on General Affairs and Policy in 1992 and ended with the second preparatory Special Commission meeting on the Judgments Project in 1996 (before the topic of creating a Judgments Convention was officially put on the agenda of the Hague Conference during the Eighteenth Diplomatic Session in 1996).[859] In project management terms, this was the concept phase.[860] The second stage covered the phase of the Special Commission meetings from June 1997 until October 1999, during which a draft convention text which was to be considered by a Diplomatic Conference was prepared (this phase covered both the 'definition phase' and the 'implementation phase' in project management terms).[861] As will be shown in the following, the US had communicated its opposition to a strict double-convention structure (and to its regulatory density) clearly throughout both stages.

---

857 Fax from Vasco Valente, Ambassadeur Représentant Permanent du Portugal auprès de l'Union Européene, Président du Comité des Représentants Permanent, to M Van Loon, Sécrétaire-Général de la Conférence de la Haye de Droit International Privé from 27 April 2000 (on file with author) 1.

858 See above, Chapter 6.

859 Cf Special Commission on general affairs and policy of the Conference, 'Work Doc No 1 June 1992' (n 613); 'Final Act Seventeenth Session' (n 505) 43; McClean (n 574) 257–259.

860 See above, Section 4.1.

861 Ibid; Nygh/Pocar Report (n 29) 211 [3].

7.2. THE GENERAL CONCEPT DEVELOPMENT PHASE (1992–1996)

In 1992, by means of a Working Document submitted by the US delegation to the meeting of the Special Commission on General Affairs and Policy, the US already had explicitly noted that it regarded the *exhaustive* regulation of international direct jurisdiction by means of a strict (or closed) double convention as 'stultifying', an effect which could be circumvented by creating a (true) mixed convention instead of a strict double convention.[862] Under the true mixed convention, 'a participating legal system could [in principle] revise its jurisdictional practices to take into account changes in legal and economic circumstances'.[863] The Working Document also noted that this mixed-convention concept would allow States to retain 'flexibility in its jurisdictional and recognition and enforcement practices [which] permit[ed] a degree of experimentation and adaptation that seem[ed] desirable'.[864]

The US repeated that it had a strong interest in maintaining flexibility in regulating the exercise of jurisdiction during the meeting of the First Commission of the Seventeenth Session of the Hague Conference on Private International Law in May 1993,[865] when the question was discussed whether the Judgments Project should be put on the agenda of the Hague Conference.[866] In his intervention, Arthur T von Mehren, who participated in the Session as a member of the US delegation,[867] referred to the conclusions of the informal Working Group, which had recommended the conclusion of a mixed convention for the same reason.[868] To recall, according to the

862 Special Commission on general affairs and policy of the Conference, 'Work Doc No 1 June 1992' (n 613) 3.

863 Ibid.

864 Ibid [II].

865 The following 36 Hague Conference Member States participated in the Seventeenth Session of the Hague Conference, see 'List of participants', in Hague Conference on Private International Law, *Proceedings of the Seventeenth Session, 10 to 29 May 1993, Tome I, First Part, Miscellaneous Matters* (SDU Publishers 1995), 7–11: Germany, Argentina, Australia, Austria, Belgium, Canada, Chile, China (People's Republic of), Cyprus, Denmark, Egypt, Spain, United States, Finland, France, Greece, Hungary, Ireland, Israel, Italy, Japan, Luxembourg, Mexico, Nepal, Norway, the Netherlands, Poland, Portugal, Romania, the United Kingdom, Sweden, Switzerland, the Czech Republic, Turkey, Uruguay and Venezuela.

866 Cf 'Final Act Seventeenth Session' (n 505) 43, [B2a].

867 'List of participants Seventeenth Session' (n 865) 9.

868 'Intervention Mr von Mehren', in 'Minutes No 3', in Hague Conference on Private International Law, *Proceedings of the Seventeenth Session, 10 to 29 May 1993, Tome I, First Part, Miscellaneous Matters* (SDU Publishers 1995) 327, 327.

conclusions of the Working Group, 'it would be attempting too much in a worldwide context [...] to require the court of origin to assume jurisdiction only on the grounds specified in the convention [i.e., on the basis of the green list]'.[869] The Working Group had therefore 'expressed a preference for a convention which would offer some of the advantages of a double convention, while at the same time having a greater degree of flexibility than that available with a convention of the Brussels/Lugano type'.[870] Von Mehren furthermore expressly stated that the US had proposed to create a mixed convention instead of a single or double convention because a mixed convention 'would improve the present situation [regarding international direct jurisdiction], but would not interfere with practices that States might consider necessary'.[871]

It is not clear whether the US expressly reiterated its interest in creating a convention which would allow for a sufficient amount of flexibility during the first exploratory Special Commission meeting in June 1994, as no verbatim minutes were taken at the meeting.[872] The Preliminary Document drafted in preparation of the Special Commission meeting (Prel Doc No 1 of June 1994) itself, however, expressly referred to the Conclusions of the Working Group, and presupposed the 'familiarity' of the participants with its conclusions.[873] It is reasonable to assume, therefore, that the participants of the Special Commission meeting in June 1994 had been aware of the US interest in creating a convention text which would allow for enough legislative flexibility. Nevertheless, the conclusions of the Special Commission meeting in June 1994 noted a 'tendency' to reject a mixed convention, and to favour the preparation of a closed (or strict) double-convention structure instead.[874]

---

869 'Conclusions Working Group: Prel Doc No 19 November 1992' (n 28) 257.

870 Ibid 257, 258.

871 'Intervention Mr von Mehren', in 'Minutes No 3', *Proceedings of the Seventeenth Session* (n 866) 327.

872 See 'Minutes No 1', in Hague Conference on Private International Law, *Proceedings of the Eighteenth Session, 30 September to 19 October 1996, Tome I, Miscellaneous Matters*, 237, 239: '[M Bucher] souhaiterait qu'à partir de la deuxième réunion de la Commission spécial consacrée à la compétence et à la reconnaissance et l'exécution des jugements étrangers, il soit prévu faire établir des procès-verbaux *verbatim*' (Monsieur Bucher 'expressed the wish that from the second Special Commission meeting on jurisdiction and the recognition and enforcement of foreign judgments onwards, verbatim minutes should be prepared') (Translation provided by the author).

873 Permanent Bureau, 'Annotated Checklist' (n 585) 2.

874 Permanent Bureau, 'Conclusions of the Special Commission of June 1994 on the Question of the Recognition and Enforcement of Foreign Judgments in Civil and Commercial Matters: Prel Doc No 2 of December 1995' (n 201) [6]; see also above at Section 4.4.2.4.

Although the US did not support the creation of a strict double convention, abandoning the project at this early stage in 1994 would not have been a reasonable option. The Special Commission meeting of June 1994 was regarded as an exploratory meeting, tasked by the Seventeenth Session of the Hague Conference to assess whether the topic of a judgments convention should be included in the agenda of the Hague Conference in the first place.[875] Moreover, the US was very interested in the Judgments Project,[876] and would have wanted the project to continue, therefore, even if it was not possible to gather enough support among the other participants in the Special Commission meeting for a mixed convention at the time. Finally, and most importantly, the US delegation was convinced that creating a strict double convention was unfeasible. For this reason, it had expected that once the project was put on the agenda, the discussions among the experts at the Special Commission meetings would eventually lead to the elaboration of a true mixed convention.[877] As national concepts of international direct jurisdiction would prove to be too different as to allow for comprehensive regulation, the US regarded it as unlikely that the experts would be able to reach agreement on an exhaustive green list of unified grounds of international direct jurisdiction.[878]

For these reasons one may reasonably conclude that the US delegation regarded the creation of a (true) mixed convention as the only possible outcome of the Judgments Project, despite the fact that the other participants had not been supportive of a mixed convention initially. This would explain why at the end of the Special Commission meeting in 1994, the US delegation submitted a joint proposal, together with the delegations from Spain, France and Switzerland, to add work on a convention on jurisdiction and the recognition and enforcement of foreign judgments in civil and commercial matters to the agenda of the Conference at the Eighteenth Session.[879]

---

875 'Final Act Seventeenth Session' (n 505) 43.

876 See Section 3.1 above.

877 Cf Intervention Jeffrey D Kovar, in 'Views from around the world', in Lowenfeld, Silberman (n 249) 119, 134; full quote below, Section 7.3.3.

878 Von Mehren, 'Recognition of United States Judgments Abroad' (n 70) 459: '[t]he aspiration to regulate comprehensively the assumption of jurisdiction to adjudicate and recognition and enforcement is not realizable in our contemporary international order'.

879 'Work Doc No 2, submitted by the Experts of Spain, the United States, France and Switzerland', as reported in Permanent Bureau, 'Conclusions of the Special Commission of June 1994 on the Question of the Recognition and Enforcement of Foreign Judgments in Civil and Commercial Matters: Prel Doc No 2 of December 1995' (n 201) [3].

7.3. THE SPECIAL COMMISSION MEETINGS FROM JUNE 1997–NOVEMBER 1998

7.3.1. THE SPECIAL COMMISSION MEETINGS IN JUNE 1997 AND MARCH 1998

An analysis of the minutes of the subsequent Special Commission meetings and of the relevant official reports could convey the impression that during the Special Commission meetings in June 1997 and March 1998 the US had communicated their need for a flexible judgments convention less clearly. Neither the minutes of the meetings nor the relevant reports prepared by the Permanent Bureau record that the US had expressed their interest in negotiating (only) a true mixed convention. However, a possible reason for why the minutes and reports do not mention any US intervention in regard to the convention type may be that the Chair of the meeting (the expert from Canada, T Bradbrooke Smith)[880] did not allow extensive discussions about the nature of the future convention during those Special Commission meetings. In a tactical attempt to achieve an agreement on this question, the Chair steered the meeting directly into discussing the relevant jurisdictional provisions which featured in Prel Doc No 7 (the document that had been prepared in preparation of the Special Commission meeting) in June 1997.[881] On the second day of the Special Commission, one of the participating experts 'indicated that the countries of the European Union [were] in favour of a "double convention" and that the Brussels and Lugano Conventions serve[d] as good models'.[882] The Chair interrupted this discussion of the convention type, however, and suggested 'that the conversation first focus on matters of practical importance, before deciding on whether the convention should be double or not'.[883] As a result, the discussions then shifted to the potential grounds of jurisdiction that could be included into the green list.[884] The first provision that was discussed subsequently was 'jurisdiction with respect to immovable property' (which was also the first of the jurisdictional provisions discussed by Prel Doc No 7).[885]

---

880 'List of participants in the Special Commission meetings', in *Proceedings of the Twentieth Session, Tome II* (n 29) 76.

881 See above, Section 5.2.

882 Special Commission on the question of jurisdiction, recognition and enforcement of foreign judgments (17–27 June 1997), 'Report of Meeting No 2' (on file with author) 1.

883 Ibid.

884 Ibid; see also McClean (n 574) 260.

885 Special Commission June 1997, 'Report of Meeting No 2' (on file with author) 1; Kessedjian, 'Prel Doc No 7 of April 1997' (n 141) 37, [84]–[86]; Permanent Bureau,

By deliberately deferring the decision on the convention type, the Chair attempted to reconcile the group which favoured a mixed convention, and the group which favoured a strict double convention.[886] While the US (and possibly, other States)[887] were in favour of the mixed-convention concept,[888] others (in particular: the EC Member States) favoured the closed-double-convention concept in the spirit of the 1968 Brussels Convention and the 1988 Lugano Convention.[889] As noted by one of the participants,

---

'Examples of Treaty Provisions on International Jurisdiction – Info Doc June 1997' (n 298) 7; McClean (n 574) 260.

886 Preliminary Results Special Commission 1997 (n 720) [2.1]–[2.3]; the following 37 Hague Conference Member States participated in the Special Commission meeting of June 1997 and March 1998, see 'List of participants in the Special Commission meetings' (n 880) 76–78: Germany, Argentina, Australia, Austria, Belgium, Canada, China (People's Republic of), Cyprus, Republic of Korea, Croatia, Denmark, Spain, United States, Finland, France, Greece, Hungary, Ireland, Israel, Italy, Japan, Luxembourg, Morocco, Mexico, Monaco, Norway, The Netherlands, Poland, Portugal, Romania, United Kingdom of Great Britain and Northern Ireland, Slovakia, Sweden, Switzerland, Czech Republic, Uruguay and Venezuela.

887 The following experts from the following Hague Conference Member States beside the US had supported the mixed-convention model in June 1992, see 'Conclusions Working Group: Prel Doc No 19 November 1992' (n 28) [1], [3]: Mr A Boggiano from Argentina, Mr Li Haopei and Mr Zhang Kening from China (People's Republic of), Mr A Amer from Egypt, Mr G Möller from Finland (chair of the Working Group), Mr J Lemontey from France, Mr T Bán from Hungary, Mr J A C Watherston and Mr P M Beaton from the United Kingdom, Mr P H Pfund, Mr A T von Mehren and Mr P D Trooboff from the United States, and Mr G Parra-Aranguren from Venezuela. Some of these participants had apparently changed their opinion about the general desirability of creating a mixed convention during the later stages of the project: Mr Parra-Aranguren (Venezuela) stated during the First Commission of the Seventeenth Session of the Hague Conference that he 'would not insist on the need for a convention concerning recognition and enforcement of judgments, but did express the view that the subject matter is very important,' see 'Minutes No 3' (n 868) 330. Egypt was not represented at the Special Commission meetings in June 1997 and March 1998, see 'List of participants in the Special Commission meetings', in *Proceedings of the Twentieth Session, Tome II* (n 29) 76–78.

888 See, e.g., Letter Edwin D Williamson to Georges Droz (n 25) 2: '[i]t seems to us that we need not necessarily choose between a traité simple, dealing only with those judgments that are entitled to recognition and enforcement in party States, and a traité double also dealing with permissible bases of jurisdiction [...]. We believe that there should be a consideration of the possibility for party States to utilize jurisdictional bases for litigation that are not designated as permissible or exorbitant by the convention. So long as such jurisdictional bases are not excluded as exorbitant, judgments based on them would not be entitled to recognition and enforcement under the convention, but party States would remain free to recognize them under their general law'.

889 See, e.g., Special Commission on the question of jurisdiction, recognition and enforcement of foreign judgments (17–27 June 1997), 'Report of Meeting No 2' (on file with author) 1: '[o]ne expert [...] indicated that the countries of the European

'[i]n some respects the June 1997 meeting was quite extraordinary. [...] The top table, with support from a number of delegations, was still proclaiming the aim of a double Convention: the United States and others were already persuaded that this aim was unrealistic'.[890] Potentially, the approach of the Chair might have been intended to create enough support for keeping the project on the agenda in the first place by not making the Special Commission decide on any particular convention type, but by keeping both options (i.e., the closed, or strict, double convention, and the mixed convention) open, thereby not deterring those delegations that had already expressed support for a convention type. Deferring the decision about the convention type followed a recognised strategy for leading negotiations which the Chair had described in an article on achieving results in international meetings. In his article, Smith, who was very experienced in chairing international meetings,[891] advised that in case an issue proved controversial during negotiations, a possible approach in resolving the controversy could be to seek agreement on smaller issues first.[892] This strategy was a generally recognised technique for making progress in multilateral negotiations.[893] Applying this strategy could have

Union [were] in favour of a "double convention" and that the Brussels and Lugano Conventions serve[d] as good models. He stressed that the European Union Member States wish[ed] to participate in a unified manner'; during the meeting of the informal Working Group in 1992, experts from two Member States of the European Community (Mr J Lemontey from France, and Mr J A C Watherston and P M Beaton from the United Kingdom) had supported creating a true mixed convention, see 'Conclusions Working Group: Prel Doc No 19 November 1992' (n 28) [1], [5].

890 McClean (n 574) 260.

891 T Bradbrooke Smith had for example chaired the Special Commission which led to the conclusion of the 1978 Hague Convention on the Law Applicable to Agency (concluded 14 March 1978, entered into force 1 May 1992) (1977) 16 ILM 775, or the Special Commission which led to the conclusion of the 1993 Hague Convention on Intercountry Adoption, see Smith, 'Achieving Results at International Meetings' (n 68) 418.

892 Smith, 'Achieving Results at International Meetings' (n 68) 425: '[a]nother aspect of flexibility is the technique of skirting difficult issues at the earlier stages of proceedings. Seek agreement on small things. Get the momentum of agreement not disagreement. This is frequently possible by selecting manageable and less controversial issues for debate and decision. Participants get a sense of accomplishment and progress. They start to feel that some sort of conclusion can, indeed, be reached, that there is light at the end of the tunnel. [... T]he technique of discussing matters, particularly if they are going to be difficult of resolution, without seeking a decision and of coming back to them later can be productive of results'.

893 Robert A Walker, *Multilateral Conferences: Purposeful International Negotiation* (Palgrave Macmillan 2004) 185.

allowed agreement to gradually build up and secured commitment to the negotiations.[894] After sufficient agreement on smaller issues (in this case: the jurisdictional provisions of the green list and the red list) had been achieved, the discussions could then, it was thought, return to the big controversial issue (i.e., the convention type). In this way, all participants might have become sufficiently satisfied with the progress achieved thus far, and therefore be more willing to seek a compromise on the previously controversial issue of the convention type.[895]

The Chair's strategy in chairing the meeting was supported by the research conducted by the Permanent Bureau, which had confirmed that pursuing a double convention as a first priority, and keeping the possibility of creating a mixed convention as a second-best option, was a valid approach in creating a draft text for a judgments convention.[896] The (erroneous) assumption underlying this approach was that with regard to regulating international direct jurisdiction, the mixed convention constituted mainly a restricted version of a double convention:[897] as discussed in Chapter 5, the preparatory material had presented the mixed convention as being merely a double convention with the additional option for States to exercise jurisdiction on the basis of national jurisdictional provisions (within the limits of the red list).[898] As Prel Doc No 7 had recommended, by pursuing primarily a strict double convention, the meeting attempted to achieve agreement on as many jurisdictional provisions as possible first.[899] If the discussions during the meetings had shown that agreement on a broad list of direct grounds of jurisdiction was in fact unattainable, then the draft convention text elaborated until then still could, it was (erroneously) assumed, be turned into a mixed convention by merely allowing Contracting States to also exercise jurisdiction on the basis of domestic law.[900]

---

894 Smith, 'Achieving Results at International Meetings' (n 68) 425.

895 Cf 'Chairman's Report March 1998' (n 719) 3, 4; see also McClean (n 574) 260.

896 See above, Section 5.1.2.

897 'Chairman's Report March 1998' (n 719) 3, 4; Preliminary Results Special Commission 1997 (n 720) [2.1]–[2.3].

898 See above, Section 5.2.; 'Chairman's Report March 1998' (n 719) 3, 4; see also Bucher, 'Vers une convention mondiale' (n 173) 79 ('Convention double restreinte').

899 Kessedjian, 'Prel Doc No 7 of April 1997' (n 141) [156].

900 Permanent Bureau, 'Examples of Treaty Provisions on International Jurisdiction – Info Doc June 1997' (n 298) [2.1.]–[2.3.]; cf also 'Chairman's Report March 1998' (n 719) 3, 4; see also above, Section 5.2.

7.3.2. REASONS FOR THE UNITED STATES TO CONTINUE WITH THE JUDGMENTS PROJECT AFTER THE SPECIAL COMMISSION MEETING IN JUNE 1997

It would not have been a sensible choice for the US to withdraw from the project after the Special Commission meeting in June 1997, despite the fact that most of the other experts had not agreed to begin work on the judgments convention by creating a mixed convention. As previously indicated, the US regarded the true-mixed-convention model as the only realistic outcome of the Special Commission meetings.[901] In addition, those experts who favoured a double convention as a first priority had not ruled out the possibility that the project could lead to a mixed convention: according to the minutes of the first day of the Special Commission meeting in June 1997, '[s]everal experts' advocated negotiating a strict double convention (a 'double convention *strictu sensu*') in order to achieve greater certainty, but these same experts also 'stated that if this proved unattainable it would remain possible to negotiate a mixed or even a single convention'.[902] According to the preliminary conclusions of the Special Commission meeting in June 1997, the experts thus proceeded on the basis that if creating a strict double convention should fail, work of the Special Commission would then turn towards creating a mixed convention.[903]

7.3.2.1. Results of the Special Commission Discussions Concerning the Green List of Required Grounds of Jurisdiction that were Re-Usable for a True Mixed Convention

Even though the majority of the experts attending the Special Commission meetings were not attempting to create a true mixed convention during

901 See above, Section 7.2; cf also 'Views from around the world', in Lowenfeld, Silberman (n 249) 119, 134; in a letter to von Mehren dating from 5 August 1997 congratulating him on receiving the Theberge Award, Peter H Pfund, one of the participants of the US delegation in the Judgments Project, noted that it would now seem 'more than possible that [the mixed-convention concept] will ultimately be accepted for the convention that the Hague Conference Member States agreed in October of last year [sic] to seek to prepare by the conclusion of the Conference's 19th diplomatic session in October 2000', see 'Letter by Peter H Pfund, Assistant Legal Adviser for Private International Law, US Department of State' (1997) 31 Int'l L 718, 719.

902 Special Commission on the question of jurisdiction, recognition and enforcement of foreign judgments (17–27 June 1997), 'Report of Meeting No 1' (Meeting of Tuesday 17 June 1997 morning) (on file with author) 2.

903 Permanent Bureau, 'Preliminary Results Special Commission 1997' (n 718) [2.1.]–[2.3]; see also above Section 5.2.

the Special Commission meetings of June 1997, March 1998 and November 1998, their discussions nevertheless could have revealed that some grounds of direct jurisdiction existed on which the participating experts in general agreed (i.e., on which consensus existed)[904] that these grounds were clearly appropriate for exercising jurisdiction (and could be included therefore in the green list). Indeed, the green list of the November 1998 Draft, the draft convention text created by the Special Commission meeting in November 1998,[905] (mostly) contained provisions which had already been identified by the Working Group in 1992 as potentially appropriate grounds of international direct jurisdiction: two provisions providing for general jurisdiction (jurisdiction of any kind of controversy) over a defendant (defendant's forum for natural persons, November 1998 Draft, Article 3(1), and defendant's forum for legal persons, November 1998 Draft, Article 3(2));[906] provisions providing for jurisdiction based on a choice of court by the parties (November 1998 Draft, Article 4);[907] and a provision providing for jurisdiction based on the appearance of the defendant (November 1998 Draft, Article 5).[908] In addition, the November 1998 Draft provided for a series of provisions allowing for specific jurisdiction over the defendant:[909] jurisdiction in matters relating to the activities of an establishment of the defendant (November 1998 Draft, Article 9);[910] and jurisdiction for claims based on a tort or a delict (November 1998 Draft, Article 10(1)(a); Article 10(1)(b); and Article 10(2)).[911]

904 Taking decisions by consensus means to take decisions by general agreement, see, e.g., Robbie Sabel, *Procedure at International Conferences: A Study of the Rules of Procedure at the UN and at Inter-governmental Conferences* (2nd edn, CUP 2006) 338.

905 November 1998 Draft (n 309).

906 'Conclusions Working Group: Prel Doc No 19 November 1992' (n 28) 259, [8a].

907 Ibid [8f].

908 Ibid [8g].

909 Specific jurisdiction refers to the power of a court to exercise jurisdiction over a defendant only regarding specific controversies, which also provide the connecting factor for the court to exercise jurisdiction, see, e.g., von Mehren, Trautman, 'Jurisdiction to Adjudicate' (n 2) 1136, 1137.

910 Cf 'Conclusions Working Group: Prel Doc No 19 November 1992' (n 28) 259, [8b]; according to November 1998 Draft (n 309) art 9, the question of whether the provision should also provide for jurisdiction over a defendant on the basis of the activities of its employees or other representatives had been discussed.

911 Cf 'Conclusions Working Group: Prel Doc No 19 November 1992' (n 28) 259, [8e].

7.3.2.2. *Results of the Special Commission Discussions Concerning the Red List of Prohibited Grounds of Jurisdiction that were Re-Usable for a True Mixed Convention*

The Special Commission meetings from June 1997 until November 1998 had also worked on the question of whether grounds of direct jurisdiction existed that should be prohibited by adding them to the red list of the convention text. A red list was not a necessary component of a strict double convention as this convention type would have allowed the exercise of jurisdiction only on the basis of the green list anyway.[912] However, the Special Commission nevertheless devoted some part of their work to discussing grounds of direct jurisdiction which potentially could be included in this red list. This was done in order to prepare for the scenario that a strict double convention could not be drafted after all:

> [During the Special Commission meeting of June 1997, a] lengthy discussion ensued as to whether it was necessary to address exorbitant jurisdiction at this time. […] However, other experts argued that it was necessary to undertake an examination of the list of prohibited bases at this time because in the event that only a mixed convention could be agreed upon, such an essential list could not and should not be discussed at the last minute. […] In the light of this, it was decided to briefly examine the examples of exorbitant grounds of jurisdiction found in paragraph 139 of the Report [Prel Doc No 7].[913]

The discussions in the Special Commission meeting in June 1997 revealed that there was consensus to include general jurisdiction on the basis that (moveable) property of the defendant was located in forum state in the red list, i.e., to ban exercise of jurisdiction on this basis.[914] Moreover, consensus existed that general jurisdiction should not be exercised on the basis that the claimant was a national of the forum State.[915] Potentially,

912 The red list of prohibited grounds of direct jurisdiction has therefore a merely declaratory effect in a strict double convention, see, e.g., Kessedjian, 'Prel Doc No 7 of April 1997' (n 141) 51 [135].

913 Special Commission on the question of jurisdiction, recognition and enforcement of foreign judgments (17–27 June 1997), 'Report of Meeting No 10' (on file with author) 1.

914 Kessedjian, 'Synthesis of the Work of the Special Commission of June 1997 on International Jurisdiction and the Effects of Foreign Judgments in Civil and Commercial Matters: Prel Doc No 8 of November 1997' (n 288) 105 [85]; see also November 1998 Draft (n 309) art 20(1)(a).

915 Kessedjian, 'Synthesis of the Work of the Special Commission of June 1997 on International Jurisdiction and the Effects of Foreign Judgments in Civil and

the results of these discussions could have been used for creating a true mixed convention, as the consensus among the participants of the Special Commission meetings was that exercising international direct jurisdiction on these bases was clearly inappropriate.

7.3.3. UNITED STATES DELEGATION BROADLY SATISFIED WITH THE PROGRESS OF DISCUSSIONS AFTER THE SPECIAL COMMISSION MEETING OF NOVEMBER 1998

The November 1998 Draft not only contained jurisdictional provisions of which the inclusion into the green or the red list had been supported by consensus: for example, the November 1998 Draft contained provisions on jurisdiction in contractual matters (November 1998 Draft, Article 6, Variants 1 and 2). During the meeting of the Working Group in 1992, no consensus had been reached on the question of whether a provision on contract jurisdiction should be included in the draft convention text in the first place.[916] Moreover, general doing business jurisdiction and general jurisdiction on the basis of the service of a writ on a defendant, standard approaches to jurisdiction from a US point of view, were included in the red list of the November 1998 Draft (Article 20(1)(e), (f)).[917] However, these provisions had not been actively discussed during the November meeting.[918] Overall, the US delegation was satisfied in general with the discussions that had taken place. In November 1998, the US was still convinced that creating a true mixed convention during the remaining two Special Commission meetings (in June and October 1999) was the only possible outcome of the discussions, even though the work of the Special Commission had primarily focussed on creating a closed double convention. During an academic conference on the Judgments Project

Commercial Matters: Prel Doc No 8 of November 1997' (n 288) 107, [86]; see also November 1998 Draft (n 309) art 20(1)(b).

916 'Conclusions Working Group: Prel Doc No 19 November 1992' (n 28) 261 [8i].

917 November 1998 Draft (n 309).

918 November 1998 Draft (n 309) art 20 (Examples of prohibited grounds of jurisdiction); article 20 was included in square brackets, see ibid; already in 1992, the Working Group had not reached a full consensus on the question whether general doing business jurisdiction and general jurisdiction on the basis of the service of a writ on a defendant should be included into the red list or not, see

in the spring of 1999, Jeffrey D Kovar remarked that the US delegation hoped that the next Special Commission meeting in June 1999

> will finally clarify that as a practical matter, the goal of these negotiations can only be to conclude a mixed convention, [...] a convention that not only creates a new global system of required and prohibited grounds for jurisdiction, but one that also leaves room for the continuation of some types of national practice outside the convention and the flexibility to permit national practice to adapt to the future change.[919]

In his letter to Hans van Loon from February 2000, Jeffrey D Kovar noted therefore that '[n]egotiations in the Hague were proceeding in a slow and deliberate, but reasonably positive, manner until the last two sessions of the Special Commission [the Special Commission meetings of June and October 1999]'.[920] Another member of the US delegation, Peter D Trooboff, equally noted that until the Special Commission meetings in June and October 1999, the discussions of the experts had proceeded with a 'collaborative and open spirit'.[921] Although the US was broadly satisfied with the discussions during the November 1998 session, the US delegation nevertheless clearly voiced their interest in concluding a flexible judgments convention during the Special Commission meeting of November 1998. On the last day of the meeting, the US delegation made

> a lengthy intervention [...] drawing attention to the fact that the basic question of a double Convention had remained out of sight throughout the meeting, reiterating the arguments which that delegation had consistently advanced ever since 1994 for a mixed Convention.[922]

No decision on the convention type was taken, however.[923]

'Conclusions Working Group: Prel Doc No 19 November 1992' (n 28) 261 [10d]–[10e].

919 'Views from around the world', in Lowenfeld, Silberman (n 249) 119, 134.

920 Jeffrey D Kovar, Letter to Hans van Loon (n 34) 2.

921 Trooboff, 'Ten (and Probably More) Difficulties' (n 298) 276.

922 McClean (n 574) 263, see also Special Commission on International jurisdiction and the effects of foreign judgments in civil and commercial matters (10–20 November 1998), 'Report of Meeting No 53' (on file with author), 2, 3; and 'Annex to the Report of Meeting No 53: Intervention by the United States Delegation on 20 November 1998' (on file with author), with a reference to von Mehren, 'Enforcing Judgments Abroad' (n 6) 17.

923 McClean (n 574) 263; 'Report of Meeting No 53' ibid 2, 3.

7.4. THE FINAL TWO SPECIAL COMMISSION MEETINGS IN JUNE AND OCTOBER 1999

The last two Special Commission meetings in June and October 1999 inter alia still needed to discuss whether provisions on the following 14 jurisdictional topics should be included in the draft convention text, and if so, which connecting factors should be employed: jurisdiction regarding contracts with consumers (jurisdiction for claims by the consumer against their contracting party, and jurisdiction against the consumer for claims brought by their contracting party); jurisdiction regarding contracts with employees; jurisdiction regarding trusts; exclusive jurisdiction for proceedings which have as their object rights in rem in immovable property; exclusive jurisdiction for proceedings which have as their object tenancies of immovable property; exclusive jurisdiction for proceedings which have as their object the validity of the constitution, the nullity or the dissolution of legal persons or associations of natural or legal persons; exclusive jurisdiction for proceedings which have as their object the decisions of organs of legal persons or associations of natural or legal persons; exclusive jurisdiction 'with respect to public registers'; exclusive jurisdiction 'with respect to intellectual property'; exclusive jurisdiction 'with respect to the enforcement of judgments'; jurisdiction over a defendant on the basis that he is one of a number of defendants ('plurality of defendants'); jurisdiction regarding counter claims; jurisdiction regarding warranty and intervention; and jurisdiction regarding related actions.[924]

For these last two Special Commission meetings, a decision-making process through majority voting was employed in order to resolve outstanding questions and to finalise a draft convention that could be sent to the Diplomatic Conference as a basis for multilateral negotiations.[925] The results of the process of majority voting during the last two Special Commission meetings left the US deeply dissatisfied: once the experts at

---

924 Kessedjian, 'Prel Doc No 7 of April 1997' (n 141); Permanent Bureau, 'Examples of Treaty Provisions on International Jurisdiction: Info Doc June 1997' (n 298).

925 'Chairman's Report March 1998' (n 719) 3: 'what we are attempting to do is steadily and purposefully narrow and define the matters to be decided to provide a basis – and time – for broader consultation and to build into the process as much flexibility as possible. [...] During the November meeting, then, within that broad framework, we shall be taking indicative votes on many issues, while in 1999 a more formal procedure will obtain so as to resolve all outstanding matters'; cf also Nygh, 'Arthur's Baby' (n 266) 156.

the Special Commission meetings had begun to take votes on the relevant provisions, the draft convention text assumed a structure which was almost as restrictive as a strict double convention in terms of regulating the exercise of direct jurisdiction, due to the imbalance of voting power between the US and the European bloc.[926] For this reason, a member of the US delegation called these votes during the Special Commission meetings in June 1999 and October 1999 'unfortunate'.[927]

Regarding the green list, in addition to the jurisdictional provisions already included in the November 1998 Draft, the October 1999 Preliminary Draft Convention eventually also contained provisions on the following matters, all of which had a counterpart in the Brussels-Lugano regime: jurisdiction for claims brought by the consumer against the other party of the consumer contract (October 1999 Preliminary Draft Convention, Article 7(1));[928] jurisdiction for claims brought by the contracting party against the consumer (Article 7(2));[929] jurisdiction for claims brought by an employee against his/her employer (Article 8(1)(a));[930] jurisdiction for claims brought by the employer against the employee (Article 8(1)(b));[931] trusts (Article 11);[932] exclusive jurisdiction for proceedings concerning rights in rem in immovable property (Article 12(1) first alternative);[933] exclusive jurisdiction for proceedings concerning tenancies of immovable property (Article 12(2) second alternative);[934] exclusive jurisdiction in proceedings which have as their object the validity, nullity, or dissolution of a legal person (Article 12(2) Alternative 1);[935] exclusive jurisdiction for proceedings which have as their object the validity or nullity of decisions of its organs (Article 12(2) Alternative 2);[936] exclusive jurisdiction for proceedings which have as their object the validity or nullity of entries in

---

926 June 1999 Draft (n 313); October 1999 Preliminary Draft Convention (n 32); Jeffrey D Kovar, Letter to Hans van Loon (n 34) 2; Brand, 'Community Competence' (n 735) 197; see also above, Section 5.3.

927 Trooboff, 'Ten (and Probably More) Difficulties' (n 298) 276.

928 Cf 1968 Brussels Convention (as amended [1990] OJ C189/2) art 14(1); 1988 Lugano Convention (n 144) art 14 (1).

929 Cf 1968 Brussels Convention (as amended [1990] OJ C189/2) art 14(2); 1988 Lugano Convention (n 144) art 14 (2).

930 Cf 'COM (1999) 348 final' (n 315) art 19.

931 Cf ibid art 20.

932 Cf 1968 Brussels Convention (as amended [1990] OJ C189/2) art 5(6).

933 Cf ibid art 16(1)(a), first alternative.

934 Cf ibid art 16(1)(a), second alternative.

935 Cf ibid art 16(2), first alternative.

936 Cf ibid art 16(2), second alternative.

public registers (Article 12(3));[937] exclusive jurisdiction for proceedings which have as their object the registration, validity (or) nullity of patents, trademarks, designs or other similar rights required to be deposited or registered (Article 12(4));[938] multiple defendants (Article 14);[939] counter claims (Article 15);[940] and third-party claims (Article 16).[941] Unlike the draft convention text of November 1998, the October 1999 Preliminary Draft Convention text contained an extensive and therefore very restrictive green list. What is more, the October 1999 Preliminary Draft Convention also contained a very restrictive red list, and a broad, general definition of exorbitant jurisdiction.[942] As a result, the grey, unregulated area of international direct jurisdiction would have been very narrow under a judgments convention based on the October 1999 Preliminary Draft Convention. Such a convention text would have been incompatible with the goal of a true mixed convention to ensure flexibility for its Contracting States in regulating international direct jurisdiction by means of domestic legislation.[943]

7.4.1. UNITED STATES INTERVENTIONS REGARDING THE STRUCTURE

An analysis of the US interventions during the Special Commission meetings in June and October 1999 shows that the US made proposals regarding the structure and the relevant jurisdictional provisions of the green list and the red list which communicated their understanding of a true mixed convention. In order to raise awareness among the other experts that the November 1998 Draft did not properly reflect a true

---

937 Cf ibid art 16(3).

938 Cf ibid art 16(4); moreover, it was suggested that the October 1999 Preliminary Draft Convention should cover also jurisdiction concerning the revocation or infringement of patents, trademarks, designs or other similar rights required to be deposited or registered, see October 1999 Preliminary Draft Convention (n 32), art 12(4).

939 Cf 1968 Brussels Convention (as amended [1990] OJ C189/2) art 6(1).

940 Cf ibid art 6(3).

941 1968 Brussels Convention (as amended [1990] OJ C189/2) art 14(1); 1988 Lugano Convention (n 144) art 14 (1); ibid art 6(2).

942 October 1999 Preliminary Draft Convention (n 32), art 18(1), (2).

943 See Jeffrey D Kovar, Letter to Hans van Loon (n 34) 5: '[t]he grey area seems to cover little more than antitrust and anticompetition lawsuits brought in the forum were the economic injury arose'; see also Clermont, 'An Introduction to the Hague Convention' (n 291) 7.

mixed convention structure,[944] the US delegation restated its interest in concluding a flexible judgments convention in the form of a true mixed convention by submitting a proposal in form of a Working Document on the first day of the meeting of the Special Commission in June 1999.[945] This Working Document (Work Doc No 150 E) contained – besides some substantive proposals on jurisdictional provisions – a restructured version of the November 1998 Draft.[946] Inter alia, Work Doc No 150 E divided the draft convention text into four sub-chapters which reflected the structure of a true mixed convention as intended by von Mehren: 'Sub-Chapter A: Required bases of jurisdiction [i.e. the green list]'; 'Sub-Chapter B: Prohibited bases of Jurisdiction [the red list]', 'Sub-Chapter C (Article 21): Non-Convention bases of jurisdiction [the grey area]', and 'Sub-Chapter D: Other jurisdictional provisions'.[947] Article 21 of Work Doc No 150 E contained a specific proposal regarding the grey area expressing the US interest in concluding a convention which would have retained the Contracting State's legislative flexibility.[948] This proposal suggested to include the following text into the draft convention: '[the] Convention does not affect the status under the law of each Contracting Party of rules of jurisdiction or competence neither required nor prohibited by this Convention.'[949]

Since the Chair would not allow discussions on the convention type itself until almost the last day of the Special Commission meeting in June 1999, however, Work Doc No 150 E was not discussed as a structural proposal by the meeting. As a result, the US delegation had only two options in voicing their opposition to the structure the draft text was assuming: either by

---

944 During the conference on the Judgments Project in spring 1999 at the New York University, Jeffrey D Kovar expressed the hope that the future discussions among the experts would show that the November 1998 Draft bore only little resemblance with the final convention text, see 'Views from around the world', in Lowenfeld, Silberman (n 249) 119, 135.

945 Special Commission on international jurisdiction and the effects of foreign judgments in civil and commercial matters (7–18 June 1999), 'Work Doc No 150 E' (on file with author).

946 See Special Commission on international jurisdiction and the effects of foreign judgments in civil and commercial matters (7–18 June 1999),'Work Doc No 150 E: Highlighted Version' (on file with author): '[t]his document is provided as a supplement to Work Doc No 150 E in order to indicate more clearly the differences between that document and the parallel provisions of Work Doc No 144 [the November 1998 Draft]'.

947 Special Commission June 1999, 'Work Doc No 150 E' (n 945).

948 Ibid art 21.

949 Ibid.

voting against the inclusion of a provision on a certain jurisdictional topic in the first place, or by making substantive proposals on the provisions, in order to demonstrate that achieving agreement on the specific connecting factors to be employed would be difficult. Some of these interventions will be discussed in the following.

7.4.2. UNITED STATES INTERVENTIONS REGARDING THE GREEN AND THE RED LIST

One example of a US intervention regarding the green list concerned jurisdiction in consumer contracts. When the Special Commission discussed jurisdiction in consumer contracts in June 1999, the US delegation submitted a joint proposal together with the United Kingdom which suggested to replace a specific provision on jurisdiction in consumer cases with a general provision providing for activity-based jurisdiction. This general provision would have been able to cover proceedings brought by a consumer against their contracting partner.[950] The minutes of the meeting recorded that the proposal

> gave rise to many questions. [...] While some experts recognised that the proposal had merit, the general view of the meeting was that there should be a specific ground of jurisdiction to deal with consumer contracts provided that consumer protection was to be included within the scope of the Convention.[951]

The Chair deferred the final consideration of this proposal, and had the experts decide between the two other proposals on jurisdiction in consumer matters, both of which contained provisions for jurisdiction in

950 Special Commission on international jurisdiction and the effects of foreign judgments in civil and commercial matters (7–18 June 1999), 'Proposal by the delegations of the United Kingdom and the United States of America: Work Doc No 163' (on file with author): according to Work Doc No 163, a plaintiff should be able to bring a claim in the courts of a Contracting State in which the defendant had acted or in which a branch, agency or other establishment of the defendant was situated and had acted for or on behalf of the defendant in conducting commercial activity, including promotional activity directed at that State or the sale of goods or services in that State (provided that the claim related to that commercial activity).

951 Special Commission on international jurisdiction and the effects of foreign judgments in civil and commercial matters (7–18 June 1999), 'Report of Meeting No 57', 2 (on file with author).

consumer contracts.[952] Eventually, provisions for specific jurisdiction in consumer contracts were included in the June 1999 Draft.[953]

Furthermore, in a true mixed convention, the red list would have only prohibited certain jurisdictional provisions regarding which consensus existed that exercising international direct jurisdiction on these bases was clearly inappropriate.[954] A general definition of exorbitant jurisdiction would have therefore contravened the purpose and the spirit of a true mixed convention.[955] Accordingly, the US proposal for a red list in Work Doc No 150 did not contain a general definition of exorbitant jurisdiction.[956] In response to Work Doc No 150, Denmark, Spain and Switzerland submitted a Working Document which inter alia proposed to introduce a general definition of exorbitant jurisdiction.[957] This Working Document (Work Doc No 162) suggested including a new first paragraph in Article 20 (Prohibited grounds of jurisdiction), according to which jurisdiction based

---

952 Ibid 2, 3.

953 June 1999 Draft (n 313), art 7(1), art 7(2).

954 An example for such an exorbitant ground of international direct jurisdiction generally regarded as inappropriate was jurisdiction exercised on the basis of the nationality of the claimant; cf 2001 Interim Text (n 36) art 18(2)(b); Code civil (France), art 14.

955 Jeffrey D Kovar, Letter to Hans van Loon (n 34) 9: 'Article 18 (Prohibited Grounds of Jurisdiction): [t]he provisions on prohibited jurisdiction are out of balance with what we believe should be the goal of this convention. This article ties the creation in paragraph 1 of a minimum legal standard for jurisdiction to a long illustrative list in paragraph 2 of both national jurisdictional practices and new factual elements. These examples are then declared not to meet the minimum standard individually and in combination. The result is a provision that is both broad and vague, and which creates uncertainty of application. It is likely to spawn a great deal of litigation in cases that would otherwise rest in the gray area and not benefit from recognition and enforcement. This will create strong disincentives to join the convention, and foreclose the ability of the gray area to permit national courts to adapt jurisdiction to a changing world'; see also Jeffrey D Kovar, Letter to Alasdair Wallace, September 10, 2000, 5 <www.cptech.org/ecom/jurisdiction/kovarletter.html> accessed 5 April 2023: '[w]e are prepared to discuss specific grounds of jurisdiction that are known and practiced by member states and others for inclusion in the list, but are not prepared to accept a vague and unknown general standard of prohibition, or to accept illustrative factors such as those listed in paragraph'; von Mehren, 'Theory and Practice of Adjudicatory Authority' (n 141) 422.

956 Special Commission on international jurisdiction and the effects of foreign judgments in civil and commercial matters (7–18 June 1999), 'Work Doc No 162 F + E: Distribution 8 June 1999' (on file with author), art 20; the idea of including a general definition of exorbitant jurisdiction had been floated by the preparatory material of the Permanent Bureau, see Kessedjian, 'Prel Doc No 7 of April 1997' (n 141) 53, [137]–[138]; Permanent Bureau, 'Examples of Treaty Provisions on International Jurisdiction: Info Doc June 1997' (n 298) art 19.

957 'Work Doc No 162 F + E: Distribution 8 June 1999' (n 956).

on national law 'shall not exist in a Contracting State when the dispute has no substantial link with such State, considering the subject matter of the dispute and the habitual residence, respectively the seat [...] of the parties'.[958] Following this proposal, the US resubmitted Work Doc No 150 E, with its proposals highlighted in bold print to emphasise the proposed changes on 9 June 1999.[959] Additionally, this version of Work Doc No 150 E did not suggest introducing a general definition of exorbitant jurisdiction in Article 20 of the draft convention text, which equalled a rejection of such an addition. Eventually, however, the final draft resulting from the Special Commission meeting in June 1999 did include a general definition of exorbitant jurisdiction: according to Article 20(1) of the June 1999 Draft, '[t]he application of a rule of jurisdiction provided for under the national law of a Contracting State is prohibited if there is no substantial connection between that State and the dispute'.[960]

7.5. CONCLUSION

Although the US had expressed their need for creating a flexible judgments convention from the beginning of the project, the October 1999 Preliminary Draft Convention had assumed the structure of a strict double convention which would have left little room for Contracting Parties to adapt their national jurisdictional provisions to new developments. When the US voiced concerns about the structure during the Special Commission meetings from November 1998 until October 1999, these concerns were either not being heard because the chair would not allow a decision on the convention type, or they were overruled because of the use of majority voting for the decision-making process. Despite the US concerns that had been communicated to the other participants in the project, the convention text organically assumed the structure of a strict double convention, which made the October 1999 Preliminary Draft Convention unacceptable to the US.

958 Ibid.
959 'Work Doc No 150 E: Highlighted Version' (n 946).
960 June 1999 Draft (n 313) art 20(1).

CHAPTER 8

DID THE JUDGMENTS PROJECT FAIL BECAUSE THE OPPOSITION OF THE EUROPEAN BLOC TOWARDS A TRUE MIXED CONVENTION WOULD HAVE BEEN IMPOSSIBLE TO OVERCOME?

The final question which must be addressed in order to understand why the Hague Judgments Project failed is why the EC and its Member States clung to the structure of the October 1999 Preliminary Draft Convention during the Diplomatic Session and were not in general willing to diverge substantially from it.[961]

8.1. THE EUROPEAN COMMUNITY'S INTEREST IN MAINTAINING A BROAD GREEN LIST

As discussed above in Chapter 3, the European bloc had an interest in filling the gap in the rules on international direct jurisdiction left by the 1968 Brussels Convention regarding defendants who were domiciled in a third State.[962] Creating unified rules on international direct jurisdiction on a global level could have helped to create a level playing field for claimants in EC Member States with regard to proceedings against defendants without a domicile in an EC Member State, and foster equal access to justice. It is likely that the EC also had another hidden interest in maintaining a broad green list reflecting the jurisdictional provisions of the 1968 Brussels Convention (or of the proposal for the Brussels I Regulation (hereafter

961 There was some movement on the part of the European bloc in reducing the green list during the first part of the Diplomatic Session: during the Diplomatic Session of 2001, consensus was reached to remove Article 14 (Multiple defendants) and Article 16 (Third party claims) from the green list, see 2001 Interim Text (n 36) 633, 635.

962 Section 3.2.2.

COM (1999) 348 final) intended to replace the Brussels Convention).[963] A Hague Judgments Convention with jurisdictional provisions drafted according to the Brussels regime would have expanded the geographical influence of the European regime to a considerable extent: a judgment rendered in one of the EC Member States could have been recognised and declared enforceable on a potentially worldwide scale under the Hague Judgments Convention if the judgment had fulfilled its requirements for recognition and enforcement.[964] According to Article 25(1) of the October 1999 Preliminary Draft Convention, the main condition for recognition and enforcement was the question of indirect jurisdiction, i.e., that the judgment was rendered on the basis of a ground of jurisdiction provided for in Articles 3–14, or that it was 'consistent with any such ground'.[965] By incorporating jurisdictional provisions reflecting the Brussels regime, the Hague Convention would have enabled judgments rendered under the European instruments to be recognised and enforced on a potentially worldwide scale.[966] In other words, the more jurisdictional provisions in the green list of the Hague Judgments Convention would have matched a jurisdictional provision of the 1968 Brussels Convention (or its successor, the Brussels I Regulation), the more European judgments could have circulated worldwide under a new Hague Judgments Convention.

The EC also had reason to believe that a majority of the jurisdictional standards used by the Brussels regime were indeed acceptable to many non-EC States, and that these States would be prepared to accept these grounds of direct jurisdiction as part of the Hague Judgments Convention

---

963 'COM (1999) 348 final' (n 315); this proposal was approved by the Council on 22 December 2000, and entered into force on 1 March 2002 as Council Regulation (EC) No 44/2001 of 22 December 2000 on jurisdiction and the recognition and enforcement of judgments in civil and commercial matters [2001] OJ L12/1 (Brussels I Regulation), see Pocar Report (n 192) [5]. This Regulation has been recast again into what is commonly referred to as the Brussels Ibis Regulation (Regulation (EU) No 1215/2012 of the European Parliament and of the Council of 12 December 2012 on jurisdiction and the recognition and enforcement of judgments in civil and commercial matters, [2012] OJ L351/1).

964 Von Mehren, 'Theory and Practice of Adjudicatory Authority' (n 141) 411: '[t]he strong attraction that the [strict] double convention model had for so many of the negotiators at The Hague is explainable on many grounds. […] Secondly, Brussels and Lugano countries had a stake in enlarging the scope and influence of their instruments'.

965 October 1999 Preliminary Draft Convention (n 32), art 25(1); 2001 Interim Text (n 36), art 25(1).

966 None of the disconnection clauses that had been proposed suggested to remove judgments rendered under the Brussels-Lugano regime from the recognition and enforcement regime provided for by the Hague Convention, see 2001 Interim Text (n 36) Annex I.

at a Diplomatic Conference.[967] Some of the jurisdictional provisions of the October 1999 Preliminary Draft Convention which reflected the Brussels approach to international direct jurisdiction had been accepted by large majorities, providing evidence that these provisions were acceptable to more delegations than only the delegations from the EC Member States.[968] For example, Article 6(a) and (b) of the October 1999 Preliminary Draft Convention allowed for jurisdiction in contractual matters in the courts of the State in which either the goods were supplied in whole or in part (in matters relating to the supply of goods), or (in matters relating to the provision of services) the services were provided in whole or in part. This approach to contract jurisdiction partly reflected the approach suggested by the proposal for what became the Brussels I Regulation (COM (1999) 348 final),[969] since it allowed for jurisdiction in contractual matters at the place where the characteristic obligation (i.e., the delivery of the goods and the performance of services) had in fact taken place.[970]

---

967 Cf Nygh, 'Arthur's Baby' (n 266) 159; Wagner, 'Gerichtsstandsvereinbarungen' (n 19) 104, 105.

968 Others only by a narrow majority, see, e.g., the discussions on whether jurisdiction in employment contracts should be included in the draft convention text, Section 4.4.5.; in June 1999, there were 47 Member States of the Hague Conference, see 'Statute of the Hague Conference on Private International Law: Status table' (n 72); 28 Hague Conference Member States were present during the Special Commission in June 1999; 14 out of these States were also Contracting Parties to the 1968 Brussels Convention, see above, Chapter 5 (n 748).

969 'COM (1999) 348 final' (n 315) 32, art 5(1)(b), first and second indent; later Brussels I Regulation (n 315), art 5(1)(b), first and second indent; see also 2007 Lugano Convention, art 5(1)(b), first and second indent.

970 Nygh/Pocar Report (n 29) 237, [102]–[103]; the approach to contract jurisdiction as reflected in 'COM (1999) 348 final' (n 315) and the Brussels I Regulation was insofar narrower than the October 1999 Preliminary Draft Convention since the relevant connecting factor in these instruments was the place of performance of the characteristic obligation as determined by the terms of the contract. On the other hand, the Brussels approach was broader than the October 1999 Preliminary Draft Convention since it allowed for contractual jurisdiction for these two types of contracts also in cases of non-performance ('should have been delivered', and 'should have been performed'), see 'COM (1999) 348 final', 32, art 5(1)(b), first and second indent, and Brussels I Regulation, art 5(1)(b), first and second indent. Finally, according to the chapeau of Article 5 in 'COM (1999) 348 final', 32, and of the Brussels I Regulation, the connecting factor of the place of performance of the characteristic obligation under the contract could be abrogated by the parties ('unless otherwise agreed'; later confirmed in Case C-381/08 *Car Trim GmbH* EU:C:2010:90, [2010] OJ C100/4, [46]). Despite these differences, in general judgments rendered on the basis of the European instrument would have circulated under a Hague Judgments Convention according to the October 1999 Preliminary Draft Convention (n 32), art 6(a), (b), if they had been rendered by courts in the State of the actual performance of the characteristic obligation (i.e., where the actual place of performance was the one agreed upon by the parties), cf Case C-381/08 *Car Trim GmbH* EU:C:2010:90, [2010] OJ C100/4, [46].

During the June 1999 meeting of the Special Commission, when votes were taken on the proposal, it was accepted with 24 votes in favour, and 1 against.[971] The proposal became Article 6(a), (b) of the June 1999 Draft (later Article 6(a), (b) of the October 1999 Preliminary Draft Convention).[972] Equally, the Special Commission meeting in June 1999 voted to include the following jurisdictional provision, which allowed for specific jurisdiction in matters relating to a branch, with 22 votes in favour, 1 against, and 1 abstention:[973] 'the plaintiff may bring an action in the courts for the place in a Contracting State where a branch, agency or any other establishment of the defendant is situated, provided that the dispute relates directly to the activity of that branch, agency or establishment'.[974] This approach also reflected the approach to jurisdiction in matters relating to a branch as contained in the Brussels regime.[975] What is more, the Special Commission in June 1999 decided to include an exclusive ground of jurisdiction for proceedings concerning rights in rem in immovable property with 20 votes in favour of this inclusion, 0 against, and 2 abstentions (see June 1999 Draft,[976] Article 13(1), first alternative).[977] This general rule contained in the June 1999 Draft Article 13(1), reflected the 1968 Brussels Convention,

---

971 Special Commission on international jurisdiction and the effects of foreign judgments in civil and commercial matters (7–18 June 1999), 'Report of Meeting No 58' (on file with author) at 2; an alternative proposal made by the United States of America which would have paid regard to the due process standard of the US constitution (Special Commission on international jurisdiction and the effects of foreign judgments in civil and commercial matters (7–18 June 1999, 'Work Doc No 150 E: Proposal by the delegation of the United States of America' [on file with author]), was not taken forward by the Drafting Committee, cf Special Commission on international jurisdiction and the effects of foreign judgments in civil and commercial matters (7–18 June 1999), 'Report of Meeting No 57' (on file with author), 1, 2.

972 Special Commission on international jurisdiction and the effects of foreign judgments in civil and commercial matters (7–18 June 1999), 'Work Doc No 164: Proposal by the Working Group on Contracts' (on file with author).

973 'Report of Meeting No 58' (on file with author) 3.

974 Special Commission on international jurisdiction and the effects of foreign judgments in civil and commercial matters (7–18 June 1999), 'Work Doc No 148: Proposal by the delegations of Germany and France' (on file with author), 4; June 1999 Draft (n 313) art 9; October 1999 Preliminary Draft Convention (n 32), art 9.

975 Brussels I Regulation (n 315), art 5(5); see also 2007 Lugano Convention, art 5(5).

976 June 1999 Draft (n 313).

977 Special Commission on international jurisdiction and the effects of foreign judgments in civil and commercial matters (7–18 June 1999), 'Report of Meeting No 61' (on file with author) 1; regarding the question whether a ground of exclusive jurisdiction for proceedings which have as their object tenancies in immovable property should be included in the draft convention text, only 15 votes were cast in favour of the proposal, 7 against, with 2 abstentions, see ibid.

Article 16(1)(a), first alternative. Regarding whether the convention should provide for a provision attributing exclusive jurisdiction in proceedings which have as their object the validity, nullity or dissolution of legal entities, 20 votes were cast in favour of this proposal, 2 against, with 2 abstentions.[978] This provision contained in the June 1999 Draft, Article 13(2), first alternative, broadly reflected 1968 Brussels Convention, Article 16(2), first alternative.[979]

These interests of the EC that essentially aimed at expanding the influence of the Brussels regime on a global level could further explain why the EC rushed the adoption of the Brussels I Regulation. By adopting the Regulation, the EC seemed to have acquired external competence for negotiating and concluding a future Hague Judgments Convention, based on ECJ case law.[980] Admittedly, it was not clear at the time whether the adoption of the Brussels I Regulation as a Community instrument would result in exclusive external competence of the EC. After the entry into force of the Treaty of Amsterdam, the EC had acquired internal competence to adopt secondary Community law in the area of judicial cooperation in civil matters having cross-border implications, insofar as necessary for the proper functioning of the internal market.[981] These measures included 'improving and simplifying [...] the recognition and enforcement of decisions in civil and commercial cases', and 'promoting the compatibility of the rules applicable in the Member States concerning the conflict of laws of jurisdiction'.[982] Case law of the ECJ suggested, however, that this internal competence also entailed the external competence to conclude international

978 Ibid 1; however, only 12 votes were cast in favour of also providing for exclusive jurisdiction in matters relating to the validity or nullity of the decisions of the organs of a legal entity, 9 against, with 3 abstentions, ibid.

979 Regarding the question of whether the provision should be narrowed down to cover only legal persons, and not legal entities in general, only 14 votes were cast in favour, however, 6 against, with 2 abstentions, see ibid 1, 2.

980 Case C-22/70 *Commission v. Council (AETR)* EU:C:1971:32, [1971] OJ C51/15, [30]–[31]; Paul Beaumont, 'The Brussels Convention becomes a Regulation: Implications for Legal Basis, External Competence, and Contract Jurisdiction', in James Fawcett (ed), *Reform and Development in Private International Law: Essays in Honour of Sir Peter North* (OUP 2002) 9, 25.

981 Treaty establishing the European Community (Amsterdam consolidated version) [1997] OJ C340/173 (EC Treaty), art 61(c), 65 (a) and (b); van Loon, Schulz, 'The European Community and the Hague Conference on Private International Law' (n 100) 260; Fausto Pocar, 'The Drafting of a World-Wide Convention on Jurisdiction and the Enforcement of Judgments: Which Format for the Negotiations in The Hague?', in Nafziger, Symeonides (eds), *Law and Justice in a Multistate World* (n 266) 191, 192.

982 EC Treaty ibid art 65(a) and (b).

treaties in this area with third States if the Community had made use of this competence and enacted a measure of secondary Community law in this area which had also entered into force, and if the relevant international treaty could adversely affect the Community legislation.[983] The Brussels I Regulation was a measure of secondary Community law.[984] Moreover, it was also the view of the Legal Service of the Council (the body in the European Community representing its Member States)[985] in 1999 that the adoption of the Brussels I Regulation would lead to an *exclusive* external competence of the EC:[986] the Legal Service noted that 'once the Community has exercised its internal competences adopting positions by which common rules are fixed [pursuant to Article 65 of the EC Treaty],[987] the Community competence becomes exclusive in the sense that the Member States lose the right to contract, individually and even collectively, obligations with third countries which affect the said rules'.[988]

In fact, the adoption of the Brussels I Regulation was so rushed that it had interrupted the revision process of the Brussels Convention and the Lugano

983 Case C-22/70 *Commission v. Council (AETR)* EU:C:1971:32, [1971] OJ C51/15, [30]–[31]. Some have argued that the EC had acquired external competence already with the adoption of the Brussels I Regulation on 22 December 2000, according to the principle of duty of loyalty according to EC Treaty (n 981), art 10, see, e.g., Wagner, 'Vergemeinschaftung Gesetzgebungskompetenz' (n 713) 219, 220; Schulz, 'Accession' (n 101) 942. Others have reported that it was originally questionable whether the EC Member States had lost their external competence to conclude international treaties also in regard of the recognition and enforcement of foreign judgments since the Brussels I Regulation only covered the recognition and enforcement of judgments in civil and commercial matters rendered in the EC Member States, and not in third States, see Beaumont, 'The Brussels Convention becomes a Regulation' (n 980) 26. Others argued that a future Hague Judgments Convention would not have affected the rules of the Brussels I Regulation regarding the mutual recognition and enforcement of judgments between the EC Member States, since the EC Member States had insisted on including a disconnection clause in the text of a future Hague Judgments Convention, ensuring that these judgments would only be covered by the Brussels regime; see Wagner, 'Vergemeinschaftung Gesetzgebungskompetenz' (n 713) 220.

984 See now TFEU (n 209), art 288 (1), (2).

985 EC Treaty (n 981), art 203(1).

986 Ronald A Brand, 'Evolving Competence for Private International Law in Europe: The External Effects of Internal Developments', in Gabriella Venturini, Stefania Bariatti (eds), *New Instruments of Private International Law – Liber Fausto Pocar* (Giuffrè Editore 2009) 163, 168, 169.

987 EC Treaty (n 981), art 65.

988 Legal Service of the Council, 'Report of 5 February 1999', as reported in Alegría Borrás, 'The Effect of the Adoption of Brussels I and Rome I on the External Competences of the EC and the Member States', in Johan Meeusen et al (eds), *Enforcement of International Contracts in the European Union* (Intersentia 2004) 99, 100.

Convention that was underway at the time.[989] From 1997 until 1999, the Brussels-Lugano Member States had been working on the simultaneous revision of both instruments by means of an ad hoc working party.[990] The working party had concluded its work in April 1999 with the adoption of a text for the revision of both instruments, which had been accepted by general agreement.[991] After the entry into force of the Treaty of Amsterdam on 1 May 1999, however, this text was '"frozen" by the Council on 12 May 1999' until such time as the European Commission presented the proposal for the draft Brussels I Regulation (COM (1999) 348 final) (the successor of the 1968 Brussels Convention.).[992] This proposal was submitted to the Council of the European Union just two months later on 14 July 1999, and was adopted by the Council on 22 December 2000 as the Brussels I Regulation.[993]

These reasons and hidden agendas stood in the way of the European bloc accepting US proposals for creating a true mixed convention. Finally, another factor that most likely prevented the European bloc from accepting US proposals for creating a true mixed convention was that the change of approach might have been regarded as too big a concession to the US. Since originally the primary goal of the Special Commission meetings had been to create a strict double convention, the European Hague Conference Member States had regarded it as accommodating US interests when the draft convention text was changed from a strict double convention to a text that was technically a mixed convention during the Special Commission meeting in June 1999.[994] This perception was unjustified, however, and

---

989 Pocar Report (n 192) [1]–[8], in particular [4]; an additional reason for transforming the 1968 Brussels Convention into a community instrument could have been to ensure that the EC Member States did not have the competence anymore to displace the 1968 Brussels Convention by means of a Hague Judgments Convention; supporting the free movement of persons by guaranteeing the free circulation of judgments within the EC was regarded as a cornerstone of EC policy in 1999, see European Council, 'Tampere European Council 15 and 16 October 1999 – Presidency Conclusions' <www.europarl.europa.eu/summits/tam_en.htm> accessed 5 April 2023, [33].

990 Pocar Report (n 192) [1]–[3].

991 Ibid [3].

992 'COM (1999) 348 final' (n 315); Pocar Report (n 192) [4].

993 The Brussels I Regulation entered into force on 1 March 2002, see Pocar Report (n 192) [5].

994 June 1999 Draft (n 313) art 19; the full text of the provision is provided in (n 729); Professor Andreas Bucher, a participant of the Swiss delegation, noted in a paper on the Judgments Project that the possibility to use domestic grounds of jurisdiction under the mixed-convention concept seemed inevitable for securing support of the convention text by the US, see Bucher, 'Vers une convention mondiale' (n 173) 80.

rooted in the lack of understanding of the mixed-convention approach, a direct result of the incomplete preparation of the mixed-convention concept during the preparatory phase of the project. As a result, there was a mismatch of expectations concerning concessions in the negotiations, which again made the process unfair from a US point of view:[995] had the true mixed convention been pursued from the beginning, then a provision allowing Contracting States to use their own domestic rules of international jurisdiction would not have been seen as a concession, but as an essential building block of a mixed convention.

8.2. WITHDRAWAL OF UNITED STATES SUPPORT FROM THE JUDGMENTS PROJECT AFTER THE DIPLOMATIC SESSION

The 2001 Diplomatic Session confirmed what had already been quite clear after the end of the drafting phase in October 1999: the European bloc (the EC and its Member States) would not accept a true mixed convention. The entry into force of the Treaty of Amsterdam and the adoption of the Brussels I Regulation had furthermore increased the imbalance of powers in the negotiation process between the US and the European bloc, and the opposition of this very powerful stakeholder must have seemed impossible to overcome to the US. During the first part of the Diplomatic Session from 6–22 June 2001, 39 Hague Conference Member States (out of 51 Member States in total)[996] participated.[997] Out of these 39, 15 were also Member States of the EC.[998] Initially, the effects of the entry into force of the Treaty of Amsterdam on 1 May 1999[999] and the adoption of the

995 Zartmann, 'Negotiation as a search for justice' (n 93) 74.

996 See 'Statue Hague Conference: Status table' (n 158).

997 Germany, Argentina, Australia, Austria, Belgium, Brazil, Bulgaria, Canada, Chile, China (People's Republic of), Republic of Korea, Croatia, Denmark, Egypt, Spain, the United States, Finland, France, Georgia, Greece, Hungary, Israel, Ireland, Italy, Japan, Luxembourg, Morocco, Mexico, Monaco, Norway, the Netherlands, Poland, Portugal, the United Kingdom, Slovakia, Sweden, Switzerland, Czech Republic, and Uruguay, see 'Members of the Second Commission', in *Proceedings of the Twentieth Session, Tome II* (n 29) 386–388.

998 In June 2001, 15 Hague Conference Member States were also Member States of the EC: Germany, Austria, Belgium, Denmark, Spain, Finland, France, Greece, Ireland, Italy, Luxembourg, the Netherlands, Portugal, the United Kingdom, and Sweden, see (n 330).

999 Treaty of Amsterdam amending the Treaty on European Union, the Treaties establishing the European Communities and certain related acts: Final Act [1997] OJ C340/115.

Brussels I Regulation on 22 December 2000 on the external competence of the EC to negotiate (and conclude) the Hague Judgments Convention were not clear.[1000] In the beginning there was great uncertainty among the EC Member States' delegations and others whether the EC had acquired exclusive external competence, or whether it shared this external competence to negotiate and conclude the Hague Judgments Convention with its Member States after the adoption of the Brussels I Regulation, as discussed above.[1001] Since the Brussels I Regulation only regulated international jurisdiction, but not the recognition and enforcement of judgments rendered in third States, the EC Member States originally assumed that they had only lost their competence to regulate international jurisdiction by means of international treaties with third States, and not the competence to conclude treaties regarding the recognition and enforcement of judgments.[1002] Eventually, the European Commission and the Council (the organ representing the EC Member States) chose not to determine the question of external competence definitely, however, but to conduct the negotiations on the Judgments Project together according to a common mandate adopted by the Council.[1003] The Member States of the EC were still allowed to make interventions, but only in accordance with a coordinated position (or on matters not covered by the common position).[1004] This mandate apparently entailed to not depart substantially from the structure of the October 1999 Preliminary Draft Convention.

1000 Beaumont, 'The Brussels Convention becomes a Regulation' (n 980) 25, 26; Wagner, 'Vergemeinschaftung Gesetzgebungskompetenz' (n 713) 218–221.

1001 Pocar, 'Which Format for the Negotiations in The Hague?' (n 981) 191, 196; Schulz, 'Accession' (n 101) 942; Wagner, 'Vergemeinschaftung Gesetzgebungskompetenz' (n 713) 218, 219.

1002 Wagner, 'Vergemeinschaftung Gesetzgebungskompetenz' (n 713) 220; Beaumont, 'The Brussels Convention becomes a Regulation' (n 980) 25, 26.

1003 Beaumont, 'The Brussels Convention becomes a Regulation' (n 980) 25, 26; Wagner, 'Vergemeinschaftung Gesetzgebungskompetenz' (n 713) 219–221; A Teun V M Struycken, 'Das Internationale Privatrecht der Europäischen Gemeinschaft im Verhältnis zu Drittstaaten und zur Haager Konferenz' (2004) ZEuP 276, 285, 286; the question of external competence was only clarified by the ECJ in its Opinion 1/03 of 7 February 2006, where the Court decided that the competence of the EC to conclude international agreements with third States in the area of international jurisdiction and the recognition and enforcement of foreign judgments was exclusive, see Opinion 1/03 of 7 February 2006 EU:C:2006:81, [2006] ECR I-01145 (Lugano Opinion) [162]–[168]; [173].

1004 Beaumont, 'The Brussels Convention becomes a Regulation' (n 980) 26; Van Loon, Schulz, 'The European Community and the Hague Conference on Private International Law' (n 100) 265; this did not apply to Denmark, however, as Denmark had not yet opted into the adoption of the Brussels I Regulation, and as a result had maintained

This can be inferred from the interventions made during the Diplomatic Session by both the EC Member States and the Swedish delegation (Sweden being the EC Member State holding the presidency of the Council at the time).[1005] In general, the EC and its Member States had rejected proposals to turn the October 1999 Preliminary Draft Convention text into a true mixed convention, as discussed above.[1006]

Another aspect which may have reinforced the decision of the US not to continue with the Judgments Project was the fact that the delegations from the EC and EFTA Member States wanted to continue to apply the Brussels-Lugano regime not only for those proceedings where all the parties were domiciled in a State where the Brussels/Lugano Convention (or the Brussels I Regulation) applied, but also when only the defendant was domiciled in a Brussels-Lugano State.[1007] That means, the Brussels/Lugano States wanted to apply the jurisdictional provisions of the Hague Convention in general only in proceedings against a defendant who was not domiciled in a Brussels/Lugano State. If implemented, it would have created a situation where the US would have had to forgo the application of domestic rules of jurisdiction for proceedings within the convention scope, while the Brussels/Lugano States would have continued to apply the rules of their regional regimes, creating an imbalance in the required

its external competence in this area, see Treaty establishing the European Community (consolidated version), Protocol (No 5) on the position of Denmark (1997) [2006] OJ C321/201, art 1, art 2; only in 2005 did Denmark opt into the adoption of the Brussels I Regulation, see Agreement between the EC and the Kingdom of Denmark on jurisdiction and the recognition and enforcement of judgments in civil and commercial matters [2005] OJ L299/62; see also Fausto Pocar, 'The Drafting of a World-Wide Convention on Jurisdiction and the Enforcement of Judgments: Which Format for the Negotiations in The Hague?', in Nafziger, Symeonides (eds), *Law and Justice in a Multistate World* (n 266) 191, 196.

1005 During the negotiations, the EC was represented by representatives of the European Commission, the Council and the European Parliament. The European Commission was represented by Anne-Marie Rouchaud, Gustaaf M Borchardt, Olivier Tell, Christian Auinger, Mirjam Söderholm and Bernd Martenczuk. The Council of the European Union was represented by Fernando R Paulino Pereira and Jan-Peter Hix (and by the Swedish delegation which held the Council presidency at the time). The European Parliament was represented by Diana Wallis and Harry Duintjer, see 'Members of the Second Commission', in *Proceedings of the Twentieth Session, Tome II* (n 29) 389.

1006 Chapter 6.

1007 See 2001 Interim Text (n 36) Annex I, art 37, Proposal 2, paragraph 2 and 3; this proposal had been introduced during the Special Commission meeting in October 1999, see October 1999 Preliminary Draft Convention (n 32), Annex; 'Work Doc No 270 of 26 October 1999: Proposal by the delegations of Denmark, Finland, France, Sweden and the United Kingdom' [on file with author].

concessions on both sides, and contributing to an outcome that could be conceived to be unfair or unjust.[1008] According to Peter Trooboff, a member of the US delegation, the opinion of the US delegation to the Judgments Project had been from the beginning that the US was negotiating for an instrument which would take precedence over regional instruments.[1009]

Equally, disagreement about how to regulate the problem of parallel proceedings subsisted between the US and other Hague Conference Member States. The 2001 Interim Text generally employed the civil-law approach to resolving a conflict of jurisdiction by obliging the court second seized to stay the proceedings before it (in proceedings between the same parties and concerning the same cause of action).[1010] At the same time, the 2001 Interim Text contained a provision that allowed a court seized first in time to exceptionally stay its proceedings under certain circumstances if exercising jurisdiction by that court would be clearly inappropriate, and another court with jurisdiction would be clearly more appropriate to hear the proceedings.[1011] The provision therefore allowed for a stay of proceedings similar to the forum-non-conveniens doctrine as applied in the US, the United Kingdom and other common-law jurisdictions.[1012] Nevertheless, the US was critical of 2001 Interim Text, Article 22, as the provision would inter alia not have applied in cases concerning consumer and employment contracts.[1013] It is submitted,

---

1008 Zartmann, 'Negotiation as a search for justice' (n 93) 68.

1009 Trooboff, 'Ten (and Probably More) Difficulties' (n 298) 274. This opinion however contradicted the statement of the French delegate speaking on behalf of the European Community during the Special Commission meeting on general affairs and policy in 1995, according to which the Brussels regime should be left 'intact' by the Hague Judgments Convention. This would have entailed the continued application of the Brussels Convention to determine jurisdiction over defendants with a domicile in an EC Member State, 'Conclusions of the Special Commission of June 1994– Annex – Extract of the Conclusions of the Special Commission of June 1995 on general affairs and policy of the Conference' (n 446), 3.

1010 2001 Interim Text (n 36), art 20(1); cf Brussels I Regulation (n 315), art 27 (now Brussels Ibis Regulation (n 963) art 29) for the civil-law approach to solving jurisdictional conflicts.

1011 2001 Interim Text (n 36), art 22.

1012 The approaches to *forum non conveniens* in the different common law jurisdictions vary for example with regard to the factors to be considered in order to assess the appropriateness of the court, see, e.g., *Gulf Oil v. Gilbert* 330 US 501 (1947) (for the US); *Spiliada Maritime Corporation v. Cansulex* [1987] AC 460 (HL) (for the UK). See also Trooboff, 'Ten (and Probably More) Difficulties' (n 298) 272.

1013 2001 Interim Text (n 36), art 22(1); Trooboff ibid; currently, finding a solution for the problem of parallel proceedings is the subject of discussions of the Hague Conference Member States in the context of the Jurisdiction Project, see Herrup, Brand, 'A Hague Convention on Parallel Proceedings' (n 56) 1, 2; see also Introduction at 10.

however, that a solution to the problem of parallel proceedings would have been found if there had been consensus on creating a true mixed convention, and if the true mixed convention concept had been pursued from the outset.[1014] If the Hague Conference Member States had worked towards creating a mixed convention from the beginning of the drafting phase, and a decision-making process on the basis of consensus had been employed, the drafting process would have been a fair one from the point of view of all the participants. This equal chance to influence the outcome for all participants would have contributed to a positive and productive attitude towards the (pre-)negotiations,[1015] and would have influenced the willingness of all participants to make concessions.[1016]

8.3. REASONS FOR THE UNITED STATES TO PARTICIPATE IN THE FIRST PART OF THE DIPLOMATIC SESSION

Although the structure of the October 1999 Preliminary Draft Convention was clearly unacceptable to the US, its delegation nevertheless participated in the Diplomatic Session. Abandoning the Judgments Project completely would have been a radical step which would have deprived the US of the possibility to influence the project.[1017] Forfeiting the chance to influence the project might in fact have even worsened the situation for US citizens involved in international civil litigation as compared to the status quo. The negotiations at The Hague involved a real risk of creating unified grounds of international direct jurisdiction which could have allowed foreign courts to exercise jurisdiction over US defendants, and to render judgments against them on these bases. Indeed, one of the policies underlying the Judgments Project was to make the new convention as widely applicable as possible. Some of the jurisdictional provisions would as a result have allowed the exercise of jurisdiction over defendants not (habitually) resident in a Contracting State.[1018] For example, the

1014 Cf Beaumont, 'The revived Judgments Project (n 43) 533.
1015 I William Zartman, 'The Structure of Negotiation', in Kremenyuk (n 65) 71, 73.
1016 Albin (n 326) 257–259.
1017 cf Walker, *Multilateral Conferences* (n 893) 191.
1018 Special Commission on international jurisdiction and the effects of foreign judgments in civil and commercial matters (25–30 October 1999) 'Report of Meeting No 77' (on file with author) 1.

provision attributing jurisdiction over a defendant to the court of the State in which one of their co-defendants was (habitually) resident (October 1999 Preliminary Draft Convention, Article 14) was meant to apply also to defendants not (habitually) resident in a Contracting State of the Hague Convention.[1019] Equally, the Hague Convention could have for example created a *forum actoris* for proceedings in matters relating to consumer contracts, allowing a consumer to bring proceedings against the other party in their home forum, even if the other party was (habitually) resident in a non-Contracting State.[1020] These far-reaching (and potentially exorbitant) grounds of jurisdiction could have been employed by courts in a Contracting State to the new Hague Convention to exercise jurisdiction over US defendants. What is more, resulting judgments could have been recognised and enforced in all the Contracting States to the Hague Convention.[1021] The US not being a party to the future Hague Convention therefore would have not protected defendants habitually resident in the US against its effects.

However, during the first part of the Diplomatic Session, the consensus approach prevented a text from being adopted which would have contradicted US interests. Already the objection of only one delegation was seen as hindering consensus.[1022] This would not have been the case for the second part of the Diplomatic Session, however, during which a final convention text for a Hague Judgments Convention should have been adopted. This second part of the Diplomatic Session would have taken place on the basis of majority voting, employing the standard Rules of Procedure of the Hague Conference.[1023] Since a simple majority would then have been sufficient to adopt a proposal, this would have strongly favoured the EC and its Member States. Judging from previous voting results, it was very likely therefore that the European group could have gathered enough support for the proposals it favoured during the final part of the

1019 Ibid 1.

1020 October 1999 Preliminary Draft Convention (n 32), art 7(1). Such a *forum actoris* for consumers in matters relating to consumer contracts was later created by the Brussels Ibis Regulation (n 963), art 18(1).

1021 2001 Interim Text (n 36), art 25(1).

1022 Nygh, 'Arthur's Baby' (n 266) 161.

1023 Original Rules of Procedure (n 90), art 3: '[d]ecisions of the Conference shall be made by a majority of the votes cast by delegations present at the time of the vote; abstentions shall not be counted as votes'; von Mehren, 'Can the Hague Conference Project Succeed?' (n 31) 194.

Diplomatic Session.[1024] The opposition of the EC and its Member States to the true-mixed-convention structure, also supported by some of the other delegations such as Canada,[1025] most likely would have been impossible to overcome by the US in a second part of the Diplomatic Session.

8.4. CONCLUSION

The first part of the Diplomatic Session in June 2001 confirmed what had already emerged after the end of the Special Commission meeting in October 1999, namely that it would not be possible to adopt a true mixed convention during a second part of the Diplomatic Session. The negotiations had shown that the EC and its Member States pursued different purposes with the Hague Judgments Project than the US. The EC and its Member States continued to strive for the convention concept that had organically developed during the Special Commission meetings from June 1997 until October 1999. This convention type embodied the purposes of a strict double convention by guaranteeing as much legal certainty as possible by means of an extensive green list[1026] and an extensive red list.[1027] Moreover, the EC and its Member States rejected the true mixed-convention model not only because they wanted to achieve as much legal certainty as possible by means of a broad green list (and a broad red list), but also for political reasons since they had a stake in extending the scope of the Brussels I Regulation by means of a global Hague Judgments Convention. The opposition of the European bloc to the true mixed convention concept would have been impossible to overcome for the US during a final Diplomatic Session due to the numerical strength of the European bloc which most likely would have balanced voting results in its favour. As a result, the US withdrew its support for concluding a broad convention on jurisdiction

1024 See above, Section 8.1.

1025 See 'Intervention Ms Sanderson', in *Proceedings of the Nineteenth Session, Tome I* (n 821) 587.

1026 Ibid arts 3–16.

1027 Ibid art 18(1) and (2).

and judgments in February 2002,[1028] and the ambition to create a broad Hague Judgments Convention was consequently abandoned during the meeting of Commission I on General Affairs and Policy during the second part of the Nineteenth Diplomatic Session in 2002.[1029]

1028 Teitz, 'Another Hague Judgments Convention' (n 50) 495.

1029 During the meeting of the Commission I on General Affairs and Policy from 22–24 April 2002, it was decided to narrow the scope of the work on the Judgments Project by focusing on 'a core area of possible grounds of jurisdiction as tentatively identified by the Commission, as well as the existing provisions on recognition and enforcement upon which there is broad agreement', see Permanent Bureau, 'Commission I on General Affairs and Policy held on 22-24 April 2002' <https://www.hcch.net/en/governance/council-on-general-affairs/archive> accessed 11 January 2024 [3]: '[t]he Commission agreed that the best path forward on the Judgments Project at this point would be to have the Secretariat convene an informal working group [...] [T]he starting point for this informal process will be a discussion of a core area of possible grounds of jurisdiction as tentatively identified by the Commission, as well as the existing provisions on recognition and enforcement upon which there is broad agreement. This core area might include choice of court agreements, defendant's forum, counter-claims, branches, submission, trusts and physical injury torts'; this process eventually led to the adoption of the 2005 Hague Choice of Court Convention, which entered into force in October 2015, see 2005 Hague Choice of Court Convention (n 3); Brand, 'Community Competence' (n 735) 195.

CHAPTER 9
CONCLUSIONS
Lessons (to be) Drawn from the Failure of the Judgments Project

9.1. LESSONS FROM THE FAILURE OF THE JUDGMENTS PROJECT (1992–2001)

The original Judgments Project of the Hague Conference, which had consumed almost 10 years of work on the part of the Hague Conference Member States and the Permanent Bureau, was a missed opportunity to create an international convention regulating both the recognition and enforcement of foreign judgments *and* international direct jurisdiction. This was not due to the unsuitability of the Hague Conference as a forum for creating a global judgments convention. The Hague Conference was an entirely suitable forum due to its unique experience in and proven track record of concluding successful conventions which harmonised rules of private international law. Moreover, the Project did not fail because unifying grounds of jurisdiction on a broad scale and on a global level was impossible. Rather, the Judgments Project did not lead to the adoption of a convention text by the Hague Conference Member States because the pre-negotiation phase of the project (between 1992 and 1999) had not been prepared and managed by the Permanent Bureau with the same rigour as other Hague Conference projects.[1030]

If the Permanent Bureau had more closely adhered to well-established management practices and procedures employed for other Hague Conventions, the Special Commission meetings would not have pursued the goal of working towards an unfeasible convention type in the form of a closed double convention as a first priority. In particular, if the Permanent Bureau had conducted an analysis of the needs and interests of at least the

1030 Cf Monheim, 'Power of Process' (n 67) 376.

two most important stakeholders in the Judgments Project (the US and the EC Member States) before the Special Commission meetings in 1994 or in 1997 at the latest, this needs analysis would have shown that only a mixed convention contained the possibility to balance the competing interests of increasing legal certainty and preserving the flexibility and sovereignty of the Contracting Parties, and that only a mixed convention would have created a chance to successfully regulate international direct jurisdiction on a global level. It was clear from the documents the US delegation had submitted to the Permanent Bureau from the very beginning of the project in 1992, and from US interventions made during the official plenary meetings of the Hague Conference Member States during the whole course of the project, that the US regarded it as vital that a judgments convention should not restrict the sovereign power of its Contracting Parties to regulate international direct jurisdiction to the same extent as a strict double convention. In addition, if the Permanent Bureau had studied the feasibility of the available methods for concluding a convention on both jurisdiction and judgments, it would have ascertained that a mixed convention was the only viable way forward. A feasibility study on the basis of the then available case law and primary and secondary sources of both US law on international direct jurisdiction and the supra-nationalised approach to international direct jurisdiction of the EC Member States would have shown that the attempt to unify grounds of jurisdiction exhaustively by means of a strict double convention would be very hard, if not impossible, to achieve. Only a mixed convention would have been a viable approach to unifying grounds of international direct jurisdiction on a global level in general, and between the US and the EC Member States in particular. Due to the lack of planning by the project managers, the Special Commission meetings in 1997 made a false start by attempting to create an unwanted (from the US perspective) and also unfeasible convention type (the strict double convention). This convention type was pursued until the penultimate Special Commission meeting in June 1999.

The third shortcoming concerning the planning of the project, which directly resulted from the lack of choosing the best convention type underlying the discussions, was the failure to recognise that the true mixed convention was a convention in its own right. In order to create a true mixed convention as intended by Arthur T von Mehren, a decision-making process through the use of consensus would have been required. Since the Permanent Bureau had not developed a plan of construction for drafting a mixed convention, the mixed convention was treated as only a restricted version of a strict double convention. These shortcomings in planning for and understanding the mixed-convention type led the Special Commission to the fateful decision to pursue a strict double convention as a first priority, while the mixed convention was maintained as the fallback option. This initial pursuit of a strict double convention, coupled with the incomplete planning for a mixed convention, and a decision-making process on the basis of majority voting, led to the creation of a draft convention text which would have been almost as restrictive on the sovereignty of its Contracting States as a strict double convention. Moreover, since the October 1999 Preliminary Draft Convention had been created through a decision-making process which had been unfair for non-EC Member States as it had given priority to EC interests, the pre-negotiation phase had produced an unjust outcome.[1031] For these reasons, the October 1999 Preliminary Draft Convention text was an unacceptable basis for official multilateral negotiations during a Diplomatic Session for some non-EC states like the US. In short, the Special Commission meetings on the Judgments Project, the Hague Conferences' pre-negotiation phase, had failed to produce a viable draft convention text.

The failure of the Judgments Project cannot, however, be attributed to a failure by the US delegation to raise concerns about the directions of the discussions during the pre-negotiation phase (the Special Commission meetings). Rather, although the US delegation repeatedly made interventions concerning the convention type, these were unsuccessful in particular due to the negotiation management techniques employed during the Special Commission meetings. Since the question of the convention type had been controversial, the Chair had repeatedly deferred the final decision on this question in a strategic attempt to reconcile the groups that favoured either the strict double convention or the mixed convention. According to this strategy, the question of the convention type should only be addressed once progress regarding the relevant individual provisions of the draft convention text had been made. In this way, it was overlooked that the convention type was not only the end result of the negotiation process, but that each convention type required specific detailed planning.

The lack of preparation regarding the convention type during the pre-negotiation phase also directly contributed to the fact that until the end of the Diplomatic Session, no agreement on the purpose of the convention existed between the US and in particular the EC and its Member States. While the US pursued a convention that would

---

1031 Zartmann, 'Negotiation as a Search for Justice' (n 93) 73.

have protected legislative and jurisdictional flexibility through the true mixed convention concept, the EC and its Member States pursued the goal of jurisdictional certainty through the strict double convention concept (and later the restricted double convention concept). This lack of agreement on the type and purpose of a judgments convention led the US to abandon the Judgments Project after the Diplomatic Session in 2001. Despite the rejection of the structure of the October 1999 Preliminary Draft Convention by the US, the EC Member States and the EC itself refused to divert substantially from the structure of the October 1999 draft text. The EC had a political interest in maintaining the October 1999 Preliminary Draft Convention as it resembled the 1968 Brussels Convention and its successor, the Brussels I Regulation, not only in terms of its structure but also in terms of the content of its jurisdictional provisions. A global judgments convention closely resembling these European instruments could have helped to enlarge the scope of application of these two instruments (and of the parallel instruments of the 1968 Brussels Convention, the 1988 Lugano Convention) and also helped to unify rules on international direct jurisdiction for claimants in the EC outside of the Brussels-Lugano regime.

As the previous analysis of the work on the 1980 Child Abduction Convention, the 1993 Child Adoption Convention and the Hague Judgments Project has shown, proper management of the pre-negotiation phase of multilateral negotiations is influential on the outcome of the negotiation process and the adoption of a convention text. The analysis has also shown that it is likely that the management of the pre-negotiation phase of the Judgments Project, which did not reflect Hague Conference practice, contributed to its failure. The analysis therefore adds weight to the argument that negotiation management, i.e., the management of the negotiation process as such, is influential on the success of multilateral negotiations and that there is indeed a 'power of process' in international negotiations.[1032] Even if proper preparation of multilateral negotiations through managing the pre-negotiation phase cannot guarantee their successful outcome, a lack of proper preparation in this phase is likely to contribute to their failure.[1033] Finally, as has been shown, proper management of the (pre-)negotiation phase can also have an influence on how fair and just negotiation processes are regarded to be by the participants.

[1032] Monheim, 'Power of Process' (n 67) 376.

[1033] Ibid; Frame, *Managing Projects in Organizations* (n 60) 22.

9.2. LESSONS (TO BE) DRAWN FOR THE REVIVED JUDGMENTS PROJECT

In reaction to the failure of the original Judgments Project, the Hague Conference amended its Statute and its Rules of Procedures during the Twentieth Diplomatic Session in June 2005.[1034] The first change made was to adopt a decision-making process on the basis of consensus as the official standard for taking decisions.[1035] This change was intended to address fears of Hague Conference Member States that the EC or its Member States would be able to outvote other States under a decision-making process on the basis of voting (i.e., it was intended to improve the fairness of the decision-making process).[1036] Furthermore, the Hague Conference Member States enabled the EC to become a member of the Hague Conference in its own right so that it could officially take part in the plenary meetings of the Hague Conference, and so that the EC's role in the negations was clarified.[1037] According to the amended Statute of the Conference, the EC could become a Member of the organisation as a 'Regional Economic Integration

1034 Statute Hague Conference (n 18), the amendments of the statute entered into force on 1 July 2007, see ibid; Rules of Procedure (as amended in 2005), partially reproduced in Hague Conference on Private International Law, *Proceedings of the Twentieth Session, 14 to 30 June 2005, Tome I, Miscellaneous Matters* (Intersentia 2015), 57 (2005 Rules of Procedure); the latest revisions of the Rules of Procedure of the Hague Conference took place in 2020 and entered into force on 6 March 2020, see Rules of Procedure of The Hague Conference on Private International Law (HCCH) (2020 Rules of Procedure), fn 1 <https://assets.hcch.net/docs/52b9ea0d-dce2-4528-aeda-77a746f5fa14.pdf> accessed 5 April 2023.

1035 Statute Hague Conference (n 18) art 8(2); 2005 Rules of Procedure (n 1034), art 1A, first sentence: '[t]o the furthest extent possible, all decisions shall be taken by consensus'; now 2020 Rules of Procedure (n 1034), art II H(3).

1036 Rolf Wagner, 'Principle of Consensus and European Union Legislative Competence in Relation to Judicial Cooperation in Civil Matters: Challenges Facing the Hague Conference on Private International Law', in The Permanent Bureau of the Hague Conference on Private International Law (eds), *A Commitment to Private International Law: Essays in Honour of Hans van Loon* (Intersentia 2013) 643, 646, 647. Decision-making on the basis of voting was still possible under the amended Rules of Procedure, but only as a last resort, see 2005 Rules of Procedure (n 1034), art 1A, first sentence, now 2020 Rules of Procedure (n 1034) art II H(4); according to Statute Hague Conference (n 18) art 3(8), the EC had as many votes as it had Member States in cases where the EC had exclusive competence. See also 2005 Rules of Procedure (n 1034), art 2(2); this latter provision has no equivalent in the revised Rules of Procedures of 2020, see 2020 Rules of Procedure (n 1034).

1037 Van Loon, Schulz, 'The European Community and the Hague Conference on Private International Law' (n 100) 283.

Organisation (REIO).'[1038] As the previous analysis of the failure of the original Hague Judgments Project has shown, however, there are more lessons to be drawn. Both the decision-making process on the basis of majority voting and the acquisition of external competence by what was then the EC to conclude treaties in private international law contributed to the failure. However, that the pre-negotiation phase (the Special Commission meetings) had not been prepared with the same rigour as the pre-negotiation phases of previous convention projects is likely to have been a major factor that led to the abandonment of the project. Unlike for other successful Hague Conventions, the Permanent Bureau had not developed a viable strategy through conceptual and detailed planning for creating a global judgments convention. In this way, the Permanent Bureau and the Hague Conference Member States had overlooked the fact that the true mixed convention as developed by Arthur von Mehren was the only convention type with a realistic chance of creating a global convention that unified rules on both judgments *and* jurisdiction. Since the true mixed convention concept had not been fully understood and developed properly, a draft convention text was created during the implementation phase (the Special Commission meetings from 1997–1999) that was not acceptable to, in particular, the US delegation, a key stakeholder in the project. The October 1999 Preliminary Draft Convention text was a mixed convention, but only in a technical sense, and it was substantially different from a true mixed convention in its regulatory content. Since the October 1999 Preliminary Draft Convention was produced by following a conceptual strategy to create a strict double convention as a first priority from the beginning of its drafting phase at the Special Commission meeting in 1997, the October 1999 Preliminary Draft Convention more resembled a strict double convention than a mixed convention, and had therefore been described as a 'restricted double convention'. The two key stakeholders (the US and the EC Member States) continued to pursue two different versions of a mixed convention, the true mixed-convention concept on the US side, and the 'restricted double convention'-type of a mixed convention on the European side. For this reason, it was also impossible for those stakeholders to reach consensus on a text for a Hague Judgments Convention during the first part of the Diplomatic Session in 2001, since the two convention

---

[1038] Statute Hague Conference (n 18) art 3(1), art 3(9); the EC became a Member of the Hague Conference on 3 April 2007, see, e.g., van Loon, Schulz, 'The European Community and the Hague Conference on Private International Law' (n 100) 279, 280; see also Wagner, 'Vergemeinschaftung Gesetzgebungskompetenz' (n 713) 223, 224.

types pursued different purposes (flexibility and protection of sovereignty under the true-mixed-convention concept; as much legal certainty as possible under the strict-double-convention concept). Since the question of this difference in understanding of the mixed convention had not been addressed, or the consequences of this difference in understanding had not been fully appreciated, the attempt to create a broad Hague Judgments Convention was ultimately abandoned in 2002.

Finally, the true-mixed-convention concept does not seem to have been considered for the revived Judgments Project when the Permanent Bureau began to reflect on whether work on the broad Project should be resumed in 2010.[1039] Originally, work on both international direct jurisdiction and the recognition and enforcement of judgments was discussed.[1040] The first document prepared by the Permanent Bureau leading to the revival of the Judgments Project (the 'Background Note') discussed the three convention types which are available for concluding a Hague Judgments Convention (i.e., a single convention focussing only on the recognition and enforcement of foreign judgments, a strict double convention, and a mixed convention).[1041] However, in the Background Note, the mixed-convention concept was equated with the October 1999 Preliminary Draft Convention.[1042] This Note was prepared for the attention of an informal Expert Group which met in The Hague in April 2012.[1043] On the basis of this document, the Expert Group was to assess whether there was 'sufficient interest among States to pursue a future instrument on cross-border litigation in civil and commercial matters [...] and [...] whether there was sufficient willingness among States to invest the resources needed for the development of a future instrument'.[1044]

1039 Permanent Bureau, 'Process Paper on the Continuation of the Judgments Project: August 2013' (n 43) [1], [6]–[9] <https://assets.hcch.net/docs/79c4fd67-6f1e-4bf8-bf18-01e589862f45.pdf> accessed 5 April 2023; Council on General Affairs and Policy, 'Conclusions and Recommendations 2011' (n 43) [15]; see also Beaumont, 'The revived Judgments Project' (n 43) 535; see also Introduction.

1040 Permanent Bureau, 'Background Note: Expert Group (April 2012)' (n 45), [35], [36]; [40]–[72].

1041 ibid [40]–[42], and [43]–[72].

1042 Ibid [40] and fn 66.

1043 Permanent Bureau, 'Conclusions and Recommendations of the Expert Group on Possible Future Work on Cross-Border Litigation in Civil and Commercial Matters: The Hague, 12–14 April 2012' <https://assets.hcch.net/docs/0e110725-5eef-429c-9fe3-24d8d4e7e87a.pdf> accessed 5 April 2023; a list of participants is not publicly available; according to Louise Ellen Teitz, approximately 25 experts participated in the meeting, 'representing different legal traditions and geographic diversity', see Teitz, 'Another Hague Judgments Convention' (n 50) 499.

1044 Permanent Bureau, 'Background Note: Expert Group (April 2012)' (n 45), [2].

The US declined to participate in the work on international direct jurisdiction from the outset, although it had been this delegation that had originally proposed to create unified grounds of international direct jurisdiction in the context of the old Judgments Project.[1045] This strong opposition by the US first led to the split of the work of the Experts' Group (which focussed on direct jurisdiction) and the Working Group (which focussed on the recognition and enforcement of foreign judgments),[1046] and eventually channelled the revived Judgments Project towards creating a single convention on the recognition and enforcement of foreign judgments only. In a document prepared in August 2013 (the 'Process Paper'), the Permanent Bureau suggested solely advancing the work on the recognition and enforcement of foreign judgments, and suspending the work on international direct jurisdiction.[1047] According to the Process Paper, this decision was based on the evaluation that only work on the recognition and enforcement of foreign judgments would likely lead to a 'successful outcome'.[1048] Focussing on the recognition and enforcement of foreign judgments was seen as 'the more practically achievable' task as compared to attempting to unify grounds of international direct jurisdiction as well.[1049] Subsequently, from 2014 onward, only work on the recognition and enforcement of foreign judgments continued, and the work on international direct jurisdiction was postponed.[1050] Work on the recognition and enforcement of foreign judgments was concluded successfully in 2019 with the adoption of the Convention on the Recognition and Enforcement of Foreign Judgments in Civil and Commercial Matters.[1051]

1045 Teitz noted in 'Another Hague Judgments Convention' (n 50) at 499, 500 that 'the most critical issue [during the meeting of the Expert Group in 2012] was the scope of any judgments convention', and that '[t]here was strong pressure by most of the experts for a convention addressing direct jurisdiction as well as recognition and enforcement, especially from some European members. The U.S. strongly opposed such an approach after the disastrous results of the 2001 draft and even rejected a two-track or protocol approach of simultaneous work'.

1046 Permanent Bureau, 'Process Paper on the Continuation of the Judgments Project – August 2013' (n 43) [1], [6]–[9] <https://assets.hcch.net/docs/79c4fd67-6f1e-4bf8-bf18-01e589862f45.pdf> accessed 5 April 2023.

1047 Ibid [20].

1048 Ibid [17].

1049 Ibid.

1050 Cf ibid [17], [20]; Permanent Bureau, 'Prel Doc No 7A – January 2015 – Ongoing Work on Judgments – Choice of Court Convention and the Judgments Project' [6]–[9] <https://assets.hcch.net/upload/wop/gap2015pd07a_en.pdf> accessed 5 April 2023; Beaumont/Walker, 'Hague Judgments Project' (n 46) 43.

1051 2019 Hague Judgments Convention (n 53).

The current work in the context of the Hague Jurisdiction Project focusses on parallel proceedings.[1052] Work on international jurisdiction is, however, still a possibility. In order to fulfil a main interest of the EU in the revived Judgments Project, namely the unification of direct grounds of jurisdiction on an international level, the Permanent Bureau should consider the creation of a Hague instrument following the spirit of a true mixed convention, possibly by creating a Hague Protocol on jurisdiction that accompanies the 2019 Hague Judgments Convention.[1053] The interest in creating unified rules on international direct jurisdiction was the main reason why the EU agreed to revive the Judgments Project. In 2009, the European Commission expressly noted its interest in creating unified rules of jurisdiction applicable to non-EU-domiciled defendants, in order to create a level playing field for EU-based claimants.[1054] During the revision process of the Brussels I Regulation, the European Commission originally suggested extending the application of the jurisdictional provisions of the Brussels I Regulation to non-EU-domiciled defendants in general.[1055] The European Parliament was of the view, however, that such an extension should not be pursued without further consultations and political debate not only on a regional, but also on a global level.[1056] For this reason, the European Parliament mandated the European Commission 'to use its best endeavours to revive [the Judgments Project of the Hague Conference]' in this context.[1057] This interest in creating

1052 See, e.g., 'Report of the Working Group on Jurisdiction: Prel. Doc. No 7 of February 2022, Annex I' <https://assets.hcch.net/docs/d05583b3-ec71-4a5b-829c-103a834173bf.pdf> accessed 5 April 2023.

1053 See further below, Section 9.3.

1054 See Commission of the European Communities, 'Green Paper on the Review of the Council Regulation (EC) No 44/2001 on Jurisdiction and the Recognition and Enforcement of Judgments in Civil and Commercial Matters, 21 April 2009: COM(2009) 175 final', <https://eur-lex.europa.eu/legal-content/EN/TXT/PDF/?uri=CELEX:52009DC0175&from=EN> accessed 5 April 2023, 3.

1055 Ibid.

1056 European Parliament, 'European Parliament resolution of 7 September 2010 on the implementation and review of Council Regulation (EC) No 44/2001 on jurisdiction and the recognition and enforcement of judgments in civil and commercial matters', <https://www.europarl.europa.eu/sides/getDoc.do?pubRef=-//EP//NONSGML+TA+P7-TA-2010–0304+0+DOC+PDF+V0//EN> accessed 5 April 2023, [15].

1057 Ibid; in the interim period, only jurisdictional rules concerning consumer and employment contracts were extended to cover also non-EU-domiciled defendants in order to protect consumers and employees, see Brussels Ibis Regulation (n 963), art 18(1), art 21(2), Recital 14; see also European Parliament, 'Report on the proposal for a regulation of the European Parliament and of the Council on jurisdiction and the recognition and enforcement of judgments in civil and commercial matters (recast) of 15 October 2012: Explanatory Statement', [2] <https://www.europarl.europa.eu/sides/getDoc.do?pubRef=-//EP//NONSGML+REPORT+A7-2012–0320+0+DOC+PDF+V0//EN> accessed 5 April 2023.

unified rules of international direct jurisdiction should have existed in particular regarding the two main extra-EU trading partners in 2010, the US and China.[1058]

In order to regain the support of the US in working towards a Hague regime that regulates both judgments *and* jurisdiction, it may be necessary for the Permanent Bureau to distance itself from the notion that the October 1999 Preliminary Draft Convention was a mixed convention as envisaged by von Mehren,[1059] after the from a US point of view 'disastrous results'[1060] of the old Judgments Project. Furthermore, the Permanent Bureau should consider developing a concept for creating an instrument on jurisdiction in the spirit of a true mixed convention, as only this convention type has the potential to successfully combine rules securing the recognition and enforcement of foreign judgments and unified rules on international direct jurisdiction in one single regime. The question of how the 2019 Hague Judgments Convention could be turned into a true mixed convention regime will be discussed in the next and final part.

9.3. TURNING THE 2019 HAGUE JUDGMENTS CONVENTION INTO A MIXED CONVENTION

Although the Hague Conference began the work on the revived Judgments Project with a focus on creating a single convention, the unification of rules of international direct jurisdiction is still possible. Despite this possibility not being described in the Preliminary Documents of the Permanent Bureau, it is still viable to create a workable mixed convention regime on the basis of the 2019 Hague Judgments Convention. Although this Convention only focusses on the recognition and enforcement

---

1058 In 2010, EU exports to the US had a total value of 243.3 billion Euros (as compared to a total value of EU exports to China of 113.3 billion Euros), and EU imports from the US had a value of 170.4 billion Euros (as compared total value of EU imports from China of 282.5 billion Euros), see European Commission, *External and intra-EU trade: A statistical yearbook – Data 1958–2010* (eurostat Statistical books 2011) 31, 32 <https://ec.europa.eu/eurostat/documents/3217494/5729733/KS-GI-11-001-EN.PDF/9e06d19b-bdce-49e0-a766-65fbbfc78081> accessed 5 April 2023.

1059 Permanent Bureau, 'Background Note: Expert Group (April 2012)' (n 45), [40] and fn 66.

1060 Teitz, 'Another Hague Judgments Convention' (n 50) 500; Teitz was a member of the US delegation during the Diplomatic Session in 2001, see 'Members of the Second Commission', in *Proceedings of the Twentieth Session, Tome II* (n 29) 386, 387.

of foreign judgments, the Hague Conference can still choose to work towards the conclusion of a binding instrument on international direct jurisdiction which would complement the rules of the 2019 Hague Judgments Convention.[1061] This new Hague instrument on international direct jurisdiction would then include jurisdictional provisions which are regarded as generally appropriate for exercising jurisdiction.[1062] The 2019 Hague Judgments Convention already contains a green list of unified grounds of indirect jurisdiction, developed on the basis of consensus.[1063] Due to the intrinsic connection between direct and indirect jurisdiction, the green list of indirect grounds of jurisdiction contained in the convention sets the limits for creating unified grounds of direct jurisdiction, and would be the starting point for discussions.[1064] In order to create an instrument in the spirit of a true mixed convention, those provisions on direct jurisdiction on which the Hague Conference Members can achieve consensus would be included in the green list of acceptable jurisdictional provisions in a new Hague instrument on direct jurisdiction.[1065] The result of this process could be an asymmetric convention in case not every ground of indirect jurisdiction contained in the 2019 Hague Judgments Convention is also regarded as an appropriate ground for exercising international direct jurisdiction.[1066] That means, the result of the Hague Jurisdiction Project could be an instrument with a green list of grounds of direct jurisdiction which is shorter than the green list of grounds of indirect jurisdiction (also called jurisdictional filters) contained in the 2019 Hague Judgments Convention.[1067] In this way, the 2019 Hague Judgments Convention and the new Hague instrument on international direct jurisdiction would create what has been described

---

1061 Due to the intrinsic connection between the two instruments, the name 'Protocol' seems appropriate, see, e.g., United Nations, *Treaty Handbook* (rev edn, United Nations Publication 2012) 69 <https://treaties.un.org/doc/source/publications/THB/English.pdf> accessed 5 April 2023.

1062 Von Mehren, 'New Approach' (n 1) 287; von Mehren, 'Enforcing Judgments Abroad' (n 6) 19.

1063 2019 Hague Judgments Convention (n 53) arts 5, 6; cf Garcimartín, Saumier, 'Judgments Convention: Revised Draft Explanatory Report' (n 48) [16].

1064 Eva Jueptner, 'The Hague Jurisdiction Project – What options for the Hague Conference?' (2020) 16 JPIL 247, 265–269.

1065 See above, Section 2.1.

1066 The concept of an asymmetric mixed convention is discussed above in Section 2.3.2.2.

1067 Cf Michaels, 'Some Fundamental Conceptions as Applied in Judgment Conventions' (n 152) 38, 39, 61; von Mehren, 'Recognition and Enforcement of Foreign Judgments – General Theory' (n 204) 56, 57.

as an 'asymmetric mixed convention' by Arthur T von Mehren and Ralf Michaels.[1068]

Creating a legal regime following the spirit of a true mixed convention in the context of the Hague Jurisdiction Project would not only be desirable from the point of view of the EU, but also of all litigants involved in international civil and commercial litigation. Even if the mixed-convention regime created by a new Hague instrument on international direct jurisdiction only unified some rules of jurisdiction, this limited unification would still constitute a significant improvement as compared to the status quo, where no unified rules of international direct jurisdiction regarding proceedings in civil and commercial matters in general exist on a global level.[1069] If the Permanent Bureau recommends the creation of a mixed-convention regime following Arthur T von Mehren's idea of a true mixed convention, the unification of grounds of jurisdiction on a global level seems to be a real possibility. Otherwise, the opportunity to create a global regime on both judgments *and* jurisdiction in the context of the revived Judgments Project might be lost again for the foreseeable future.

[1068] Von Mehren, 'Enforcing Judgments Abroad' (n 6) fn 16; von Mehren, 'Jurisdictional Requirements' (n 250) A-39, A-40; see also von Mehren, 'Can the Hague Conference Project Succeed?' (n 31) 198, 199.

[1069] Von Mehren, 'The Case for a Convention-mixte Approach' (n 266) 92; Nygh, 'Arthur's Baby' (n 266) 162; see also Goddard, 'Rethinking the Hague Judgments Convention' (n 7) 29.

BIBLIOGRAPHY

PREPARATORY LEGISLATIVE MATERIAL: EUROPEAN UNION

Commission of the European Communities, 'Proposal for a Council Regulation (EC) on jurisdiction and the recognition and enforcement of judgments in civil and commercial matters: COM(1999) 348 final' <http://aei.pitt.edu/47831/1/COM_(99)_348_final.pdf>

Commission of the European Communities, 'Green Paper on the Review of the Council Regulation (EC) No 44/2001 on Jurisdiction and the Recognition and Enforcement of Judgments in Civil and Commercial Matters, 21 April 2009: COM(2009) 175 final' <https://eur-lex.europa.eu/legal-content/EN/TXT/PDF/?uri=CELEX:52009DC0175&from=EN>

European Parliament, 'European Parliament resolution of 7 September 2010 on the implementation and review of Council Regulation (EC) No 44/2001 on jurisdiction and the recognition and enforcement of judgments in civil and commercial matters' <https://www.europarl.europa.eu/sides/getDoc.do?pubRef=-//EP//NONSGML+TA+P7-TA-2010-0304+0+DOC+PDF+V0//EN>

——, 'Report on the proposal for a regulation of the European Parliament and of the Council on jurisdiction and the recognition and enforcement of judgments in civil and commercial matters (recast) of 15 October 2012: Explanatory Statement' <https://www.europarl.europa.eu/sides/getDoc.do?pubRef=-//EP//NONSGML+REPORT+A7-2012-0320+0+DOC+PDF+V0//EN>

PROCEEDINGS OF THE HAGUE CONFERENCE ON PRIVATE INTERNATIONAL LAW

Actes de la Conférence de la Haye chargée de réglementer diverses matières de droit international privé (12–27 septembre 1893), Première partie (Imprimerie Nationale 1893)

Conférence de la Haye de Droit International Privé/Hague Conference on Private International Law, *Actes de la Cinquième Session, tenue du 12 octobre au 7 novembre 1925* (Imprimerie Nationale 1926)

——, *Actes de la Dixième Session – 7 au 28 octobre 1964, Tome Premier* (Imprimerie Nationale 1965)

——, *Actes et Documents de la Dixième Session - 7 au 28 octobre 1964, Tome III, Notification* (Imprimerie Nationale 1965)

——, *Actes et Documents de la Session Extraordinaire - 13 au 26 avril 1966* (Imprimerie National 1969)

——, *Actes et Documents de la Treizième Session - 4 au 23 octobre 1976, Tome I, Miscellaneous Matters* (Imprimerie Nationale 1978)

——, *Actes et Documents de la Quatorzième Session - 6 au 25 octobre 1980, Tome III, Child Abduction* (Imprimerie Nationale 1982)

——, *Actes et Documents de la Quinzième Session - 8 au 20 octobre 1984, Tome I, Miscellaneous Matters* (Imprimerie Nationale 1986)

Garcimartín F, Saumier G, 'Judgments Convention: Revised Draft Explanatory Report - Preliminary Document No 1 of December 2018' <https://assets.hcch.net/docs/7d2ae3f7-e8c6-4ef3-807c-15f112aa483d.pdf>

Hague Conference on Private International Law, Council on General Affairs and Policy of the Conference (5–7 April 2011), 'Conclusions and Recommendations adopted by the Council' <www.hcch.net/en/governance/council-on-general-affairs/archive>

——, Council on General Affairs and Policy of the Conference (17–20 April 2012), 'Conclusions and Recommendations adopted by the Council' <www.hcch.net/en/governance/council-on-general-affairs/archive>

——, Council on General Affairs and Policy of the Conference (13–15 March 2018), 'Conclusions and Recommendations adopted by the Council' <https://assets.hcch.net/docs/715fc166-2d40-4902-8c6c-e98b3def3b92.pdf>

——, Council on General Affairs and Policy of the Conference (3–6 March 2020), 'Conclusions and Recommendations adopted by the Council' <https://assets.hcch.net/docs/70458042-f771-4e94-9c56-df3257a1e5ff.pdf>

——, Council on General Affairs and Policy 2023 (March 2023), 'Conclusions & Decisions' <https://assets.hcch.net/docs/5f9999b9-09a3-44a7-863d-1dddd4f9c6b8.pdf>

——, 'List of participants, Special Commission on international jurisdiction and the effects of foreign judgments in civil and commercial matters, 7–18 June 1999' (on file with author)

——, *Proceedings of the Sixteenth Session, 3 to 20 October 1988, Tome I, Miscellaneous Matters* (SDU Publishers 1991)

——, *Proceedings of the Seventeenth Session, 10 to 29 May 1993, Tome I, First Part, Miscellaneous Matters* (SDU Publishers 1995)

——, *Proceedings of the Seventeenth Session, 10 to 29 May 1993, Tome II, Adoption* (SDU Publishers 1994)

——, *Proceedings of the Eighteenth Session, 30 September to 19 October 1996, Tome I, Miscellaneous Matters* (SDU Publishers 1999)

——, *Proceedings of the Nineteenth Session, 6 to 22 June 2001 - Part One, 2 to 13 December 2002 - Part Two, Tome I, Miscellaneous Matters* (Koninklijke Brill NV 2008)

——, *Proceedings of the Twentieth Session, 14 to 30 June 2005, Tome I, Miscellaneous Matters* (Intersentia 2015)

——, *Proceedings of the Twentieth Session, 14 to 30 June 2005, Tome II, Judgments* (Intersentia 2013)

——, *Proceedings of the Twentieth Session, 14 to 30 June 2005, Tome III, Choice of Court* (Intersentia 2010)

Permanent Bureau, 'Report of the Second Special Commission Meeting to Review the Operation of the Hague Convention on the Civil Aspects of International Child Abduction held 18–21 January 1993', <https://assets.hcch.net/upload/abdrpt93e.pdf>

——, 'Annotated Checklist of Issues to be Discussed at the Meeting of the Special Commission on Jurisdiction and Enforcement of Judgments: Prel Doc No 1 of May 1994', <https://assets.hcch.net/docs/5a2b5a48-65bb-4272-8a01-cd43117068f3.pdf>

——, 'Conclusions of the Special Commission of June 1994 on the Question of the Recognition and Enforcement of Foreign Judgments in Civil and Commercial Matters: Prel Doc No 2 of December 1995 for the attention of the Special Commission of June 1996 on the question of the recognition and enforcement of foreign judgments in civil and commercial matters – Annex – Extract of the Conclusions of the Special Commission of June 1995 on general affairs and policy of the Conference' <https://assets.hcch.net/docs/4a144f70-bab3-4d18-85bc-646b24d7c640.pdf>

——, 'Note on the Question of 'Forum non Conveniens' in the Perspective of a Double Convention on Judicial Jurisdiction and the Enforcement of Decisions: Prel Doc No 3 of April 1996' <https://assets.hcch.net/upload/wop/jdgm_pd03(1996).pdf>

——, 'Note on the Recognition and Enforcement of Decisions in the Perspective of a Double Convention with Special Regard to Foreign Judgments Awarding Punitive or Excessive Damages: Prel Doc No 4 of May 1996 for the attention of the Special Commission of June 1996 on the question of the recognition and enforcement of foreign judgments in civil and commercial matters' <https://assets.hcch.net/upload/wop/jdgm_pd04(1996).pdf>

——, 'Conclusions of the second Special Commission meeting on the recognition and enforcement of foreign judgments in civil and commercial matters: Prel Doc No 6 of August 1996 – List of Participants in the Special Commission Meeting' <https://assets.hcch.net/docs/a0062ce0-96bb-4132-9cc3-65f0671c370f.pdf>

——, 'Examples of Treaty Provisions on International Jurisdiction: Info Doc, June 1997' (on file with author)

——, 'Preliminary Results of the Work of the Special Commission Concerning the Proposed Convention on International Jurisdiction and Foreign Judgments in Civil and Commercial Matters: Info Doc, September 1997' (on file with author)

——, 'Conclusions of the Special Commission on General Affairs and Policy of May 2000: Prel Doc No 10 of June 2000' <https://assets.hcch.net/docs/a154cf31-1583-4602-90eb-6b251d2eb7a4.pdf>

——, 'Commission I on General Affairs and Policy held on 22–24 April 2002' <https://www.hcch.net/en/governance/council-on-general-affairs/archive>
——, 'Conclusions of the Special Commission of April 2003 on General Affairs and Policy of the Conference' <https://www.hcch.net/en/governance/council-on-general-affairs/archive>
——, 'Continuation of the Judgments Project: Prel Doc No 14 of February 2010 for the attention of the Council of April 2010 on General Affairs and Policy' <https://assets.hcch.net/docs/cd5f79f4-d710-44a1-a266-af0e73a6ffb4.pdf>
——, 'Background Note: Document for the attention of the Expert Group (meeting of 12–14 April 2012)' <https://assets.hcch.net/docs/d2355e5c-fd79-4366-9caa-8a434367ba84.pdf>
——, 'Conclusions and Recommendations of the Expert Group on Possible Future Work on Cross-Border Litigation in Civil and Commercial Matters: The Hague, 12–14 April 2012' <https://assets.hcch.net/docs/0e110725-5eef-429c-9fe3-24d8d4e7e87a.pdf>
——, 'Issues Paper on Matters of Jurisdiction (Including Parallel Proceedings): January 2013 – Document for the attention of the Experts' Group (February 2013 meeting)' <https://assets.hcch.net/docs/edf2f696-2ac2-4553-afa5-d13c942b8f0d.pdf>
——, 'Ongoing work on International Litigation: Prel Doc No 3 of March 2013' <https://assets.hcch.net/docs/d00eb333-41fc-4b92-8405-e7eb20039154.pdf#report2>
——, 'Process Paper on the Continuation of the Judgments Project: Document for the attention of the Working Group and the Experts' Group – August 2013' <https://assets.hcch.net/docs/79c4fd67-6f1e-4bf8-bf18-01e589862f45.pdf>
——, 'Ongoing Work on Judgments: Choice of Court Convention and the Judgments Project – Prel Doc No 7A of January 2015' <https://assets.hcch.net/upload/wop/gap2015pd07a_en.pdf>
——, 'Working Group on Jurisdiction: Report – Prel Doc No 2 of February 2023 – Annex I: Report of the Chair of the Working Group on matters related to jurisdiction in transnational civil or commercial litigation' <https://assets.hcch.net/docs/fd997e67-381e-47f1-9ff8-74c28e2faf68.pdf>
Special Commission on general affairs and policy of the Conference (1–4 June 1992), 'Work Doc No 1 – distributed 1 June 1992 – Document submitted by the United States Delegation (Lc ON No 15(92)' (on file with author)
Special Commission on the question of jurisdiction, recognition and enforcement of foreign judgments (17–27 June 1997), 'Report of Meeting No 1' (on file with author)
——, 'Report of Meeting No 2' (on file with author)
——, 'Report of Meeting No 10' (on file with author)
——, 'Report of Meeting No 14' (on file with author)

Special Commission on the question of jurisdiction, recognition and enforcement of foreign judgments in civil and commercial matters (3–13 March 1998), 'Final list of participants' (on file with author)
——, 'Chairman's Report with respect to the meeting of 3–13 March 1998' (on file with author)
Special Commission on international jurisdiction and the effects of foreign judgments in civil and commercial matters (25–30 October 1999), 'Report of Meeting No 61' (on file with author)
——, 'Report of Meeting No 74' (on file with author)
Special Commission on international jurisdiction and the effects of foreign judgments in civil and commercial matters (10–20 November 1998), 'Report of Meeting No 53' (on file with author)
——, 'Annex to the Report of Meeting No 53: Intervention by the United States Delegation on 20 November 1998'
Special Commission on international jurisdiction and the effects of foreign judgments in civil and commercial matters (7–18 June 1999), 'Final list of participants' (on file with author)
——, 'Report of Meeting No 57' (on file with author)
——, 'Report of Meeting No 58' (on file with author)
——, 'Report of Meeting No 61' (on file with author)
——, 'Work Doc No 148: Proposal by the delegations of Germany and France' (on file with author)
——, 'Work Doc No 150 E' (on file with author)
——, 'Work Doc No 150 E: Highlighted Version' (on file with author)
——, 'Work Doc No 162 F + E' (on file with author)
——, 'Work Doc No 163: Proposal by the delegations of the United Kingdom and the United States of America' (on file with author)
——, 'Work Doc No 164: Proposal by the Working Group on Contracts' (on file with author)
Special Commission on international jurisdiction and the effects of foreign judgments in civil and commercial matters (25–30 October 1999), 'Final list of participants' (on file with author)
——, 'Report of Meeting No 74' (on file with author)
——, 'Report of Meeting No 77' (on file with author)
——, 'Work Doc No 270 of 26 October 1999: Proposal by the delegations of Denmark, Finland, France, Sweden and the United Kingdom' (on file with author)
Schulz A, 'Reflection Paper to assist in the preparation of a Convention on Jurisdiction and Recognition and Enforcement of Foreign Judgments in Civil and Commercial Matters: Prel Doc No 19 of August 2002' <https://assets.hcch.net/upload/wop/jdgm_pd19e.pdf>

MONOGRAPHS

Beaumont P R, McEleavy P E, *The Convention on International Child Abduction* (OUP 1999)

Milleker E, *Der Negative Internationale Kompetenzkonflikt* (Verlag Ernst und Werner Gieseking 1975)

Sperl H, *Eine internationale Zuständigkeitsordnung in bürgerlichen Rechtssachen* (Hölder-Pichler-Tempsky AG 1926)

COLLECTED COURSES OF THE HAGUE ACADEMY OF INTERNATIONAL LAW

Droz G A L, 'La Conférence de la Haye et l'Entraide Judiciaire Internationale' (1980) 168 Recueil des Cours de l'Académie de Droit International 159

——, 'La Conférence de La Haye de droit international privé en 1980: Évolution et Perspectives' (1980) 168 Recueil des Cours de l'Académie de Droit International 123

——, 'Régards sur le droit international privé comparé: Cours général de droit international privé' (1991) 229 Recueil des Cours de l'Académie de Droit International 9

Dyer A, 'International Child Abduction by Parents' (1980) 168 Recueil des Cours de l'Académie de Droit International 231

Van Hoogstraten M H, 'La codification par traités en droit international privé dans le cadre de la Conférence de la Haye' (1967) 122 Recueil des Cours de l'Académie de Droit International 337

Von Mehren A T, 'Recognition and Enforcement of Foreign Judgments - General Theory and the Role of Jurisdictional Requirements' (1980) 167 Recueil des Cours de l'Académie de Droit International 9

——, 'Theory and Practice of Adjudicatory Authority' (2002) 295 Recueil de Cours de l'Académie de Droit International 9

Pfund P E, 'Contributing to Progressive Development of Private International Law: The International Process and the United States Approach' (1994) 249 Recueil des Cours de l'Académie de Droit International 9

Schwind F, 'Cours général de droit international privé' (1984) 187 Recueil des Cours de l'Académie de Droit International 9

BOOKS

Aust A, *Modern Treaty Law and Practice* (3rd edn, CUP 2013)

Association for Project Management, *Introduction to Project Planning* (Association for Project Management 2008)

Barceló J J, Clermont K M (eds), *A Global Law of Jurisdiction and Judgments: Lessons from The Hague* (Kluwer Law International 2002)

Beaumont P R, McEleavy P E, *Anton's Private International Law (Private International Law, A.E. Anton)* (3rd edn, W Green 2011)

Berton P, Kimura H, Zartman I W (eds), *International Negotiation: Actors, Structure/ Process, Values* (Macmillan 1999)

Binchy W, *Irish Conflicts of Law* (Butterworth (Ireland) Ltd 1988)

Borrás A et al (eds), *E Pluribus Unum: Liber Amicorum Georges A L Droz* (Martinus Nijhoff Publishers 1996)

Bos M (ed), *The Present State of International Law and Other Essays written in honour of the Centenary Celebration of the International Law Association 1873–1973* (Springer 1973)

Capelletti M, Garth B (eds), *Access to Justice Volume I: A World Survey, Book I* (Sijthoff and Noordhoff/Dottore A Giuffrè 1978)

——, *Access to Justice Volume III: Emerging Issues and Perspectives* (Sijthoff and Noordhoff/Dottore A Giuffrè 1979)

Carmody C, Iwasawa Y, Rhodes S (eds), *Trilateral Perspectives on International Legal Issues: Conflict and Coherence* (Cadmus-Port City Press Division 2003)

Cheng B, Brown E D (eds), *Contemporary Problems of International Law: Essays in Honour of Georg Schwarzenberger on his Eightieth Birthday* (Stevens & Sons Limited 1988)

Doek J et al (eds), *Children on the Move: How to Implement Their Right to Family Life* (Kluwer Law International 1999)

Fawcett J (ed), *Reform and Development of Private International Law: Essays in Honour of Sir Peter North* (OUP 2002)

Frame J D, *Managing Projects in Organizations* (1995 Jossey-Bass Inc)

Gottschalk E et al (eds) *Conflict of Laws in a Globalized World: A Tribute to Arthur von Mehren* (CUP 2007)

Hartley T C, *International Commercial Litigation* (3rd edn, CUP 2020)

Jeong H-W, *International Negotiation: Process and Strategies* (CUP 2016)

Kremenyuk V A (ed), *International Negotiation – Analysis, Approaches, Issues* (2nd edn, Jossey-Bass 2002)

Lowenfeld A F, Silberman L J (eds), *The Hague Convention on Jurisdiction and Judgments: Records of the Conference Held at New York University School of Law on the Proposed Convention, April 30–May 1, 1999* (Juris Publishing Inc 2001)

Lutz R E, *A Lawyer's Handbook for Enforcing Foreign Judgments in the United States and Abroad* (CUP 2007)

Markus A R, *Internationales Zivilprozessrecht* (Stämpfli Verlag 2014)

Martenczuk B, van Thiel S (eds), *Justice, Liberty, Security: New Challenges for EU External Relations* (BUP 2008)

Meeusen J et al (eds), *Enforcement of International Contracts in the European Union* (Intersentia 2004)

Nafziger J A R, Symeonides S (eds), *Law and Justice in a Multistate World: Essays in Honour of Arthur T von Mehren* (Transnational Publishers Inc 2002)

——, *Commitment to Private International Law: Essays in Honour of Hans van Loon* (Intersentia 2013)

Platto C (ed), *Enforcement of Foreign Judgments Worldwide* (Graham & Trotman and International Bar Association 1989)

Platto C and Horton W G (eds), *Enforcement of Foreign Judgments Worldwide* (2nd edn, Springer 1993)

Project Management Institute (PMI), *A Guide to the Project Management Body of Knowledge (PMBOK Guide)* (6th edn, Project Management Institute, Inc 2017)

Sabel R, *Procedure at International Conferences: A Study of the Rules of Procedure at the UN and at Inter-governmental Conferences* (2nd edn, CUP 2006)

Scoles EF, Hay P, *Conflict of Laws* (2nd edn, West Publishing Co 1992)

United Nations, *Treaty Handbook* (rev edn, United Nations Publication 2012) <https://treaties.un.org/doc/source/publications/THB/English.pdf>

Venturini G, Bariatti S (eds), *New Instruments of Private International Law – Liber Fausto Pocar* (Giuffrè Editore 2009)

Walker R A, *Multilateral Conferences: Purposeful International Negotiation* (Palgrave Macmillan 2004)

——, *Manual for UN Delegates* (EBSCO Publishing 2011)

Walter G, Baumgartner S (eds), *Recognition and Enforcement of Foreign Judgments Outside the Scope of the Brussels and Lugano Conventions* (Kluwer Law International 2000)

Zartman I W, *Negotiation and Conflict Management: Essays on Theory and Practice* (Routledge 2008)

ENCYCLOPAEDIAS

Basedow J et al (eds), *Encyclopedia of Private International Law, Volume 3* (Edward Elgar Publishing 2017)

Wolfrum R, (ed), *Max Planck Encyclopedia of Public International Law* (2009)

JOURNAL ARTICLES

Adler M A, 'If we build it, will they come? – The Need for a Multilateral Convention on the Recognition and Enforcement of Civil Monetary Judgments' (1994–1995) 26 Law & Pol'y Int'l Bus 79

Adler M A and Zarychta M C, 'The Hague Convention on Choice of Court Agreements: The United States Joins the Judgment Enforcement Band' (2006) 27 Nw J Int'l L & Bus 1

Albin C, Druckman D, 'Procedures Matter: Justice and Effectiveness in International Trade Negotiations' (2014) 20(4) European Journal of International Relations 1014

Baumgartner S P, 'Understanding the Obstacles to the Recognition and Enforcement of US Judgments Abroad' (2013) 45 NYUJ Int'l L & Pol 965

Beaumont P R, 'A United Kingdom Perspective on The Proposed Hague Judgments Convention' (1998) 24 Brook J Int'l L 75

——, 'The Hague Choice of Court Agreement Convention 2005: Background, Negotiations, Analysis and Current Status' (2009) 5 JPIL 125

——, 'The revived Judgments Project in The Hague' (2014) 4 NiPR 532

Beaumont P R and Walker L, 'Recognition and enforcement of judgments in civil and commercial matters in the Brussels I Recast and some lessons from it and the recent Hague Conventions for the Hague Judgments Project' (2015) 11 JPIL 31

Behr V, 'Enforcement of United States Money Judgments in Germany' (1994) 13 JL & Com 211

Borchers P, 'Comparing Personal Jurisdiction' (1992) 40 Am J Comp L 121

Brand R A, 'Enforcement of Foreign Money-Judgments in the United States: In Search of Uniformity and International Acceptance' (1991) 67 Notre Dame Law Review 253

——, 'Enforcement of Judgments in the United States and Europe' (1994) 13 JL & Com 193

——, 'Due Process, Jurisdiction, and a Hague Judgments Project' (1998) 60 U Pitt L Rev 661

——, 'Community Competence for Matters of Judicial Cooperation at the Hague Conference on Private International Law: A View from the United States' (2002) 21 JL & Com 191

Bucher A, 'Vers une convention mondiale sur la compétence et les jugements étrangers' (2000) 2 La Semaine Judiciaire 77

Von Bülow A, 'Vereinheitlichtes Internationales Zivilprozessrecht in der Europäischen Wirtschaftsgemeinschaft: Der Entwurf eines Abkommens über die internationale Zuständigkeit, die Anerkennung und die Vollstreckung gerichtlicher Entscheidungen' (1965) 29 RabelsZ 473

Clermont K M, 'Jurisdictional Salvation and the Hague Treaty' (1999–2000) 85 Cornell L Rev 89

——, 'A Global View of Jurisdiction and Judgments: Views from the United States and Japan' (2004) 37 Cornell Int'l LJ 1

Danford B B, 'The Enforcement of Foreign Money Judgments in the United States and Europe: How Can We Achieve a Comprehensive Treaty?' (2004) 23 Rev Litig 381

Droz G A L, 'A Comment on the Role of the Hague Conference on Private International Law' (1994) 57 Law & Contemp Probs 3

Goddard D, 'Rethinking the Hague Judgments Convention: A Pacific Perspective' (2001) 3 Yearbook of Private International Law 27

Graupner R, 'Some Recent Aspects of the Recognition and Enforcement of Foreign Judgments in Western Europe' (1963) 12 ICLQ 367

Graveson R H, 'The International Unification of Law' (1968) 16 Am J Comp L 4

Halpern J, 'Exorbitant Jurisdiction and the Brussels Convention: Toward a Theory of Restraint' (1983) 9 Yale J World Pub Ord 369

Herrup P, Brand RA, 'A Hague Convention on Parallel Proceedings' (2022) 63 Harvard International Law Journal Online 1
Herzog P, 'Common Market Convention on Jurisdiction and the Enforcement of Judgments: An Interim Update' (1976-1977) 17 Va J Int'l L 417
Hollander-Blumoff R, Tyler T R, 'Procedural Justice in Negotiation: Procedural Fairness, Outcome Acceptance, and Integrative Potential' (2003) 33(2) Law & Social Inquiry 473
Juenger F K, 'The Recognition of Money Judgments in Civil and Commercial Matters' (1988) 26 Am J Comp L 1
——, 'A Shoe Unfit for Globetrotting' (1995) 28 U C Davis L Rev 1027
Jueptner E, 'The Hague Jurisdiction Project – What options for the Hague Conference?' (2020) 16 JPIL 247
Lechler T G, Cohen M, 'Exploring the role of steering committees in realizing value from project management' (2009) 40 PMJ 42
Lenhoff A, 'International Law and Rules on International Jurisdiction' (1964) 50 Cornell Law Review 5
Lipstein K, 'One Hundred Years of Hague Conferences on Private International Law' (1993) 42 ICLQ 553
Lowenfeld A F, 'Transatlantic Business Transactions: Some Questions for the Lawyers' (2004) 26 Hous J Int'l L 251
Maier H G, 'A Hague Conference Judgments Convention and United States Courts: A Problem and a Possibility' (1998) 61 Alb L Rev 207
Mancini P S, 'Négociations Diplomatiques du Gouvernement Italien avec les Différentes Puissances Relativement à la Fixation par Traite de Certaines Règles de Droit International Privé et à l'Exécution des Jugements Etrangers' (1886) 13 J Dr Int'l Prive & Juris Comparee 35
Martiny D, 'Recognition and Enforcement of Foreign Money Judgments in the Federal Republic of Germany' (1987) 35 Am J Comp L 721
Von Mehren A T, 'Adjudicatory Jurisdiction: General Theories Compared and Evaluated' (1983) 63 BU L Rev 279
——, 'Recognition of United States Judgments Abroad and Foreign Judgments in the United States: Would an International Convention Be Useful?' (1993) 57 RabelsZ 449
——, 'Recognition and Enforcement of Foreign Judgments: A New Approach for the Hague Conference?' (1994) 57 Law & Contemp Probs 271
——, 'The Case for a Convention-mixte Approach to Jurisdiction to Adjudicate and Recognition and Enforcement of Foreign Judgments' (1997) 61 RabelsZ 86
——, 'Enforcing Judgments Abroad: Reflections on the Design of Recognition Conventions' (1998) 24 Brook J Int'l L 17
——, 'The Hague Jurisdiction and Enforcement Convention Project Faces an Impasse – A Diagnosis and Guidelines for a Cure' (2000) IPRax 465
——, 'Drafting a Convention on International Jurisdiction and the Effects of Foreign Judgments Acceptable World-wide: Can the Hague Conference Project Succeed?' (2001) 29 Am J Comp L 191

Michaels R, 'Recognition and Enforcement of Foreign Judgments' (2009) <https://scholarship.law.duke.edu/faculty_scholarship/2076/>

Monheim K, 'The "Power of Process": How Negotiation Management Influences Multilateral Cooperation' (2016) 21 International Negotiation 345

Morse C G J, 'International Shoe v. Brussels and Lugano: Principles and Pitfalls in the Law of Personal Jurisdiction' (1995) 28 UC Davis L Rev 999

Nadelmann K H, 'Ignored State Interests: The Federal Government and International Efforts to Unify Rules of Private Law' (1954) 102 U Pa L Rev

——, 'The United States joins the Hague Conference on Private International Law: A "History" with Comments' (1965) 30 Law & Contemp Probs 291

North P M, 'The Draft U.K./U.S. Judgments Convention: A British Viewpoint' (1979) 1 Nw J Int'l L & Bus 219

Pfund P H, 'Letter by Peter H Pfund, Assistant Legal Adviser for Private International Law, US Department of State' (1997) 31 Int'l L 718

——, 'The Project of the Hague Conference on Private International Law to Prepare a Convention on Jurisdiction and the Recognition/Enforcement of Judgments in Civil and Commercial Matters' (1998–1999) 24 Brook J Int'l L 7

Pfund P H and Trautman D T, 'Jurisdiction to Adjudicate: A Suggested Analysis' (1966) 79 Harv L Rev 1121

Schack H, 'Hundert Jahre Haager Konferenz für IPR' (1993) 53 RabelsZ 224

Schulz A, 'The Accession of the European Community to the Hague Conference on Private International Law' (2007) ICLQ 939

Schütze R A, 'The Recognition and Enforcement of American Civil Judgments Containing Punitive Damages in the Federal Republic of Germany' (1990) 11 U Pa J Int'l Bus L 581

Shelburne R C, Schoepfle G K, 'The European Community 1992 program and US workers' (1990) Monthly Lab Rev 22

Smit H, 'Common and Civil Law Rules of in Personam Adjudicatory Authority: An Analysis of Underlying Policies' (1972) 21 ICLQ 335

——, 'International Control of International Litigation: Who Benefits?' (1994) 57 Law & Contemp Probs 25

Struycken A T V M, 'Das Internationale Privatrecht der Europäischen Gemeinschaft im Verhältnis zu Drittstaaten und zur Haager Konferenz' (2004) ZEuP 276

Teitz L E, 'Another Hague Judgments Convention: Bucking the Past to Provide for the Future' (2019) 29 Duke J Comp & Int'l L 491

Tell O, 'La construction de l'espace unique européen en matière de justice face à l'harmonisation universelle de la procédure civile: propos réalistes d'un acteur européen' (2003) 8 Unif L Rev 453

Wagner R, 'Die Bemühungen der Haager Konferenz für Internationales Privatrecht um ein Übereinkommen über die gerichtliche Zuständigkeit und ausländische Entscheidungen in Zivil- und Handelssachen – Ein Sachstandsbericht nach dem 1. Teil der Diplomatischen Konferenz (2001) 6 IPRax 533

——,'Das Haager Übereinkommen vom 30.6.2005 über Gerichtsstandsvereinbarungen' (2009) 73 RabelsZ 100

——, 'Die Haager Konferenz für Internationales Privatrecht zehn Jahre nach der Vergemeinschaftung der Gesetzgebungskompetenz in der justiziellen Zusammenarbeit in Zivilsachen' (2009) 73 RabelsZ 215

Weintraub R J, 'How substantial is our need for a judgments-recognition convention and what should we bargain away to get it?' (1998–1999) 24 Brook J Int'l L 167

Weser M, 'Les conflits de juridictions dans le cadre du Marché Commun. Difficultés et remèdes' (1959) RCDIP 613–649

——, 'Les conflits de juridictions dans le cadre du Marché Commun. Difficultés et remèdes' (1960) RCDIP 21–41; 151–172; 314–333; 533–556

——, 'Les conflits de juridictions dans le cadre du Marché Commun. Difficultés et remèdes' (1961) RCDIP 105–129

——, 'Les conflits de juridictions dans le cadre du Marché Commun. Difficultés et remèdes (suite et fin)' (1961) RCDIP 105

——, 'Bases of Judicial Jurisdiction in the Common Market Countries' (1961) 10 Am J Comp L 331

Woodward D L, 'Reciprocal Recognition and Enforcement of Civil Judgments in the United States, the United Kingdom and the European Economic Community' (1982) 8 NCJ Int'l L & Com Reg 299

Wurmnest W, 'Recognition and Enforcement of U.S. Money Judgments in Germany' (2005) 23 Berkeley J Int'l L 175

Yang I, 'International Enforcement of Punitive Damages Awards' (2014) 9 J Comp L 353

Yuan A A, 'Enforcing and Collecting Money Judgments in China from a US Judgment's Creditor's Perspective' (2004) Geo Wash Intl' L Rev 757

Zekoll J, 'The Role and Status of American Law in the Hague Judgments Project' (1998) 61 Alb L Rev 1283

REPORTS AND STUDIES

Beaumont P, 'UK Position on the Hague Preliminary Draft Convention on Jurisdiction and Foreign Judgments in Civil and Commercial Matters adopted by the Special Commission on 30 October 1999' (on file with author)

Committee on Foreign and Comparative Law – Association of the Bar of the City of New York, 'Survey on Foreign Recognition of US Money Judgments' (July 31 2001) <www.cptech.org/ecom/jurisdiction/CFCL.rtf>

European Commission, *External and intra-EU trade: Statistical yearbook – Data 1958–2006* (eurostat Statistical books 2008) <https://ec.europa.eu/eurostat/documents/3217494/5729733/KS-GI-11-001-EN.PDF/9e06d19b-bdce-49e0-a766-65fbbfc78081>

——, *External and intra-EU trade: A statistical yearbook – Data 1958 –2010* (eurostat Statisticalbooks2011) <https://ec.europa.eu/eurostat/documents/3217494/5729733/KS-GI-11-001-EN.PDF/9e06d19b-bdce-49e0-a766-65fbbfc78081>

Jenard P, 'Report on the Convention on jurisdiction and the enforcement of judgments in civil and commercial matters' [1979] OJ C59/1 (Jenard Report)

Jones Day, 'Comparative Study of Jurisdictional Gaps and Their Effect on the Judgments Project (July 1, 2015)' <https://assets.hcch.net/docs/7ebd2982-351a-4ca7-b6b3-356c8cdc1778.pdf>

Koppenol-Laforce M, Vermeulen F, 'Comparative Study of "Residual Jurisdiction" in Civil and Commercial Disputes in the EU – National Report for: Netherlands' (on file with author)

McEleavy P E, 'Towards a Worldwide Convention on Jurisdiction and Foreign Judgments in Civil and Commercial Matters: Edinburgh Informal Meeting 23–26 April 2001 – Scottish Executive Justice Department & Lord Chancellor's Department – Report on the Proceedings' (McEleavy Report) (on file with author)

Pocar F, 'Convention on jurisdiction and the recognition and enforcement of judgments in civil and commercial matters, signed in Lugano on 30 October 2007 – Explanatory Report' [2009] OJ C319/1 (Pocar Report)

Raoul-Duval P, Stoyanov M, 'Comparative Study of "Residual Jurisdiction" in Civil and Commercial Disputes in the EU – National Report for: France' (on file with author)

Schlosser P, 'Report on the Convention on the Association of the Kingdom of Denmark, Ireland and the United Kingdom of Great Britain and Northern Ireland to the Convention on jurisdiction and the enforcement of judgments in civil and commercial matters and to the Protocol on its interpretation by the Court of Justice' [1979] OJ C59/71 (Schlosser Report)

Statistisches Bundesamt, 'Export, Import, Globalisierung – Deutscher Außenhandel und Welthandel, 1990–2008' (Destatis 2010)

UNGA 'Documents A/6369 and Add 1 and 2, Report of the Secretary General' (23 September 1966) 21st Session (1966) Annexes (Schmitthoff Report)

UNGA, 'Review of the Multilateral Treaty-Making Process' UNGA 35th Session UN Doc A/35/312 (1980)

WTO, International Trade Statistics 2015 <https://www.wto.org/english/res_e/statis_e/its2015_e/its15_toc_e.htm>

POLICY DOCUMENTS

European Council, 'Tampere European Council 15 and 16 October 1999: Presidency Conclusions' <www.europarl.europa.eu/summits/tam_en.htm>

European Parliament, 'European Parliament resolution of 7 September 2010 on the implementation and review of Council Regulation (EC) No 44/2001 on jurisdiction and the recognition and enforcement of judgments in civil and commercial matters' <https://www.europarl.europa.eu/sides/getDoc.do?pubRef=-//EP//NONSGML+TA+P7-TA-2010-0304+0+DOC+PDF+V0//EN>

——, 'Report on the proposal for a regulation of the European Parliament and of the Council on jurisdiction and the recognition and enforcement of judgments in civil and commercial matters (recast) of 15 October 2012: Explanatory Statement' <https://www.europarl.europa.eu/sides/getDoc.do?pubRef=-//EP//NONSGML+REPORT+A7-2012-0320+0+DOC+PDF+V0//EN>

WEBSITES AND BLOGS

Delić A, 'The Birth of Modern Private International Law: The Treaties of Montevideo (1889, amended 1940)' <https://opil.ouplaw.com/page/Treaties-Montevideo/the-birth-of-modern-private-international-law-the-treaties-of-montevideo-1889-amended-1940>

EDA, 'Convention concernant la compétence judiciaire et l'exécution des décisions en matière civile et commerciale faite à Lugano le 16 septembre 1988: Parties' <https://www.eda.admin.ch/dam/eda/fr/documents/aussenpolitik/voelkerrecht/autres-conventions/lugano1/Lugano-1-parties_fr.pdf>

European Union, 'Country Profiles' <https://europa.eu/european-union/about-eu/countries_en#tab-0-1>

Hague Conference on Private International Law, 'Statute of the Hague Conference on Private International Law: Status table' <https://www.hcch.net/en/instruments/conventions/status-table/?cid=29>

——, 'Convention of 15 April 1958 on the jurisdiction of the selected forum in the case of international sales of goods: Status table' <https://www.hcch.net/en/instruments/conventions/status-table/?cid=34>

——, 'Convention of 15 November 1965 on Jurisdiction, Applicable Law and Recognition of Decrees Relating to Adoptions: Status table' <https://www.hcch.net/en/instruments/conventions/status-table/?cid=75>

——, 'Convention of 1 February 1971 on the Recognition and Enforcement of Foreign Judgments in Civil and Commercial Matters: Status table' <https://www.hcch.net/en/instruments/conventions/status-table/?cid=78>

——, 'Convention of 25 October 1980 on the Civil Aspects of International Child Abduction: Status table' <www.hcch.net/en/instruments/conventions/status-table/?cid=24>

——, 'Convention of 29 May 1993 on Protection of Children and Co-operation in Respect of Intercountry Adoption: Status table' <www.hcch.net/en/instruments/conventions/status-table/?cid=69>

——, 'Convention of 30 June 2005 on Choice of Court Agreements: Status table' <https://www.hcch.net/en/instruments/conventions/status-table/?cid=98>

——, Convention of 2 July 2019 on the Recognition and Enforcement of Foreign Judgments in Civil or Commercial Matters: Status table' <https://www.hcch.net/en/instruments/conventions/status-table/?cid=137>

——, 'Jurisdiction Project' <https://www.hcch.net/en/projects/legislative-projects/jurisdiction-project>

——, 'Meetings of the Special Commission' <https://www.hcch.net/en/publications-and-studies/details4/?pid=6644&dtid=61>

WITS, 'Trade Summary for Germany 1992' <http://wits.worldbank.org/CountryProfile/en/Country/DEU/Year/1992/SummaryText>

——, 'United States Trade Summary 1992' <https://wits.worldbank.org/CountryProfile/en/Country/USA/Year/1992/SummaryText>

OTHER

Dogauchi M, 'The Draft Convention on Jurisdiction and Foreign Judgments in Civil and Commercial Matters – A View from the Far East – The Hague Draft Convention from the Perspective of Japan', UIA Seminar Edinburgh, April 20–21 2000 <www.cptech.org/ecom/jurisdiction/Dogauchi.pdf>

EFTA Secretariat, 'The EFTA Convention: The Free Trade Association of Iceland, Liechtenstein, Norway and Switzerland (2017) <www.efta.int/sites/default/files/publications/fact-sheets/EFTA-Convention-guide/EFTA-Convention-brochure.pdf>

Kovar J D, Letter to Hans van Loon, 22 February 2000, regarding Preliminary Draft Hague Convention on Jurisdiction and the Enforcement of Civil Judgments <www.cptech.org/ecom/hague/kovar2loon22022000.pdf>

——, Letter to Alasdair Wallace, September 10, 2000' <www.cptech.org/ecom/jurisdiction/kovarletter.html>

Die Regierungen des Königreichs Belgien, der Bundesrepublik Deutschland, der Französischen Republik, der Italienischen Republik, des Großherzogtums Luxemburg und des Königreichs der Niederlande, 'Gemeinsame Erklärung' [1972] OJ L299/45

UNGA Res 2205 (XXI) 1966 (17 December 1966)

US Department of State, 'Papers relating to the foreign relations of the United States, transmitted to Congress, with the annual message of the President, December 7, 1874: No 509' <https://history.state.gov/historicaldocuments/frus1874/pg_794>

Valente V, Ambassadeur Représentant Permanent du Portugal auprès de l'Union Européene, Président du Comité des Représentants Permanent, fax to M Van Loon, Sécrétaire-Général de la Conférence de la Haye de Droit International Privé, from 27 April 2000 (on file with author)

Williamson E D (Legal Advisor, US Department of State), Letter to Georges Droz, Secretary General of the Hague Conference, May 5 1992 (on file with author)

INDEX

D

E

ABOUT THE AUTHOR

DR EVA JUEPTNER is a Lecturer in Law and Baxter Fellow at the University of Dundee (Scotland, United Kingdom). Prior to joining the University of Dundee, Eva worked at the Institute for Private International Law and Civil Procedure at the University of Bern (Switzerland). Eva's research focuses on private international law in general, and on issues of international jurisdiction and the recognition and enforcement of foreign judgments in civil and commercial matters in particular.

www.ingramcontent.com/pod-product-compliance
Ingram Content Group UK Ltd.
Pitfield, Milton Keynes, MK11 3LW, UK
UKHW021845100926
8556IPUK00019B/1054

9 781839 704321